Clean Architecture with Python

Implement scalable and maintainable applications using proven architectural principles

Sam Keen

Clean Architecture with Python

Portfolio Director: Kunal Chaudhari

Relationship Lead: Samriddhi Murarka

Project Manager: Ashwin Dinesh Kharwa

Content Engineer: Alexander Powell

Technical Editor: Seemanjay Ameriya

Copy Editor: Safis Editing

Indexer: Manju Arasan

Proofreader: Alexander Powell

Production Designer: Jyoti Kadam

Growth Lead: Sayantani Saha

First published: June 2025

Production reference: 2290126

Published by Packt Publishing Ltd.

Grosvenor House

11 St Paul's Square

Birmingham

B3 1RB, UK.

ISBN 978-1-83664-289-3

www.packtpub.com

To my loving wife, Jin, whose unwavering support, patience, and encouragement made this book possible. Your belief in me through countless weekends spent coding and writing has been my greatest source of strength.

— Sam Keen

Contributors

About the author

Sam Keen is a software engineering leader with over 25 years of experience. He is a polyglot developer who's leveraged Python in varied contexts, from small start-ups to industry giants including AWS, Lululemon, and Nike. His expertise spans cloud architecture, continuous delivery, and building scalable systems. At Lululemon, Sam pioneered the company's first cloud-native application development team, setting standards for distributed cloud architecture within the company. Currently, Sam leverages Python to design and implement internal platform engineering solutions for AWS focusing on Clean Architecture principles and maintainable code. Sam resides in the US Pacific Northwest with his loving wife and two very spoiled cats.

I want to express my gratitude to the team at Packt for their guidance and support throughout the writing process. Special thanks to the editors and reviewers whose feedback was invaluable in refining the concepts presented in this book. I'm also grateful to the open source community whose tools and libraries make Python development such a joy. Finally, thank you to my family for their unwavering support during the long hours of writing and coding.

About the reviewer

Aindrila Ghorai is a lead architect with over 17 years of experience in software development, specializing in PEGA technology, artificial intelligence, and healthcare solutions. She has driven strategic, enterprise-wide BPM initiatives and contributed to operational excellence through Agile-Scrum and iterative methodologies. Aindrila has authored several peer-reviewed papers and served as a judge for prestigious awards including the Globee Awards, NCWIT, and Technovation Girls. Passionate about innovation and mentorship, she is dedicated to delivering transformative, sustainable solutions by leveraging emerging technologies and best practices.

Table of Contents

Chapter 2: SOLID Foundations: Building Robust Python Applications   25

Chapter 3: Type-Enhanced Python: Strengthening Clean Architecture   55

Part 2: Implementing Clean Architecture in Python 77

Chapter 4: Domain-Driven Design: Crafting the Core Business Logic 79

Chapter 6: The Interface Adapters Layer: Controllers and Presenters 133

Part 3: Applying Clean Architecture in Python

Chapter 9: Adding Web UI: Clean Architecture's Interface Flexibility   219

Chapter 12: Your Clean Architecture Journey: Next Steps 299

Preface

Clean Architecture has become increasingly vital in modern software development, particularly as applications grow in complexity and teams need to maintain them over time. While architectural principles are often discussed in abstract terms, this book brings Clean Architecture to life through practical Python implementations, demonstrating how these concepts can transform your development approach.

Python's versatility makes it an excellent language for applying Clean Architecture principles. Its dynamic nature and extensive ecosystem enable rapid development, yet these same strengths can lead to complex, difficult-to-maintain codebases as applications evolve. Clean Architecture provides the framework needed to balance Python's flexibility with structured, maintainable design.

Throughout this book, we'll explore how to apply Clean Architecture patterns to Python projects, creating systems that are not just functional but also testable, maintainable, and adaptable. Using a task management application as our running example, we'll build a complete system from the ground up, demonstrating how proper architectural boundaries create software that can evolve gracefully over time.

Whether you're building new systems or maintaining existing ones, the principles and practices described in this book will help you create more robust and flexible Python applications. You'll learn how to separate core business logic from external concerns, create clear interfaces between system components, and implement patterns that enable your software to adapt to changing requirements.

In this book, we're going to cover the following main topics:

- Understanding Clean Architecture fundamentals and applying SOLID principles in Python applications
- Enhancing Python with type hints to strengthen architectural boundaries and interfaces
- Building robust domain models and application layers that encapsulate business logic independent of external concerns
- Creating clear interfaces between architectural layers through controllers, presenters, and adapters

- Integrating with frameworks and external systems while maintaining architectural integrity
- Applying Clean Architecture in practical scenarios: testing, web interfaces, observability, and legacy system transformation

Together, these topics form a comprehensive approach to building Python applications that can withstand the test of time. By the end of this book, you'll have both the theoretical understanding and practical skills to implement Clean Architecture in your own projects, creating systems that are more maintainable, testable, and adaptable to change.

Who this book is for

This book is for Python developers who want to create more maintainable, testable, and adaptable applications. It's ideal for developers of an intermediate level or greater who have experience with Python and are looking to improve their architectural skills. If you've struggled with codebases that resist change, suffered through tangled dependencies, or simply want to write better Python code, this book will provide you with practical strategies and patterns to overcome these challenges.

Several roles will find value in this material:

- **Software architects** seeking to implement clean, maintainable system designs in Python projects
- **Technical leads** responsible for guiding development teams and establishing coding standards
- **Backend developers** working on complex applications that need to evolve over time
- **DevOps engineers** looking to create more testable, observable Python services

While beginners can benefit from the concepts presented, some familiarity with Python and object-oriented programming principles will help you get the most from this material. Technical leads, architects, and senior developers will find valuable insights for implementing Clean Architecture in team environments and guiding architectural decisions.

What this book covers

Chapter 1, Clean Architecture Essentials: Transforming Python Development, introduces the foundational concepts of Clean Architecture and explains why these principles matter for Python developers. It establishes the core architectural layers and explores how Clean Architecture can transform Python development practices.

Chapter 2, SOLID Foundations: Building Robust Python Applications, examines how SOLID principles provide the foundation for Clean Architecture. Through practical Python examples, you'll learn how to implement Single Responsibility, Open–Closed, Liskov Substitution, Interface Segregation, and Dependency Inversion Principles.

Chapter 3, Type-Enhanced Python: Strengthening Clean Architecture, demonstrates how Python's type hints can enhance architectural boundaries. You'll explore how typing improves interface definition, supports dependency inversion, and enables better tooling for architectural validation.

Chapter 4, Domain-Driven Design: Crafting the Core Business Logic, focuses on building robust domain models. You'll learn how to identify and model entities, value objects, and domain services while ensuring they remain independent of external concerns.

Chapter 5, The Application Layer: Orchestrating Use Cases, covers the implementation of use cases that coordinate domain objects to accomplish specific tasks. You'll create clean interfaces between your domain and outer layers while maintaining proper separation of concerns.

Chapter 6, The Interface Adapters Layer: Controllers and Presenters, explores how to create controllers that translate external requests and presenters that format domain data. You'll build clean boundaries between your application core and delivery mechanisms.

Chapter 7, The Frameworks and Drivers Layer: External Interfaces, demonstrates how to integrate external frameworks and infrastructure while keeping your core business logic independent. You'll implement database adapters, web frameworks, and external services that respect Clean Architecture boundaries.

Chapter 8, Implementing Test Patterns with Clean Architecture, provides strategies for comprehensive testing across architectural boundaries. You'll create unit tests for domain objects, integration tests for use cases, and end-to-end tests that verify system behavior.

Chapter 9, Adding Web UI: Clean Architecture's Interface Flexibility, shows how to implement a web interface for your Clean Architecture application. You'll build a Flask-based web interface that demonstrates how Clean Architecture enables adding new interfaces without disrupting existing functionality.

Chapter 10, Implementing Observability: Monitoring and Verification, covers strategies for adding logging, monitoring, and architectural verification while maintaining Clean Architecture boundaries. You'll implement cross-cutting concerns without compromising architectural integrity.

Chapter 11, Legacy to Clean: Refactoring Python for Maintainability, provides practical approaches for gradually transforming legacy Python applications. You'll learn incremental refactoring techniques that improve architecture while maintaining system stability.

Chapter 12, Your Clean Architecture Journey: Next Steps, explores how to apply Clean Architecture across different system types and organizational contexts. You'll discover strategies for architectural leadership, community building, and balancing pragmatism with architectural principles.

To get the most out of this book

Basic familiarity with Python programming is assumed, including knowledge of object-oriented concepts such as classes, inheritance, and composition. Experience with web development concepts will be helpful for later chapters but is not required.

Software/hardware covered in the book	Operating system requirements
Python 3.13 or greater	Windows, macOS, or Linux

If you are using the digital version of this book, we advise you to type the code yourself or access the code from the book's GitHub repository. Doing so will help you avoid any potential errors related to the copying and pasting of code.

Download the example code files

The complete code for all examples is available in the book's GitHub repository at `https://github.com/PacktPublishing/Clean-Architecture-with-Python`. In addition, for relevant chapters, you'll find a functional implementation of our task management application at the stage corresponding to that chapter. This allows you to run, test, and explore a working version of the application as it evolves throughout the book. Each chapter builds upon the previous ones, so it's recommended to proceed through the book sequentially, although experienced developers may choose to focus on specific chapters relevant to their current challenges.

We also have other code bundles from our rich catalog of books and videos available at `https://github.com/PacktPublishing/`. Check them out!

Download the color images

We also provide a PDF file that has color images of the screenshots/diagrams used in this book. You can download it here: `https://packt.link/gbp/9781836642893`.

Conventions used

There are a number of text conventions used throughout this book.

`Code in text`: Indicates code words in text, database table names, folder names, filenames, file extensions, pathnames, dummy URLs, user input, and X/Twitter handles. Here is an example: "The `project_id` parameter comes from the URL itself (`/projects/<project_id>/tasks/new`), while form fields contain task details."

A block of code is set as follows:

```python
# cli_main.py
def main() -> int:
    """Main entry point for the CLI application."""
    app = create_application(
        notification_service=NotificationRecorder(),
        task_presenter=CliTaskPresenter(),
        project_presenter=CliProjectPresenter(),
    )
    cli = ClickCli(app)
    return cli.run()
```

Any command-line input or output is written as follows:

```
> python web_main.py
 * Serving Flask app 'todo_app.infrastructure.web.app'
 * Debug mode: on
 * Running on http://127.0.0.1:5000
Press CTRL+C to quit
 * Restarting with stat
 * Debugger is active!
 * Debugger PIN: 954-447-204
127.0.0.1 - - [05/Feb/2025 13:58:57] "GET / HTTP/1.1" 200 -
```

Bold: Indicates a new term, an important word, or words that you see on the screen. For instance, words in menus or dialog boxes appear in the text like this. For example: "**Bounded contexts** are conceptual boundaries that define where specific domain models apply."

 Warnings or important notes appear like this.

 Tips and tricks appear like this.

Get in touch

Feedback from our readers is always welcome.

General feedback: Email `feedback@packtpub.com` and mention the book's title in the subject of your message. If you have questions about any aspect of this book, please email us at `questions@packtpub.com`.

Errata: Although we have taken every care to ensure the accuracy of our content, mistakes do happen. If you have found a mistake in this book, we would be grateful if you reported this to us. Please visit `http://www.packtpub.com/submit-errata`, click **Submit Errata**, and fill in the form.

Piracy: If you come across any illegal copies of our works in any form on the internet, we would be grateful if you would provide us with the location address or website name. Please contact us at `copyright@packtpub.com` with a link to the material.

If you are interested in becoming an author: If there is a topic that you have expertise in and you are interested in either writing or contributing to a book, please visit `http://authors.packtpub.com/`.

Share your thoughts

Once you've read *Clean Architecture with Python*, we'd love to hear your thoughts! Scan the QR code below to go straight to the Amazon review page for this book and share your feedback.

`https://packt.link/r/183664289X`

Your review is important to us and the tech community and will help us make sure we're delivering excellent quality content.

Free benefits with your book

This book comes with free benefits to support your learning. Activate them now for instant access (see the "*How to Unlock*" section for instructions).

Here's a quick overview of what you can instantly unlock with your purchase:

DRM-Free PDF Version

Download DRM-free PDF and ePub copies of this book.

7-Day Packt Library Access

Get 7-day unlimited access to 8,000+ books and videos. No credit card required.

Available for first-time Packt+ trial users only.

Next-Gen Reader Access

Read this book on Packt Reader with progress sync, dark mode and note-taking.

How to Unlock

Scan the QR code (or go to `packtpub.com/unlock`). Search for this book by name, confirm the edition, and then follow the steps on the page.

Note: Keep your invoice handy. Purchases made directly from Packt don't require one

Part 1

Foundations of Clean Architecture in Python

This part establishes the fundamental principles and patterns of Clean Architecture in the Python context. You'll gain a comprehensive understanding of the core architectural concepts, SOLID principles, and how Python's type system can enhance your architectural implementations. These chapters provide the essential knowledge foundation upon which the rest of the book builds, setting you up for success in implementing Clean Architecture in your own Python projects.

This part of the book includes the following chapters:

- *Chapter 1, Clean Architecture Essentials: Transforming Python Development*
- *Chapter 2, SOLID Foundations: Building Robust Python Applications*
- *Chapter 3, Type-Enhanced Python: Strengthening Clean Architecture*

1

Clean Architecture Essentials: Transforming Python Development

As Python developers, we apply best practices such as writing clean functions, using descriptive variable names, and striving for modularity. Yet, as our applications grow, we often struggle to maintain this clarity and adaptability at scale. Python's simplicity and versatility make it popular for projects ranging from web development to data science, but these strengths can become challenges as applications become more complex. We find ourselves lacking a master plan, an overarching architecture to guide our decisions and keep our projects maintainable as they evolve. This is where **Clean Architecture** comes into play, offering a structured approach to building Python applications that balance planning and agility, providing the architectural guidance we need for sustainable, large-scale development.

Clean Architecture, introduced by Robert C. Martin in 2012 (`https://blog.cleancoder.com/uncle-bob/2012/08/13/the-clean-architecture.html`), synthesizes decades of software design wisdom into a cohesive set of principles. It addresses persistent challenges in software development, such as managing complexity and accommodating change. By applying Clean Architecture principles to Python projects, developers can create systems that are not only functional but also maintainable, testable, and adaptable over time.

In this chapter, we'll explore the essence of Clean Architecture and its relevance to Python development. We'll examine how Clean Architecture principles align with Python's philosophy of simplicity and readability, creating a natural synergy that enhances Python's strengths. You'll learn how Clean Architecture can help you build Python applications that are easier to understand, modify, and extend, even as they grow in complexity.

By the end of this chapter, you'll have an overview of Clean Architecture principles and their potential benefits for Python development. You'll be introduced to how this approach can address common challenges in software development, particularly as Python projects grow in scale and complexity. This foundational understanding of Clean Architecture will be essential as we delve deeper into its implementation and best practices in Python throughout the rest of the book.

In this chapter, we're going to cover the following main topics:

- Why Clean Architecture in Python: the benefits of balancing planning and agility
- What is Clean Architecture?
- Clean Architecture and Python: a natural fit

Technical requirements

The code snippets in this chapter are for demonstration purposes only, showing the application of some of the topics and practices noted in the chapter. Future chapters will feature more involved examples of code with specific requirements noted when applicable. All code for all chapters can be found in the book's accompanying GitHub repository at `https://github.com/PacktPublishing/Clean-Architecture-with-Python`.

Why Clean Architecture in Python: the benefits of balancing planning and agility

In this section, we'll explore the critical balance between planning and agility in Python development and how Clean Architecture can help achieve this balance. We'll examine the challenges posed by increasing complexity in modern Python applications and the imperative for agility in today's fast-paced business environment. We'll then discuss the trade-offs between planning and flexibility, and how architectural thinking can provide a framework for managing these trade-offs. Finally, we'll look at the role of architecture in managing complexity and setting the stage for long-term success. Through these discussions, you'll gain insight into why Clean Architecture is particularly valuable for Python developers striving to create maintainable, adaptable, and efficient applications.

Let's begin by examining the complex challenges facing modern Python development.

The complexity challenge in modern Python development

As Python's popularity soars, so do the scale and complexity of applications built with it. From web services to data science pipelines, Python projects are growing larger and more intricate. This growth brings significant challenges that every Python developer must grapple with.

The increasing complexity of systems makes them harder to understand, modify, and maintain. This complexity can severely limit your ability to add new features or respond to changing requirements. The maintenance burden of complex Python systems can overwhelm development teams, slowing down progress and innovation. Even small changes in large, complex systems can have far-reaching consequences, making modifications expensive and risky.

Consider a fictitious large Python-based e-commerce site: PyShop. The business decides to implement a seemingly simple feature: adding gift-wrapping options to orders. However, this straightforward addition quickly cascades into a complex project:

- The order processing module needs updates to include gift-wrapping choices
- The inventory system requires modification to track gift-wrapping supplies
- The pricing engine needs adjustments to calculate additional costs
- The user interface (UI) must be updated to present gift-wrapping options
- The fulfillment system needs changes to include gift-wrapping instructions

What was estimated as a two-week-long task stretches into a multi-month project. Each change potentially impacts other system parts: adjustments in order processing affect reporting, inventory changes influence supply chain management, and UI modifications require extensive user experience testing.

This example highlights how interconnected modules in a complex system can turn a simple feature addition into a significant undertaking, emphasizing the need for an architecture that allows for more isolated changes and easier testing processes.

Moreover, as Python projects grow, developers often struggle with abstractions, a critical aspect that Clean Architecture helps address. Without proper guidance, codebases can suffer from extremes: either becoming a tangled mess of deeply nested class hierarchies that are hard to understand and modify or devolving into monolithic *do-everything* classes that lack any meaningful abstraction. In the former case, developers may create too-complex inheritance structures to maximize code reuse, resulting in a fragile system where changes in one place have unforeseen consequences elsewhere. In the latter case, the lack of abstraction leads to massive, unwieldy classes and rampant code duplication, making it nearly impossible to maintain consistency or make systemic changes. Both scenarios result in codebases that are difficult to understand, maintain, and extend, which is precisely the issues that a well-planned architecture helps prevent.

Furthermore, in today's rapidly evolving tech landscape, complex, tightly coupled systems struggle to take advantage of new technologies. This limitation can significantly impact your ability to stay competitive in a field where technological agility is crucial.

The agility imperative

In our fast-paced business environment, agility is not just an advantage—it's a necessity. With every company essentially becoming a technology company, the pressure to deliver quickly has never been higher. Python's simplicity and extensive ecosystem make it an excellent choice for rapid development.

However, sustainable agility requires more than just initial speed, it demands architectural decisions that support ongoing evolution. It's akin to building a high-performance race car: without proper design fundamentals, what starts as impressive acceleration quickly becomes limited by poor handling and maintenance challenges.

In rapidly evolving Python applications, this principle becomes starkly evident. Without a cohesive architecture, quick feature additions can create a tangled web of dependencies. What starts as a nimble codebase can, within months, become rigid and fragile. Developers find themselves spending more time deciphering existing code than writing new features. When it's not immediately clear where new code should be added or how it should interact with existing components, developers under pressure may make hasty decisions, leading to suboptimal implementations and introducing bugs. These quick fixes further complicate the codebase, making future changes even more challenging. The initial velocity becomes unsustainable, not because of the speed itself, but due to the lack of a sturdy architectural foundation that can guide rapid changes and provide clear pathways for new feature integration.

Requirements change, often unpredictably. Your Python projects need to be structured in a way that allows for easy adaptation to these changes. This adaptability is crucial for long-term success in software development.

Striking a balance: the planning–agility trade-off

Finding the right balance between planning and agility is crucial in Python development. As Dave Thomas wisely said, *"Big design up front is dumb. Doing no design up front is even dumber."* The key is finding the middle ground that allows for both structure and flexibility.

Good architecture helps you postpone decisions. It gives you the flexibility to push decisions to later stages when you have more information to make the correct choice. This approach is particularly valuable in Python development, where the language's flexibility can sometimes lead to decision paralysis.

Introducing architectural thinking in Python development means considering the long-term structure of your project from the start, without over-engineering. It's about creating a framework that guides development while remaining adaptable to change.

The role of architecture in managing complexity

Effective architecture is your best tool for managing complexity in Python systems. Good architecture simplifies complex systems by providing a clear structure and **separation of concerns (SoC)**. One of the first steps in architecting a new system is determining how to divide it, keeping things that change for the same reason together and things that change for different reasons apart.

Consider two Python-based **content management systems (CMSs)** for media companies, both tasked with implementing a new AI-powered content tagging feature. In the well-architected system, this feature is implemented as a standalone module with clear interfaces. It integrates smoothly with the existing content creation and search modules through well-defined APIs. Developers can build and test the AI tagging service independently, and then connect it to the content database and UI with minimal disruption. Conversely, in a poorly structured system, adding this feature requires changes across the entire stack—from database schemas to frontend code—leading to unexpected bugs and performance issues. What takes a sprint in the well-architected system becomes a months-long refactoring project in the poorly structured one, demonstrating how thoughtful initial architecture can dramatically improve development efficiency and system adaptability.

The architectural decisions you make early on have a profound impact on the long-term development costs and flexibility of your Python projects. A well-architected system can significantly reduce the cost of change over time, allowing your team to respond more quickly to new requirements or technological changes.

Preparing for Clean Architecture

As we move toward discussing Clean Architecture, it's important to understand that it offers a systematic approach to balancing planning and agility in Python projects. Architectural principles provide powerful tools for managing and reducing complexity in your Python systems.

At its core, Clean Architecture is about strategic SoC in your Python applications. It advocates for a structure where the essential business logic is insulated from external factors such as UIs, databases, and third-party integrations. This separation creates clear boundaries between different parts of your application, each with its own responsibilities. By doing so, Clean Architecture allows your core business rules to remain pure and unaffected by the implementation details of **input/output (I/O)** mechanisms or **data management systems (DMSs)**.

By understanding these challenges and principles, you'll be better prepared to appreciate the benefits that Clean Architecture can bring to your Python projects. In the next sections, we'll delve into what Clean Architecture is and how it specifically applies to Python development, providing you with the tools to combat complexity and reduce the cost of change in your software systems.

What is Clean Architecture?

Having explored the challenges of managing complexity in Python development and the need for balancing planning with agility, the goal of this section is to give you a high-level overview of Clean Architecture. We'll be covering several key concepts and principles in quick succession to provide a broad understanding. Don't worry if you don't grasp every detail immediately. This is just the beginning of our journey. Each of these topics will be explored in depth in the chapters to come, where we'll dive into practical Python implementations and real-world scenarios.

Clean Architecture synthesizes many ideas from previous architectural styles, but it is built around a fundamental concept: the separation of software elements into ring levels, with a strict rule that code dependencies can only move inward from outer levels. This principle is formally known as the **Dependency Rule**, one of the most critical aspects of Clean Architecture. The Dependency Rule states that source code dependencies must only point inward, toward higher-level policies. Inner circles must know nothing about outer circles, while outer circles must depend on and adapt to inner circles. This ensures that changes to external elements (like databases, UI, or frameworks) don't impact the core business logic. The aim is to create software systems that are not only functional but also maintainable and adaptable over time. To illustrate this, let's consider a simple Python application for a library management system:

1. At the core, we have the Book class, representing the basic data structure.
2. Moving outward, we have a BookInventory class that manages operations on books.
3. In the outer ring, we have a BookInterface class that handles user interactions related to books.

In this structure, the Book class knows nothing about the BookInventory or BookInterface classes. The BookInventory class might use the Book class but doesn't know about the interface. This separation ensures that the core logic remains unaffected by external concerns.

Crucially, this structure allows us to modify or even replace outer layers without affecting the inner layers. For instance, we could change the UI from a **command-line interface (CLI)** to a web interface by modifying the BookInterface class, without needing to alter the Book or BookInventory classes. This flexibility is a key advantage of the Clean Architecture approach.

This structure is designed to produce systems that embody the key principles we introduced earlier:

*   SoC
*   Independence of external details
*   **Testability** and **maintainability**

Let's explore further how Clean Architecture achieves these goals and the benefits it brings to software development.

The onion architecture concept

Let's visualize the ring levels mentioned earlier and add another level of detail as to the purpose of each ring. Clean Architecture is often visualized as a series of concentric circles, like an onion. Each circle represents a different layer of software, and the Dependency Rule we discussed ensures that dependencies only flow inward across these boundaries. The core layers contain business logic (entities), while the external layers contain interface and implementation details (*see Figure 1.1*):

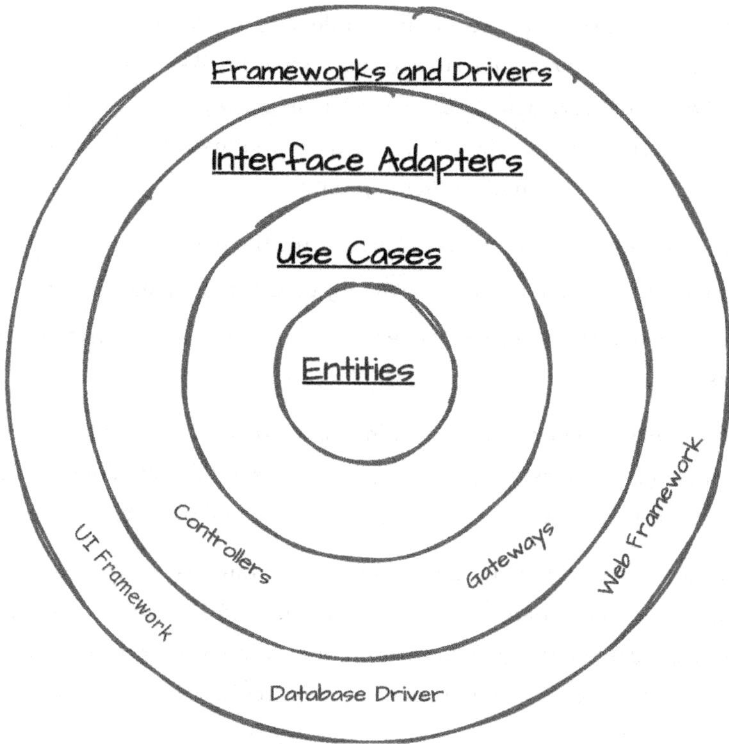

Figure 1.1: Clean Architecture: a series of concentric layers

Figure 1.1 demonstrates the separation of inner core business logic progressing out to external interfaces:

- **Entities**: At the center are entities, which encapsulate enterprise-wide business rules. Entities in this context are the primary *nouns* of your product, the core business objects that would exist even without software. For example, in an e-commerce system, entities might include *Customer*, *Product*, and *Order*. In a task management application, they could be *User*, *Task*, and *Project*. These entities contain the most basic, universal rules about how these objects behave and interact.

- **Use Cases:** The next layer contains use cases, which orchestrate the flow of data to and from entities. A use case represents a specific way the system is used. It's essentially a description of how the system should behave for a particular scenario. For instance, in a task management app, use cases might include *Create New Task*, *Complete Task*, or *Assign Task*. Use cases contain application-specific business rules and control how and when entities are used to fulfill the goals of the application.

- **Interface Adapters**: Further out, we find interface adapters, which convert data between use cases and external agencies. This layer acts as a set of translators between the inner layers (entities and use cases) and the outer layer. It might include things such as controllers that handle HTTP requests, presenters that format data for display, and gateways that transform data for persistence. In a Python web application, this might include your view functions or classes that handle routing and request processing. A key point of this layer is that it allows us to decouple from frameworks.

- **Frameworks and Drivers**: The outermost layer contains frameworks and drivers, where the *external agencies* reside. By *drivers*, we mean the specific tools, frameworks, and delivery mechanisms that are used to run the system but aren't core to the business logic. In a Python context, examples might include the following:

  - Web frameworks such as Django or Flask

  - Database drivers such as `psycopg2` for PostgreSQL or `pymongo` for MongoDB

  - External libraries for tasks such as sending emails (for example, `smtplib`) or processing payments

  - UI frameworks if you're building a desktop or mobile app (for example, PyQt)

  - System utilities for tasks such as logging or configuration management

  This outermost layer is the most volatile, as it's where we interact with the outside world and where technologies are most likely to change over time. By keeping it separate from our core business logic, we can more easily swap out these external tools without affecting the heart of our application.

This layered structure of Clean Architecture promotes SoC, establishing a clear organizational framework for software systems. Now that we have an idea of the fundamental structure of Clean Architecture, let's further investigate its broader benefits.

Benefits of Clean Architecture

One of the primary advantages of Clean Architecture is its focus on protecting and isolating your core business logic, the domain objects that represent the foundation of your business. While external details such as web frameworks and persistence engines come and go, the true value to your business lies in the time invested in designing and implementing these core domain objects. Clean Architecture recognizes this and provides a structure that insulates these crucial components from the volatility of external technologies.

This architectural approach protects your investment in domain logic from the need to move away from a given framework or technology. For example, if a framework you're using moves from an open source model to a proprietary one, Clean Architecture allows you to replace it without rewriting your core business logic. This separation significantly reduces the cost and risk of changes over time, allowing your system to evolve more easily as requirements change or as you need to adapt to new technologies. In essence, Clean Architecture ensures that the most valuable and stable part of your application, your business logic, remains unaffected by the often turbulent world of external technologies and frameworks.

Another key benefit is enhanced testability across all layers of the application. The independence of the core business logic from external details makes it much easier to write comprehensive unit tests. You can test business rules in isolation, without the need to spin up a database or web server or build cumbersome mocks. This leads to more thorough testing and, consequently, more robust software. It also encourages developers to write more tests, as the process becomes simpler and more straightforward.

Clean Architecture also provides flexibility in technology choices. Because the core of the application isn't dependent on external frameworks or tools, you have the freedom to swap out these elements as needed. This is particularly valuable in the fast-moving world of technology, where today's popular framework might be obsolete tomorrow. Similarly, you might start with a CLI for internal use, then add a web interface for broader access, all without altering your core business rules' code. Your core business logic remains stable, while you have the flexibility to adopt new technologies in the outer layers as they emerge. Lastly, Clean Architecture promotes long-term agility in development and leads to what Robert C. Martin calls a *Screaming Architecture* (`https://blog.cleancoder.com/uncle-bob/2011/09/30/Screaming-Architecture.html`). Its focus on separating concerns and managing dependencies results in a codebase that's easier to understand and modify. The concept of Screaming Architecture suggests that when you look at the structure of your system, it should scream its purpose and use cases, not its frameworks or tools. For instance, your architecture should scream *online bookstore*, not *Django application*. This clear, purpose-driven structure allows new team members to quickly grasp the system's intent and make contributions. The architecture itself becomes a form of documentation, revealing the system's core purpose and functionality at a glance. Such clarity and flexibility translate to increased development speed over the long term, even as the system grows in complexity. It also ensures that your system remains focused on its core business logic, rather than being tied to specific technical implementations.

Clean Architecture in context

To fully appreciate the value of Clean Architecture, it's important to understand its place in the broader context of software development practices and methodologies.

Clean Architecture represents an evolution from traditional layered architecture. While it builds upon the concept of layers, it places a stronger emphasis on SoC and enforces the Dependency Rule more strictly than traditional architectures. Unlike traditional layered architectures where lower layers often depend on persistence or infrastructure concerns, Clean Architecture keeps the inner layers pure and focused on business logic. This shift in focus allows for greater flexibility and resilience to change.

Clean Architecture complements modern development practices such as Agile and DevOps. It aligns well with Agile methodologies by facilitating **continuous delivery (CD)** and making it easier to respond to change. The clear SoC supports iterative development and makes it easier to modify or extend functionality in response to changing requirements. In terms of DevOps, Clean Architecture supports practices such as **continuous integration and deployment (CI/CD)** by making systems more testable and modular. The clear boundaries between components can also help in scaling development across teams, as different teams can work on different layers or components with minimal interference.

In conclusion, Clean Architecture offers a powerful approach to building software systems that are scalable, maintainable, and adaptable to change. By focusing on SoC and managing dependencies, it provides a structure that can withstand the test of time and the pressures of evolving technology and business needs. As we move into the next section, we'll explore how these principles align particularly well with Python development practices.

Clean Architecture and Python: a natural fit

As we've explored the principles and benefits of Clean Architecture, you might be wondering how well these concepts align with Python development. In this section, we'll discover that Clean Architecture and Python share a natural affinity, making Python an excellent language for implementing Clean Architecture principles.

Python's philosophy, as embodied in *The Zen of Python* (`https://peps.python.org/pep-0020/`) aligns remarkably well with Clean Architecture principles. Both emphasize simplicity, readability, and the importance of well-structured code. Python's focus on creating clear, maintainable, and adaptable code provides a strong foundation for implementing Clean Architecture. As we delve deeper into this section, we'll explore how Python language features can be leveraged to create robust, maintainable systems that adhere to Clean Architecture principles.

Implementing Clean Architecture in Python

Python's dynamic nature, combined with its strong support for **object-oriented programming (OOP)** and functional programming paradigms, allows developers to implement Clean Architecture concepts with less boilerplate and greater clarity than many other languages.

Note on code examples

Throughout this book, you'll notice type annotations in our code examples (e.g., `def function(parameter: type) -> return_type`). These type hints enhance code clarity and help enforce Clean Architecture boundaries. We'll explore this powerful feature in depth in *Chapter 3*.

A key principle of Clean Architecture is the reliance on abstractions rather than concrete implementations. This principle directly supports the Dependency Rule we discussed earlier: dependencies should only point inward. Let's see how this works in practice using Python's **abstract base classes (ABCs)**.

Consider the following example, which models a notification system:

```python
from abc import ABC, abstractmethod


class Notifier(ABC):
    @abstractmethod
    def send_notification(self, message: str) -> None:
        pass


class EmailNotifier(Notifier):
    def send_notification(self, message: str) -> None:
        print(f"Sending email: {message}")


class SMSNotifier(Notifier):
    def send_notification(self, message: str) -> None:
        print(f"Sending SMS: {message}")


class NotificationService:
    def __init__(self, notifier: Notifier):
        self.notifier = notifier
```

```python
    def notify(self, message: str) -> None:
        self.notifier.send_notification(message)

# Usage
email_notifier = EmailNotifier()
email_service = NotificationService(email_notifier)
email_service.notify("Hello via email")
```

This example demonstrates key concepts of Clean Architecture using Python's ABCs:

1. **ABC**: The `Notifier` class is an ABC, defining an interface that all notifier classes must follow. This represents an inner ring in our Clean Architecture structure.

2. **Abstract method**: The `send_notification` method in `Notifier` is marked with @ abstractmethod, enforcing implementation in subclasses.

3. **Concrete implementations**: `EmailNotifier` and `SMSNotifier` are concrete classes in an outer ring. They inherit from `Notifier` and provide specific implementations.

4. **Dependency inversion**: The `NotificationService` class depends on the abstract `Notifier` class, not on concrete implementations. This adheres to the Dependency Rule, as the abstract `Notifier` class (inner ring) doesn't depend on the concrete notifiers (outer ring). We'll dive deeper into dependency inversion in the next chapter.

This structure embodies the Clean Architecture principles we've discussed:

- **It respects the Dependency Rule**: The abstract `Notifier` class (inner ring) knows nothing about the concrete notifiers or the `NotificationService` class (outer rings)

- **It allows for easy extension**: We can add new types of notifiers (such as `PushNotifier`) without changing the `NotificationService` class

- **It promotes flexibility and maintainability**: The core business logic (sending a notification) is separated from the implementation details (how the notification is sent)

By structuring our code this way, we create a system that's not only flexible and maintainable but also adheres to the fundamental principles of Clean Architecture. The abstract `Notifier` class represents our core business rules, while the concrete notifiers and the `NotificationService` class represent the more volatile outer layers. This separation allows us to easily swap or add new notification methods without affecting the core logic of our application.

So, we've seen a simple ABC example, but this is where Python truly shines. We can implement the same Clean Architecture principles without using a class hierarchy, instead relying on Python's support for **duck typing** (https://en.wikipedia.org/wiki/Duck_typing). This flexibility is one of Python's strengths, allowing developers to choose the approach that best fits their project's needs while still adhering to Clean Architecture principles.

Duck typing is a programming concept where the suitability of an object is determined by the presence of certain methods or properties, rather than its explicit type. The name comes from the saying, "If it walks like a duck and quacks like a duck, then it must be a duck." In duck typing, we don't care about the object's type; we care about whether it can do what we need it to do.

This approach aligns well with Clean Architecture's emphasis on abstractions and interfaces. If you'd prefer to stay away from rigid class hierarchies, Python's Protocol feature, introduced in Python 3.8 (https://peps.python.org/pep-0544/), offers the best of both worlds: duck typing with type hinting. Here's an example that implements the same notification system using protocols:

```python
from typing import Protocol
class Notifier(Protocol):
    def send_notification(self, message: str) -> None:
        ...


class EmailNotifier:  # Note: no explicit inheritance
    def send_notification(self, message: str) -> None:
        print(f"Sending email: {message}")


class SMSNotifier:  # Note: no explicit inheritance
    def send_notification(self, message: str) -> None:
        print(f"Sending SMS: {message}")


class NotificationService:
    # Still able to use type hinting
    def __init__(self, notifier: Notifier):
        self.notifier = notifier

    def notify(self, message: str) -> None:
        self.notifier.send_notification(message)
```

```
# Usage
sms_notifier = SMSNotifier()
sms_service = NotificationService(sms_notifier)
sms_service.notify("Hello via SMS")
```

This example demonstrates the same notification system as before but using Python's Protocol feature instead of ABCs. Let's break down the key differences and their implications for Clean Architecture:

- **Protocol versus ABC**: The `Notifier` class is now a `Protocol` class instead of an ABC class. It defines a structural subtyping interface rather than requiring explicit inheritance.

- **Implicit conformance**: The `EmailNotifier` and `SMSNotifier` classes don't explicitly inherit from the `Notifier` class, but they conform to its interface by implementing the `send_notification` method.

- **Duck typing with type hinting**: This approach combines Python's duck typing flexibility with the benefits of static type checking, aligning with Clean Architecture's emphasis on loose coupling.

- **Concrete implementations**: The `NotificationService` class still depends on the abstract `Notifier` protocol, not concrete implementations, adhering to Clean Architecture principles.

This protocol-based approach offers a flexible, Pythonic implementation of Clean Architecture concepts, balancing type safety with reduced class hierarchy rigidity. It demonstrates how to align Clean Architecture principles with Python's philosophy, promoting adaptable and maintainable code.

We highly recommend the use of type hinting via either ABCs or protocols when implementing Clean Architecture. This approach, as opposed to simple implicit interfaces without type hinting, offers significant advantages:

- Improved code readability
- Enhanced IDE support and earlier error detection
- Better alignment with Clean Architecture goals

In the remaining parts of the book, we'll primarily use ABCs in our examples as they are in greater use in existing Python codebases. However, the principles discussed are equally applicable to protocol-based implementations, and readers can adapt the examples to use protocols if preferred.

Practical example: a glimpse of Clean Architecture in a Python project

To illustrate the concepts we've discussed, let's examine the basic structure of a Clean Architecture Python project. This structure embodies the principles we've covered and demonstrates how they translate into a practical file organization. We'll stay at a high level here; later chapters will cover real-world examples in full detail:

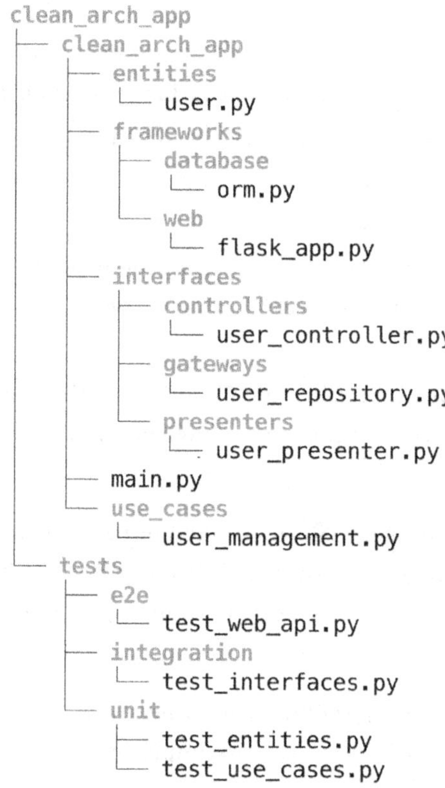

Figure 1.2: A potential layout for a Clean Architecture Python web application

This file structure in *Figure 1.2* exemplifies the Clean Architecture principles we've discussed:

1. **SoC**: Each directory represents a distinct layer of the application, aligning with the concentric circles we saw in *Figure 1.1.*

2. **Dependency Rule**: The structure enforces the Dependency Rule we discussed earlier. If we were to investigate the inner layers (`entities` and `use_cases`), we would not see any imports from the outer layers.

3. **Entities layer**: The `entities` directory contains the core business objects, such as `user.py`. These are at the center of our Clean Architecture diagram and have no dependencies on outer layers.

4. **Use Cases layer**: The `use_cases` directory holds the application-specific business rules. It depends on the entities but is independent of the outer layers.

5. **Interface Adapters layer**: The `interfaces` directory contains controllers, presenters, and gateways. These adapt data between use cases and external agencies (such as web frameworks or databases).

6. **Frameworks layer**: The outermost `frameworks` directory contains implementations of external interfaces, such as database **object-relational mappers (ORMs)** or web frameworks.

7. **Straightforward testing**: The `tests` directory structure mirrors the application structure, allowing for comprehensive testing at all levels.

This structure supports the key benefits of Clean Architecture we discussed:

- **Maintainability**: Changes to external components (in the `frameworks` directory) don't affect the core business logic in entities and use cases
- **Flexibility**: We can easily swap out the database or web framework in the `frameworks` directory without touching the business logic
- **Testability**: The clear separation allows for easy unit testing of core components and integration testing of interfaces

Remember our discussion about abstractions? The `interfaces` directory is where we'd implement the ABCs or protocols we talked about. For instance, `user_repository.py` might define an abstract `UserRepository` class, which is then implemented concretely in the `frameworks/database/orm.py` file.

This structure also facilitates the *master plan* we mentioned earlier. It provides a clear roadmap for where new code should be placed, helping developers make consistent decisions even as the project grows and evolves.

By organizing our Python project this way, we're setting ourselves up for long-term success, creating a codebase that's not just functional but also maintainable, flexible, and aligned with Clean Architecture principles.

Python-specific considerations and potential pitfalls

While Clean Architecture and Python are highly compatible, there are some important considerations to be aware of when implementing these principles in Python projects. Throughout this book, we'll guide you through mitigating these concerns, providing practical solutions and best practices.

Balancing Pythonic code with architectural principles

Python's *batteries included* philosophy and an extensive standard library can sometimes tempt developers to bypass architectural boundaries for the sake of convenience. However, maintaining a clean architecture often involves creating abstractions around even standard library functions to maintain SoC. For example, instead of directly using Python's `smtplib` library in your use cases, consider creating an abstraction layer for sending notifications.

As we progress through this book, we'll demonstrate how this effort of creating abstractions pays off in terms of maintainability, flexibility, and testability. You'll see that the initial investment in Clean Architecture principles yields significant long-term benefits.

Python's ease of importing can sometimes lead to messy dependency structures, as all packages are effectively public. We'll show you how to be vigilant about maintaining the Dependency Rule, ensuring that inner layers don't depend on outer layers. In *Chapter 2*, we'll explore techniques and tools to help you maintain clean dependency structures in your Python projects.

Scaling Clean Architecture in Python projects

The application of Clean Architecture principles should be tailored to the size and complexity of your Python project.

For instance, in small projects or quick prototypes, it's perfectly fine to have a simple, monolithic architecture. However, even in these cases, building in a thoughtful, modular manner can set the stage for future growth. You might start with a simple structure:

```
small_project
├── main.py
├── models.py
├── utils.py
└── views.py
```

Figure 1.3: Quick prototype Python project

In this small project, you can still apply Clean Architecture principles by doing the following:

- Keeping business logic in `models.py` separate from presentation logic in `views.py`
- Using **dependency injection** (**DI**) to make components more modular and testable
- Defining clear interfaces between modules

As your project grows, you can gradually evolve toward a more comprehensive Clean Architecture structure. This evolution might involve the following:

1. Separating core business logic (entities and use cases) into their own modules
2. Introducing interfaces to abstract away framework-specific code
3. Organizing tests to align with the architectural layers

This book takes a hands-on approach, starting with a basic application and a pragmatic application of Clean Architecture principles. As we progress, the complexity of our example application will increase, demonstrating how to evolve the Clean Architecture approach as the codebase grows.

Clean Architecture is a spectrum, not a binary choice. The patterns we'll explore represent a comprehensive implementation designed to showcase Clean Architecture's full capabilities, but in practice, you might choose to implement only the patterns that provide clear value for your specific context. A small API might benefit from clean controller patterns without needing full presenter abstractions, while a data processing script might adopt domain entities while skipping interface adapters entirely. You'll learn how to apply these principles judiciously, avoiding over-engineering in smaller projects while leveraging the full power of Clean Architecture in larger systems. The key is understanding what each pattern provides so you can make informed decisions about which architectural boundaries matter most for your project.

Leveraging Python's dynamic nature appropriately

While Python's dynamic nature is powerful, it can also lead to issues if not used carefully. *Chapter 3* is devoted to aspects of Python's dynamic nature, including duck typing, the use of type hints, and newer features such as protocols. By the end of this chapter, you'll have a solid foundation on how to best leverage these language features to support a Clean Architecture approach, balancing Python's flexibility with architectural rigor.

Testing considerations

This book, as with Clean Architecture itself, strongly promotes the use of tests. Tests are essentially first-class clients of your application code, using the codebase and making assertions on the results. The same architectural considerations that apply to your main codebase also apply to your Python tests.

We'll guide you through writing tests that respect architectural boundaries. You'll learn to recognize when your tests are indicating potential issues in your architecture, such as when they require excessive setup or mocking. In the test cases for each chapter's code examples and culminating in *Chapter 8*, we'll explore these concepts in depth, showing you how to use tests not just for verification, but as a tool for maintaining and improving your architecture.

By being aware of these considerations and potential pitfalls and following the guidance provided throughout this book, you can create Python systems that are both clean and practical, leveraging the strengths of both Clean Architecture and Python. Remember, the key is to apply these principles thoughtfully, always with an eye toward creating maintainable, testable, and flexible Python code.

Summary

In this chapter, we introduced Clean Architecture at a high level and its relevance to Python development. We gave you context by exploring the evolution of software architecture, from Waterfall to Agile, highlighting persistent challenges in managing complexity, accommodating change, and maintaining long-term productivity.

We introduced Clean Architecture's core principles:

- Separation of concerns (SoC)
- Independence of external details
- Testability and maintainability

We examined Clean Architecture's general structure, from core entities and use cases to outer layers of interface adapters, frameworks, and drivers, emphasizing how this structure promotes maintainability and flexibility. We discussed the benefits of Clean Architecture, including improved adaptability, enhanced testability, and long-term development agility, and how it complements modern development practices such as Agile and DevOps.

Furthermore, we explored the natural fit between Clean Architecture and Python, addressing how Python's features can be leveraged to implement Clean Architecture effectively. We also highlighted Python-specific considerations and potential pitfalls, emphasizing the need to balance Pythonic code with architectural principles and adapt Clean Architecture to different project sizes.

In this chapter, we introduced the primary goals of Clean Architecture and explored its natural fit with Python development. We saw how Clean Architecture principles can be implemented using Python's features such as ABCs and protocols, providing a foundation for creating maintainable and flexible software systems.

In the next chapter, we'll build upon this foundation by diving into the SOLID principles. These principles, which form the bedrock of Clean Architecture, will be explored in depth with practical Python examples, showing how they contribute to robust and extensible application design.

Further reading

To learn more about the topics that were covered in this chapter, take a look at the following resources:

- *Clean Architecture: A Craftsman's Guide to Software Structure and Design* by Robert C. Martin. This book provides a comprehensive look at Clean Architecture from its originator.

- *Domain-Driven Design: Tackling Complexity in the Heart of Software* by Eric Evans. While not specific to Clean Architecture, this book provides valuable insights into designing software around business domains.

- *Agile Software Development, Principles, Patterns, and Practices* by Robert C. Martin. This book covers many of the principles that underpin Clean Architecture in the context of Agile development.

- *The Pragmatic Programmer: Your Journey to Mastery* by Andrew Hunt and David Thomas. This classic book offers practical advice on software design and development that aligns well with Clean Architecture principles.

Get this book's PDF version and more

Scan the QR code (or go to `packtpub.com/unlock`). Search for this book by name, confirm the edition, and then follow the steps on the page.

Note: Keep your invoice handy. Purchases made directly from Packt don't require an invoice.

2

SOLID Foundations: Building Robust Python Applications

In the previous chapter, we explored Clean Architecture, a powerful approach to building maintainable, flexible, and scalable Python applications. We learned how it separates concerns into distinct layers, from core business logic to external interfaces, promoting independence and testability. Now, we'll dive deeper into a set of principles that form the foundation of Clean Architecture. These are known as the **SOLID** principles.

The acronym SOLID (https://en.wikipedia.org/wiki/SOLID) represents five key principles of object-oriented programming and design. These principles, when applied correctly, help developers create software structures that are more understandable, flexible, and maintainable. In this chapter, we'll explore each of these principles in depth, focusing on their application in Python and how they support the goals of Clean Architecture we discussed earlier.

By the end of this chapter, you'll have a clear understanding of the following aspects:

- The **Single Responsibility Principle (SRP)** and its role in creating focused, maintainable code
- The **Open–Closed Principle (OCP)** and how it enables building extensible systems
- The **Interface Segregation Principle (ISP)** and its application in Python's duck-typed
- environment
- The **Liskov Substitution Principle (LSP)** and its importance in designing robust abstractions
- The **Dependency Inversion Principle (DIP)** and its crucial role in supporting the Dependency Rule of Clean Architecture

We'll examine each principle through the lens of Python development, providing practical examples and best practices. You'll learn how to apply these principles so that you can write cleaner, more maintainable Python code, setting a strong foundation for implementing Clean Architecture in your projects.

Technical requirements

The code examples presented in this chapter and throughout the rest of the book are tested with Python 3.13. For brevity, code examples in the chapter may be partially implemented. Complete versions of all examples can be found in the book's accompanying GitHub repository at `https://github.com/PacktPublishing/Clean-Architecture-with-Python`.

A note about the order in which we'll cover the SOLID principles

While the SOLID principles are traditionally presented in the order of their acronyms, this book adopts a more strategic sequence. We'll cover SRP, OCP, then ISP, followed by LSP, and finally DIP. The start of each section will detail the relationship between its topic and the ones before. This order creates a natural progression from writing clean, modular code to designing flexible, maintainable systems, directly supporting the goals of Clean Architecture.

Crafting focused, maintainable code: the power of single responsibility

In the hierarchy of software design, we have high-level architecture at the top, followed by components, modules, classes, and, finally, functions. The SOLID principles primarily operate at the module level, providing guidelines for creating well-structured, maintainable code. These module-level practices form the foundation for good architecture in general, including Clean Architecture. By applying SOLID principles, we can create loosely coupled, highly cohesive components that are easier to test, modify, and extend. These qualities are fundamental attributes of Clean Architecture.

Understanding single responsibility

The Single Responsibility Principle (SRP) states that each software module should have one and only one reason to change (`https://blog.cleancoder.com/uncle-bob/2014/05/08/SingleReponsibilityPrinciple.html`).

At first glance, the concept of *single responsibility* might seem straightforward. However, in practice, it can be challenging to define and implement. Let's consider a simple example to illustrate this principle.

Let's consider a User class intended to serve as an entity in a social media application. Recall that entities in Clean Architecture should represent core business objects with the most general rules:

```python
class User:
    def __init__(self, user_id: str, username: str, email: str):
        self.user_id = user_id
        self.username = username
        self.email = email
        self.posts = []

    def create_post(self, content: str) -> dict:
        post = {
            "id": len(self.posts) + 1,
            "content": content,
            "likes": 0            }
        self.posts.append(post)
        return post

    def get_timeline(self) -> list:
        # Fetch and return the user's timeline
        # This might involve complex logic to fetch and
        # sort posts from followed users
        pass

    def update_profile(self, new_username: str = None,
                       new_email: str = None):
        if new_username:
            self.username = new_username
        if new_email:
            self.email = new_email
```

Initially, this `User` class might seem reasonable. It encapsulates user data and provides methods for common user actions in a social media application. However, while intended to be an entity, it deviates significantly from the Clean Architecture concept introduced in *Chapter 1*. Remember, entities should represent core business objects that encapsulate the most general and high-level rules, independent of specific application behaviors or external concerns. Our current `User` class violates these principles by taking on too many responsibilities:

- User data management (handling `user_id`, `username`, and `email`)
- Post-creation and management
- Timeline generation
- Profile updates

This structure combines core user data with application-specific behaviors, violating both SRP and the entity concept. As the product grows, this class could become a bottleneck, leading to development challenges, merge conflicts, and unintended side effects.

When identifying and separating responsibilities, consider these tips:

- Look for groups of methods operating on different subsets of the class's data
- Consider which aspects would be affected by different types of changes or requirements
- Use the *reason to change* heuristic: if you can think of more than one reason for the class to change, consider splitting it

Let's refactor our `User` class so that it adheres to SRP and the entity concept:

```python
class User:
    def __init__(self, user_id: str, username: str, email: str):
        self.user_id = user_id
        self.username = username
        self.email = email


class PostManager:
    def create_post(self, user: User, content: str):
        post = {
            "id": self.generate_post_id(),
            "user_id": user.user_id,
            "content": content,
            "likes": 0
        }
```

```python
        # Logic to save the post
        return post

    def generate_post_id(self):
        # Logic to generate a unique post ID
        pass

class TimelineService:
    def get_timeline(self, user: User) -> list:
        # Fetch and return the user's timeline
        # This might involve complex logic to fetch and
        # sort posts from followed users
        pass

class ProfileManager:
    def update_profile(self, user: User, new_username: str = None,
                       new_email: str = None):
        if new_username:
            user.username = new_username
        if new_email:
            user.email = new_email
        # Additional logic for profile updates,
        # like triggering email verification
```

This refactored version not only adheres more closely to SRP but also aligns with the concept of entities in Clean Architecture. Let's break down the changes and their implications:

- `User`: Now stripped down to its essence, the User class truly embodies an entity. It encapsulates the most general and high-level rules, independent of specific application behaviors. It has a single responsibility: managing core user data.
- `PostManager`: This takes on the focused responsibility of creating and managing posts.
- `TimelineService`: This handles timeline generation logic independently.
- `ProfileManager`: This manages profile updates, further reducing the User class's responsibilities.

Each of these classes now has a clear, focused role that adheres to SRP and promotes separation of concerns. This refactoring brings several benefits:

- **Improved maintainability and testability**: Each class has a single, well-defined purpose, making it easier to understand, modify, and test independently
- **Greater flexibility and reduced coupling**: We can extend or modify one aspect of the system without affecting others, making our codebase more resilient to change

This modular and flexible design aligns well with Clean Architecture principles, creating clear boundaries between different components of our system. While it might seem like overkill for a small application, it sets a foundation for a more maintainable and scalable system as it grows.

Remember, most of us work on applications we intend to be successful. With success come feature requests, pivots, and scaling challenges. Preparing for this growth from the start by applying SRP judiciously can save significant refactoring effort later, creating a structure that's both flexible and comprehensible as your system evolves.

SRP and testing

Classes with a single responsibility are generally easier to test as they have fewer dependencies and edge cases. This facilitates the creation of testable systems, a key tenet of Clean Architecture. For example, testing `PostManager` becomes straightforward:

```python
import unittest
from post_manager import PostManager
from user import User


class TestPostManager(unittest.TestCase):
    def test_create_post(self):
        user = User("123", "testuser", "test@example.com")
        post_manager = PostManager()
        post = post_manager.create_post(user, "Hello, world!")

        self.assertEqual(post["user_id"], "123")
        self.assertEqual(post["content"], "Hello, world!")
        self.assertEqual(post["likes"], 0)
        self.assertIn("id", post)
```

This test case showcases the clarity SRP brings to unit testing. Here, `PostManager`, with its single responsibility, is easily tested in isolation without complex setup or mocking. We can verify all essential aspects of post-creation straightforwardly. This simplicity in testing is a direct benefit of SRP and aligns with Clean Architecture principles. As systems become more complex, the ability to test individual responsibilities in isolation becomes crucial. It allows us to maintain high code quality, catch issues early, and evolve our test suite alongside the system, ensuring the correctness of each focused component without the need to resort to complex integration tests.

Balancing the SRP

While SRP is a powerful principle, it's important not to take it to extremes. Over-applying SRP can lead to an explosion of tiny classes and functions, which can make the overall system harder to understand and navigate. Misinterpreting SRP *as a class or module that should do only one thing* can lead to the creation of too many tiny classes. The principle is about single reasons to change, not strictly about single actions performed.

The key is to find a balance, where each unit of code (be it a class, function, or module) has a clear, cohesive purpose, without becoming so granular that the overall structure becomes fragmented. Remember, the goal of SRP is to make your code more maintainable and understandable. If splitting a class or function makes the overall system harder to understand, it might not be the right move. Use your judgment and always consider the context of your specific application.

In summary, SRP provides a powerful foundation for creating maintainable and flexible code. By ensuring each module or class has a single, well-defined purpose, we can set the stage for systems that are easier to understand, modify, and extend. As we've seen, the key is finding the right balance for your specific context to avoid the extremes of overly complex classes or an explosion of tiny, fragmented components.

This principle of balanced application extends throughout Clean Architecture. Each pattern and abstraction layer we explore offers specific benefits like improved testability, easier maintenance, and enhanced flexibility, but also adds complexity. As you progress through this book, consider each pattern through the lens of your specific needs. A startup building an MVP might defer some abstractions until growth demands them, while an enterprise system might benefit from the full architectural approach from day one. With SRP as our starting point, we're now ready to explore how OCP builds upon this foundation.

Building extensible systems: embracing open–closed design in Python

Having explored SRP and its role in creating focused, maintainable classes, we'll turn our attention to another crucial aspect of robust software design: extensibility. The Open–Closed Principle (OCP), introduced by Bertrand Meyer in 1988 (`https://en.wikipedia.org/wiki/Open%E2%80%93closed_principle`), builds upon the foundation laid by SRP. It guides us in creating systems that are said to be *open for extension but closed for modification*. This means that we should be able to add new functionality without changing existing code, essentially extending our system's behavior through new code rather than modifying what's already in place.

OCP is a powerful tool in our SOLID principles toolkit as it works in harmony with SRP to create modular, flexible code. It addresses a common challenge in software development: how to add new features or behaviors without altering existing, tested code. By adhering to OCP, we can design our Python classes and modules so that they can be easily extended, reducing the risk of introducing bugs when adding new functionality.

In the context of Clean Architecture, OCP plays a vital role in creating systems that can accommodate change over time. It supports the creation of stable, core business logic that remains untouched as we add new features or adapt to new technologies. As we explore OCP in Python, we'll see how it contributes to building maintainable, scalable applications that align with Clean Architecture principles.

Let's explore this principle using a practical example of an area calculator for different shapes. Consider the following initial implementation:

```python
class Rectangle:
    def __init__(self, width, height):
        self.width = width
        self.height = height


class Circle:
    def __init__(self, radius):
        self.radius = radius


class AreaCalculator:
    def calculate_area(self, shape):
        if isinstance(shape, Rectangle):
            return shape.width * shape.height
```

```python
        elif isinstance(shape, Circle):
            return 3.14 * shape.radius ** 2
        else:
            raise ValueError("Unsupported shape")


# Usage
rectangle = Rectangle(5, 4)
circle = Circle(3)


calculator = AreaCalculator()
print(f"Rectangle area: {calculator.calculate_area(rectangle)}")
print(f"Circle area: {calculator.calculate_area(circle)}")
```

Here, we have a simple `AreaCalculator` class that can calculate the area of rectangles and circles. However, this design violates OCP. If we want to add support for a new shape, such as a triangle, we'd need to modify the `calculate_area` method of the `AreaCalculator` class. This modification could potentially introduce bugs in the existing working code.

To adhere to OCP, we need to restructure our code so that we can add new shapes without modifying the existing `AreaCalculator` class. Here's how we can refactor this code so that it embraces OCP:

```python
from abc import ABC, abstractmethod
import math


class Shape(ABC):
    @abstractmethod
    def area(self):
        pass


class Rectangle(Shape):
    def __init__(self, width, height):
        self.width = width
        self.height = height


    def area(self):
        return self.width * self.height


class Circle(Shape):
```

```python
    def __init__(self, radius):
        self.radius = radius

    def area(self):
        return math.pi * self.radius ** 2

class AreaCalculator:
    def calculate_area(self, shape: Shape):
        return shape.area()

# Usage
rectangle = Rectangle(5, 4)
circle = Circle(3)

calculator = AreaCalculator()
print(f"Rectangle area: {calculator.calculate_area(rectangle)}")
print(f"Circle area: {calculator.calculate_area(circle)}")

# Adding a new shape without modifying AreaCalculator
class Triangle(Shape):
    def __init__(self, base, height):
        self.base = base
        self.height = height

    def area(self):
        return 0.5 * self.base * self.height

triangle = Triangle(6, 4)
print(f"Triangle area: {calculator.calculate_area(triangle)}")
```

In this refactored version, we've made several key changes to adhere to the concept of OCP:

- We introduced an abstract Shape class with an area method. This serves as the interface that all shapes must implement.

- Each concrete shape (Rectangle, Circle, and now Triangle) inherits from Shape and implements its own area method.

- The `AreaCalculator` class now depends on the abstract `Shape` class rather than concrete implementations. It calls the area method on any shape object it receives, without needing to know the specific type of shape.

- We can now add new shapes (such as `Triangle`) without modifying the `AreaCalculator` class. The system is open for extension but closed for modification.

This refactored design exemplifies OCP in action, while also maintaining adherence to SRP. Let's examine the key aspects:

- **Open for extension**: We can add new shapes (such as `Triangle`) without modifying existing code. Each shape class has the single responsibility of defining its properties and calculating its own area.

- **Closed for modification**: The core `AreaCalculator` class remains unchanged when adding new shapes, demonstrating closure to modification.

- **Polymorphism**: By using an abstract `Shape` class, we can treat different shape objects uniformly. This allows `AreaCalculator` to work with any shape through a common interface, without knowing specific implementations.

This design aligns perfectly with Clean Architecture's goals:

- **Extensibility**: New requirements (such as adding shapes) can be met without disturbing existing, tested code

- **Isolation of core logic**: Each shape's area calculation is protected from external changes

- **Testability**: The clear separation of responsibilities facilitates straightforward unit testing

By combining OCP and SRP, we've created a foundation for building larger, more complex systems that can evolve without becoming brittle. This example, though small, demonstrates how Clean Architecture principles can be applied effectively in Python to create systems that are well-organized, maintainable, and adaptable to changing requirements.

ISP: tailoring interfaces to clients

As we delve deeper into the SOLID principles, we've seen how SRP promotes focused classes and OCP enables extensibility. Now, we'll turn our attention to the interfaces these classes expose to the world. The Interface Segregation Principle (ISP) (`https://en.wikipedia.org/wiki/Interface_segregation_principle`) guides us in creating lean, purpose-specific interfaces that cater to the exact needs of their clients. This principle is crucial for developing flexible, modular Python code that's easy to understand and maintain.

ISP not only builds upon the concept of single responsibility introduced by SRP but also applies it at the interface level. It advocates for designing interfaces that are narrowly focused on specific tasks, rather than interfaces that attempt to encompass too many responsibilities. This approach leads to more flexible and maintainable systems as clients only depend on the methods they actually use.

To illustrate the importance of ISP and how it relates to classes doing too much, let's consider an example of a multimedia player system:

```python
from abc import ABC, abstractmethod


class MultimediaPlayer(ABC):
    @abstractmethod
    def play_media(self, file: str) -> None:
        pass


    @abstractmethod
    def stop_media(self) -> None:
        pass


    @abstractmethod
    def display_lyrics(self, file: str) -> None:
        pass


    @abstractmethod
    def apply_video_filter(self, filter: str) -> None:
        pass


class MusicPlayer(MultimediaPlayer):
    def play_media(self, file: str) -> None:
        # Implementation for playing music
        print(f"Playing music: {file}")


    def stop_media(self) -> None:
        # Implementation for stopping music
        print("Stopping music")


    def display_lyrics(self, file: str) -> None:
```

```python
        # Implementation for displaying lyrics
        print(f"Displaying lyrics for: {file}")

    def apply_video_filter(self, filter: str) -> None:
        # This method doesn't make sense for a MusicPlayer
        raise NotImplementedError(
            "MusicPlayer does not support video filters")


class VideoPlayer(MultimediaPlayer):
    # Implementation for video player
    ...
```

This design violates ISP by trying to do too much (excess of methods). Let's examine the issues that arise from this approach:

- **Unnecessary methods and a confusing API**: Here, `MusicPlayer` is forced to implement `apply_video_filter`, which doesn't make sense for an audio-only player. This leads to awkward implementations and potential runtime errors. Moreover, users of the `MusicPlayer` class see methods such as `apply_video_filter` in the interface, which can lead to confusion about what the class can actually do. This lack of clarity makes the class harder to use correctly and increases the risk of misuse.

- **Lack of modularity**: The interface doesn't allow for easy creation of specialized players. For instance, we can't easily create a lyrics-only display without also implementing media playback methods. This rigid structure limits extensibility and reuse, making it difficult to adapt the system to new requirements or use cases.

- **Increased maintenance burden**: If we want to add more video-specific features to the `MultimediaPlayer` interface later, we'll need to update all implementing classes each time, even though these features aren't relevant to some of them. This makes the system more difficult to evolve and increases the risk of introducing bugs when making changes.

These issues demonstrate how violating ISP can lead to inflexible, confusing, and hard-to-maintain code. By addressing these problems, we can create a more modular, flexible, and easy-to-use design.

Let's refactor this design so that it adheres to ISP:

```python
from abc import ABC, abstractmethod


class MediaPlayable(ABC):
    @abstractmethod
```

```python
    def play_media(self, file: str) -> None:
        pass


    @abstractmethod
    def stop_media(self) -> None:
        pass

class LyricsDisplayable(ABC):
    @abstractmethod
    def display_lyrics(self, file: str) -> None:
        pass


class VideoFilterable(ABC):
    @abstractmethod
    def apply_video_filter(self, filter: str) -> None:
        pass

class MusicPlayer(MediaPlayable, LyricsDisplayable):
    def play_media(self, file: str) -> None:
        print(f"Playing music: {file}")

    def stop_media(self) -> None:
        print("Stopping music")

    def display_lyrics(self, file: str) -> None:
        print(f"Displaying lyrics for: {file}")

class VideoPlayer(MediaPlayable, VideoFilterable):
    def play_media(self, file: str) -> None:
        print(f"Playing video: {file}")

    def stop_media(self) -> None:
        print("Stopping video")

    def apply_video_filter(self, filter: str) -> None:
        print(f"Applying video filter: {filter}")
```

```python
class BasicAudioPlayer(MediaPlayable):
    def play_media(self, file: str) -> None:
        print(f"Playing audio: {file}")

    def stop_media(self) -> None:
        print("Stopping audio")
```

In this refactored design, we've leveraged Python's **abstract base classes (ABCs)** to create a set of focused interfaces. This approach allows us to define clear contracts for different functionalities without forcing classes to implement methods they don't need. By breaking down the original monolithic interface into smaller, more specific ones, we've created a flexible structure that adheres to ISP. Let's examine the key components of this refactored design:

- `MediaPlayable`: This interface focuses solely on playing and stopping media, a core functionality shared by all media players

- `LyricsDisplayable`: By separating the lyrics display into its own interface, we've ensured that classes that don't support lyrics (such as `VideoPlayer`) aren't forced to implement unnecessary methods

- `VideoFilterable`: This interface isolates video-specific functionality, preventing audio-only players from implementing irrelevant methods

The concrete classes (`MusicPlayer`, `VideoPlayer`, and `BasicAudioPlayer`) now implement only the interfaces relevant to their functionality. This design allows for easy creation and use of different types of media player. For example, `MusicPlayer` can play media and display lyrics, while `BasicAudioPlayer` only needs to implement media playback. This flexibility makes it simple to create new types of player by combining the relevant interfaces, without the burden of implementing unnecessary methods.

Let's summarize the overall benefits of ISP:

- **Reduced coupling**: Classes depend only on the methods they actually use

- **Improved maintainability**: Changes to one aspect (for example, video filtering) don't affect unrelated classes

- **Enhanced flexibility**: We can easily create new types of player by combining relevant interfaces

- **Better testability**: We can mock interfaces more easily by focusing tests on specific functionalities

This ISP-driven design supports Clean Architecture by creating clear, focused interfaces that align with specific use cases. Recall from *Chapter 1* that use cases in Clean Architecture represent application-specific business rules, describing how and when the system uses entities to achieve its goals. ISP facilitates this by allowing us to define precise interfaces for each use case. For instance, the `LyricsDisplayable` interface directly supports a *display lyrics* use case without burdening other player types. This approach allows for a more modular system where components can evolve independently, making it easier to implement new use cases or modify existing ones without affecting unrelated parts of the system. As a result, our application can adapt more readily to changing requirements while maintaining the integrity of its core business logic.

In conclusion, ISP guides us in creating more flexible, maintainable systems by encouraging the design of focused, specific interfaces. By applying ISP alongside SRP and OCP, we can create Python code that's easier to understand, test, and extend. ISP helps us avoid the pitfall of classes trying to *do too much*, just as OCP helps us avoid classes trying to *be too many things*. Together, these principles support Clean Architecture's goals, helping us create systems that can adapt to changing requirements while maintaining a clear, modular structure.

From rigid to flexible: rethinking inheritance and interfaces in Python

As we've explored the Single Responsibility, Open–Closed, and Interface Segregation Principles, we've built a foundation for creating modular, extensible, and focused code. These principles guide us in structuring our classes and interfaces to be more maintainable and adaptable. Now, we turn our attention to the Liskov Substitution Principle (LSP), which complements and reinforces the principles we've discussed.

While SRP guides us in creating focused, cohesive classes, OCP allows us to extend our code without modifying existing components, and ISP promotes the creation of specific, client-tailored interfaces. LSP ensures that our abstractions are well-formed, and our components are truly interchangeable. This principle is crucial for creating robust, flexible systems by ensuring that our inheritance hierarchies behave predictably.

In the context of Clean Architecture, LSP plays a vital role in supporting the flexibility promised by OCP and the focused design encouraged by SRP and ISP. As we delve into LSP, we'll see how it works in concert with the other SOLID principles to create a system that's not just modular, but also reliable and intuitive to use and extend.

Understanding LSP

The Liskov Substitution Principle (LSP), introduced by Barbara Liskov in 1987 (`https://en.wikipedia.org/wiki/Liskov_substitution_principle`), provides a guideline for creating inheritance hierarchies that behave predictably and intuitively. At its core, LSP is about maintaining the integrity of a base class's contract throughout its inheritance hierarchy.

Here's what LSP tells us:

- A base class defines a contract that users of the class can rely on. This contract consists of a set of behaviors and properties.
- Subclasses shouldn't alter or be destructive to this contract. They must honor the promises made by the base class.
- Subclasses can extend or refine the contract, making it more specific to themselves, but they can't reduce or violate the original contract.

In other words, if we have a base class, any of its subclasses should be able to stand in for that base class without breaking the program or violating the expectations set by the base class.

This principle is crucial for several reasons:

- **Predictability**: When LSP is followed, users of a base class can trust that all derived classes will behave in a way that's consistent with the base class. This makes the system more predictable and easier to reason about.
- **Flexibility**: LSP allows us to use polymorphism effectively. We can write code that works with the base class and trust that it will work correctly with any of its subclasses.
- **Extensibility**: By ensuring that subclasses respect the base class contract, we create a system that's easier to extend. New subclasses can be added without fear of breaking existing code that relies on the base class.

However, adhering to LSP isn't always straightforward. It requires careful thought about how we model our objects and their relationships. Let's look at an example to see how violating LSP can lead to problems, and how we can refactor our code to follow this principle.

The pitfalls of rigid hierarchies

Consider a system for managing different vehicle types and their fuel consumption:

```python
class Vehicle:
    def __init__(self, fuel_capacity: float):
        self._fuel_capacity = fuel_capacity
```

```python
        self._fuel_level = fuel_capacity

    def fuel_level(self) -> float:
        return self._fuel_level

    def consume_fuel(self, distance: float) -> None:
        # Assume 10 km per liter for simplicity:
        fuel_consumed = distance / 10
        if self._fuel_level - fuel_consumed < 0:
            raise ValueError("Not enough fuel to cover the distance")
        self._fuel_level -= fuel_consumed
```

This `Vehicle` class represents a typical fuel-based vehicle. Now, let's introduce an `ElectricCar` class that inherits from `Vehicle`:

```python
class ElectricCar(Vehicle):
    def __init__(self, battery_capacity: float):
        super().__init__(battery_capacity)

    def consume_fuel(self, distance: float) -> None:
        # Assume 5 km per kWh for simplicity:
        energy_consumed = distance / 5
        if self._fuel_level - energy_consumed < 0:
            raise ValueError("Not enough charge to cover the distance")
        self._fuel_level -= energy_consumed
```

At first glance, this might seem like a reasonable approach. However, it leads to several issues:

- It violates LSP because `ElectricCar` can't be substituted for `Vehicle` without causing incorrect behavior

- The `ElectricCar` class changes the meaning of *fuel consumption*, violating the contract established by `Vehicle`

- It creates a fragile design where functions that work with `Vehicle` may silently produce incorrect results with `ElectricCar`

To illustrate this, consider the following function:

```python
def drive_vehicle(vehicle: Vehicle, distance: float) -> None:
    initial_fuel = vehicle.fuel_level()
    vehicle.consume_fuel(distance)
```

```python
    fuel_consumed = initial_fuel - vehicle.fuel_level()
    print(f"Fuel consumed: {fuel_consumed:.2f} liters")

# Usage
car = Vehicle(50)  # 50 liter tank
drive_vehicle(car, 100)  # Works fine

electric_car = ElectricCar(50)  # 50 kWh battery
drive_vehicle(electric_car, 100) # This prints incorrect fuel consumption
```

This `drive_vehicle` function works correctly for `Vehicle` but produces misleading output for `ElectricCar`. These problems stem from forcing `ElectricCar` into an inheritance relationship with `Vehicle`, even though an electric car's energy consumption works differently from a fuel-based vehicle. This is a common pitfall when modeling *is-a* relationships too literally.

Embracing flexibility with LSP

Let's refactor this so that it adheres to LSP. We'll start by defining an abstract base class for power sources:

```python
from abc import ABC, abstractmethod

class PowerSource(ABC):
    def __init__(self, capacity: float):
        self._capacity = capacity
        self._level = capacity

    def level(self) -> float:
        return self._level

    @abstractmethod
    def consume(self, distance: float) -> float:
        pass
```

Now, we can create specific implementations for different types of power source:

```python
class FuelTank(PowerSource):
    def consume(self, distance: float) -> float:
        # Assume 10 km per liter for simplicity:
        fuel_consumed = distance / 10
```

```python
        if self._level - fuel_consumed < 0:
            raise ValueError("Not enough fuel to cover the distance")
        self._level -= fuel_consumed
        return fuel_consumed


class Battery(PowerSource):
    def consume(self, distance: float) -> float:
        # Assume 5 km per kWh for simplicity:
        energy_consumed = distance / 5
        if self._level - energy_consumed < 0:
            raise ValueError("Not enough charge to cover the distance")
        self._level -= energy_consumed
        return energy_consumed
```

With these power sources defined, we can create a more flexible `Vehicle` class:

```python
class Vehicle:
    def __init__(self, power_source: PowerSource):
        self._power_source = power_source


    def power_level(self) -> float:
        return self._power_source.level()


    def drive(self, distance: float) -> float:
        return self._power_source.consume(distance)
```

Finally, we can update our `drive_vehicle` function so that it works with this new design:

```python
def drive_vehicle(vehicle: Vehicle, distance: float) -> None:
    try:
        energy_consumed = vehicle.drive(distance)
        print(f"Energy consumed: {energy_consumed:.2f} units")
    except ValueError as e:
        print(f"Unable to complete journey: {e}")


# Usage
fuel_car = Vehicle(FuelTank(50))  # 50 liter tank
drive_vehicle(fuel_car, 100)  # Prints: Energy consumed: 10.00 units
```

```
electric_car = Vehicle(Battery(50))  # 50 kWh battery
drive_vehicle(electric_car, 100)  # Prints: Energy consumed: 20.00 units
```

This refactored design demonstrates LSP in action. The key change is the introduction of abstraction and separation of concerns. We've decoupled the concept of a power source from the vehicle itself, allowing for different types of power sources to be used interchangeably. This abstraction is achieved through the `PowerSource` base class, which defines a common interface for all types of energy sources.

Let's break down the key components of this new design:

- **The `PowerSource` abstract base class**: This defines a contract with the `level` and `consume` methods that all power sources must fulfill. It establishes a common interface for different types of energy source.

- **Concrete implementations (`FuelTank` and `Battery`)**: These classes inherit from `PowerSource` and provide specific implementations of the `consume` method. Crucially, they maintain the behavioral contract defined by `PowerSource`.

- **The `Vehicle` class**: This class depends on the abstract `PowerSource` base class, not on concrete implementations. This adherence to LSP allows any subclass of `PowerSource` to be used interchangeably without affecting the behavior of `Vehicle`.

- **The `drive_vehicle` function**: This function demonstrates how LSP enables polymorphism. It can work with any `Vehicle` class, regardless of its specific power source, without modification.

LSP's impact on this design is multifaceted. It ensures behavioral consistency, allowing all power sources to be treated uniformly by the `Vehicle` class. This polymorphic flexibility enables functions like `drive_vehicle` to work with any vehicle type without knowing specific implementation details. The design improves extensibility, as new power sources (like hydrogen fuel cells) can be added by implementing the `PowerSource` interface without changing existing code. It also enhances testability by allowing us to create mock power sources for testing `Vehicle` behavior.

By adhering to LSP, we've created a flexible system where core business logic remains protected from changes in specific power source implementations. This separation is a key aspect of Clean Architecture that promotes long-term stability while enabling easy extension. LSP works harmoniously with other SOLID principles: it builds upon SRP by ensuring interfaces have clear purposes, supports OCP by allowing extension without modification, and complements ISP by promoting focused, substitutable interfaces.

This alignment enhances modularity, a cornerstone of Clean Architecture. Components like `FuelTank` and `Battery` can be swapped without affecting the rest of the system, allowing our application to evolve with minimal disruption. Clear interfaces like `PowerSource` make the system easier to understand and navigate, serving as guideposts for developers whether new to the project or returning months later.

In conclusion, LSP guides us in creating hierarchies that are both flexible and reliable. By ensuring derived classes can truly substitute for their base classes, we build more robust, extensible Python applications aligned with Clean Architecture goals. As we move forward to explore DIP, remember how LSP works with the other SOLID principles to form a powerful toolkit for creating enduring applications.

Decoupling for flexibility: inverting dependencies in Python

Upon exploring LSP and its role in creating robust abstractions, we've seen how it contributes to the flexibility and maintainability of our Python code. Now let's turn our attention to the final piece of the SOLID puzzle: the Dependency Inversion Principle (DIP).

DIP serves as a capstone to the SOLID principles, tying together and reinforcing the concepts we explored in the previous principles. It provides a powerful mechanism for structuring the relationships between different components of our system, further enhancing the flexibility and maintainability we've been building throughout our journey through SOLID.

While LSP ensures that our abstractions are well-formed and substitutable, DIP focuses on how these abstractions should relate to one another. It guides us in creating a structure where high-level modules aren't dependent on low-level modules, but both depend on abstractions. This inversion of traditional dependency structures is crucial for implementing Clean Architecture in Python as it allows us to create systems that are truly decoupled and adaptable to change.

As we delve into DIP, we'll see how it provides a practical approach to implementing the Dependency Rule, a cornerstone of Clean Architecture that we introduced in *Chapter 1*. Recall that the Dependency Rule states that source code dependencies should only point inwards, with inner circles containing high-level policies and outer circles containing implementation details. DIP offers a concrete strategy for adhering to this rule, allowing us to structure our code so that high-level modules are independent of low-level modules. Let's explore how we can invert our dependencies to create more flexible, maintainable Python systems that truly embody the principles of Clean Architecture and respect the Dependency Rule.

Understanding DIP

Before we dive into the intricacies of DIP, let's clarify what we mean by *depends on* in the context of software design. Consider this simple code example:

```python
class A:
    def __init__(self):
        self.b = B()
class B:
    def __init__(self):
        pass
```

In this case, we say that A depends on B. This dependency manifests because A knows about B. This is evident in the line that creates an instance of B: `self.b = B()`. However, B knows nothing about A. We typically represent this dependency with an arrow pointing from A to B, as shown in *Figure 2.1*:

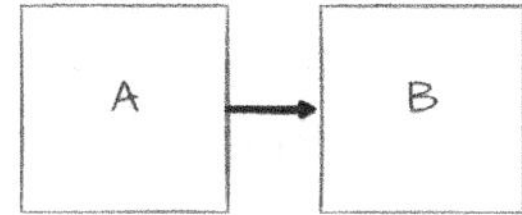

Figure 2.1: A depends on B

This simple example sets the stage for understanding the problem that DIP aims to solve. In many software systems, high-level modules (which contain the core business logic) often depend on low-level modules (which handle specific details or implementations). This can lead to inflexible designs that are difficult to modify and maintain.

To illustrate this, let's consider a more concrete example involving a `UserEntity` class that relies on a low-level detail:

```python
class UserEntity:
    def __init__(self, user_id: str):
        self.user_id = user_id
        # Direct dependency on a low-level module:
        self.database = MySQLDatabase()
    def save(self):
        self.database.insert("users", {"id": self.user_id})
class MySQLDatabase:
    def insert(self, table: str, data: dict):
        print(f"Inserting {data} into {table} table in MySQL")
```

In this example, `UserEntity` directly depends on `MySQLDatabase`, a low-level module. Now, imagine that we receive a feature request to support multiple database systems. With the current design, we'd need to modify `UserEntity` so that it can accommodate this change, violating OCP and potentially introducing bugs into our core business logic. The following are some additional problems with this design:

- The `UserEntity` class is tightly coupled to `MySQLDatabase`, making it difficult to change the database system in the future

- Testing `UserEntity` becomes challenging because we can't easily substitute a mock database for testing purposes

- The core business logic (`UserEntity`) is polluted with infrastructure concerns (database operations)

Fixing the design with DIP

DIP, introduced by Robert C. Martin (`https://en.wikipedia.org/wiki/Dependency_inversion_principle`), proposes a solution to the problems seen in the preceding example. It states the following:

- High-level modules shouldn't depend on low-level modules. Both should depend on abstractions.

- Abstractions shouldn't depend on details. Details should depend on abstractions.

These two points fundamentally change how we structure our code. Instead of having direct dependencies between high-level and low-level modules, we introduce abstractions that both depend on. However, the key insight of DIP lies in what's actually *inverted*:

- Traditionally, low-level modules define abstractions that high-level modules use

- With DIP, high-level modules define abstractions that low-level modules implement

This inversion of abstraction ownership is what gives DIP its name, not a simple reversal of dependency direction between modules. The high-level module now controls the abstraction, while low-level modules conform to it. This shift in control allows high-level modules to remain independent of low-level implementation details, promoting flexibility and maintainability in our system design.

Let's look at how this changes our dependency diagram:

Figure 2.2: A and B depend on an interface

As shown in *Figure 2.2*, the dependencies now point toward the abstraction, inverting the traditional flow. The high-level module (A) and the low-level module (B) both depend on an abstraction (Interface), rather than on each other directly. This change is profound: A no longer *knows of* B; rather, it knows of a contract that a *thing like* B will adhere to.

This shift from concrete knowledge to abstract contract has far-reaching implications:

- **Decoupling and flexibility**: Now, A is decoupled from the specifics of B, only knowing the contract it must fulfill. This allows us to easily swap or upgrade components without affecting the rest of the system, making it more adaptable to future requirements.

- **Improved testability**: We can create mock objects that implement the interface for testing purposes, allowing us to test components in isolation without a complex setup.

- **Clarity and encapsulation**: The interface clearly defines component interactions, making the code more self-documenting. Changes in implementation are contained, reducing ripple effects across the system.

- **Design by contract**: This approach encourages thinking in terms of interfaces rather than concrete implementations, promoting better-designed, more modular systems that are easier to understand and maintain.

By adhering to DIP, we're not just changing the direction of dependencies; we're fundamentally altering how different parts of our system interact. This creates a more loosely coupled, flexible, and maintainable architecture that can better withstand the test of time and changing requirements.

To align our `UserEntity` code with DIP, we need to introduce an abstraction that both the high-level and low-level modules can depend on. This abstraction typically takes the form of an interface. Let's refactor our code so that it adheres to DIP:

```python
from abc import ABC, abstractmethod
class DatabaseInterface(ABC):
    @abstractmethod
```

```python
    def insert(self, table: str, data: dict):
        pass
class UserEntity:
    def __init__(self, user_id: str, database: DatabaseInterface):
        self.user_id = user_id
        self.database = database
    def save(self):
        self.database.insert("users", {"id": self.user_id})
class MySQLDatabase(DatabaseInterface):
    def insert(self, table: str, data: dict):
        print(f"Inserting {data} into {table} table in MySQL")
class PostgreSQLDatabase(DatabaseInterface):
    def insert(self, table: str, data: dict):
        print(f"Inserting {data} into {table} table in PostgreSQL")
# Usage
mysql_db = MySQLDatabase()
user = UserEntity("123", mysql_db)
user.save()
postgres_db = PostgreSQLDatabase()
another_user = UserEntity("456", postgres_db)
another_user.save()
```

In this refactored version, we did the following:

- We introduced an abstraction (`DatabaseInterface`) that both high-level (`UserEntity`) and low-level (`MySQLDatabase`, `PostgreSQLDatabase`) modules depend on.

- The `UserEntity` class no longer creates its database dependency, instead receiving it through its constructor. This technique is known as dependency injection, which is a key practice in implementing DIP.

- We can easily add support for new database systems by creating new classes that implement `DatabaseInterface`.

Figure 2.3 represents the new state of relationships between these components:

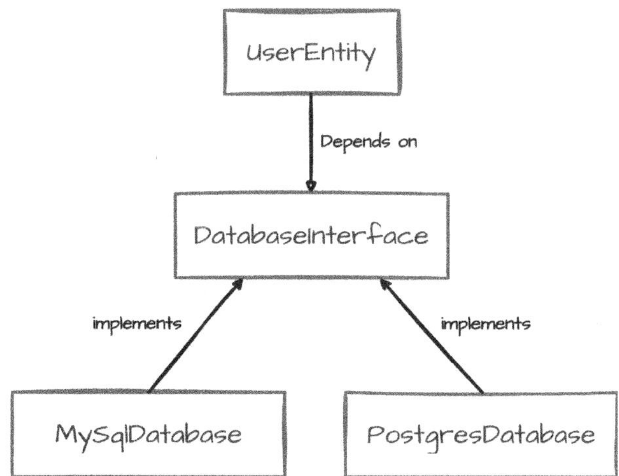

Figure 2.3: UserEntity is decoupled from the concrete storage classes

This diagram's significance lies in several key aspects:

- **Inverted dependency and abstraction as a contract**: The `UserEntity` class depends on the `DatabaseInterface` abstraction, not concrete implementations. This interface serves as a contract for any database implementation.

- **Separation of concerns**: The `UserEntity` class is decoupled from specific database operations, knowing only about the abstract operations defined in `DatabaseInterface`.

- **Extensibility and flexibility**: The design allows us to easily add new database implementations and swap between them without affecting `UserEntity`.

By applying DIP, we've created a flexible, maintainable system where our core business logic (`UserEntity`) is protected from changes in external details (database implementations). This separation is a cornerstone of Clean Architecture that promotes long-term system stability and adaptability. The preceding diagram shows how multiple implementations (`MySQLDatabase` and `PostgreSQLDatabase`) can coexist, demonstrating the power of this abstraction-based approach. We could easily add more implementations, such as `OracleDatabase` or `MongoDBAdapter`, without modifying `UserEntity`, further illustrating the extensibility benefits of DIP.

DIP's effect on testing

As we've seen with other SOLID principles, the use of dependency injection significantly aids in testing. We can now easily create a mock database for testing `UserEntity`:

```python
class MockDatabase(DatabaseInterface):
    def __init__(self):
        self.inserted_data = []
    def insert(self, table: str, data: dict):
        self.inserted_data.append((table, data))
# In a test
mock_db = MockDatabase()
user = UserEntity("test_user", mock_db)
user.save()
assert mock_db.inserted_data == [("users", {"id": "test_user"})]
```

This ability to easily substitute dependencies makes our code much more testable, allowing us to verify the behavior of `UserEntity` in isolation from any actual database implementation.

DIP in the context of SOLID and Clean Architecture

DIP serves as a cornerstone in both SOLID principles and Clean Architecture. It complements other SOLID principles by enabling the separation of interface definitions from implementations and supporting the easy extension of system behavior. In Clean Architecture, DIP is crucial for implementing the Dependency Rule, allowing inner layers to define interfaces that outer layers must adhere to. This inversion separates business logic from implementation details, creating more flexible, maintainable, and testable systems that align perfectly with Clean Architecture goals.

Summary

In this chapter, we explored the SOLID principles and their application in Python to create clean, maintainable, and flexible architectures. We learned how each principle contributes to robust software design:

- SRP for creating focused, cohesive classes

- OCP for extending behavior without modification

- LSP for ensuring well-formed, substitutable abstractions

- ISP for designing targeted, client-specific interfaces

- DIP for structuring dependencies to maximize flexibility

These principles are crucial for developing Python applications that can evolve with changing requirements, resist software entropy, and remain clear as systems grow in complexity. They form the foundation of Clean Architecture, enabling us to create more modular, testable, and adaptable code.

In the next chapter, we'll explore how to leverage Python's type system to further enhance the robustness and clarity of our Clean Architecture designs. You'll see how type hints can strengthen several SOLID principles we've just covered: creating more explicit interfaces for ISP, defining clearer contracts for DIP, and making substitutability more apparent for LSP. These typing capabilities will help us create even more maintainable and self-documenting code while maintaining Python's flexibility.

Further reading

- *SOLID Principles* (`https://realpython.com/solid-principles-python/`). This is a comprehensive tutorial that walks through each SOLID principle with Python-specific examples.

- *Agile Software Development, Principles, Patterns, and Practices* by Robert C. Martin.

- *Python Design Patterns* by Brandon Rhodes (`https://python-patterns.guide/`). While not exclusively about SOLID, this resource covers many design patterns that complement SOLID principles in Python.

- *SOLID: The First Five Principles of Object-Oriented Design* (`https://www.digitalocean.com/community/conceptual-articles/s-o-l-i-d-the-first-five-principles-of-object-oriented-design`). This comprehensive article provides a clear explanation of each SOLID principle with practical code examples. While the examples are in PHP, the concepts are universally applicable and can be easily translated into Python, making it a valuable resource for deepening your understanding of SOLID principles in object-oriented design.

Get this book's PDF version and more

Scan the QR code (or go to packtpub.com/unlock). Search for this book by name, confirm the edition, and then follow the steps on the page.

Note: Keep your invoice handy. Purchases made directly from Packt don't require an invoice.

3

Type-Enhanced Python: Strengthening Clean Architecture

In *Chapter 2* we explored the SOLID principles and their application in Python, establishing a foundation for maintainable and flexible code. Building on this, we now turn to a powerful feature in Python: **type hinting**.

While Python's dynamic typing offers flexibility, it can sometimes lead to unexpected errors in complex projects. Type hinting provides a solution, combining the benefits of dynamic typing with the robustness of static type checking.

This chapter explores how type hinting enhances Clean Architecture implementations, making code more self-documenting and less error-prone. We'll see how type hints support SOLID principles, particularly in creating clear interfaces and reinforcing the Dependency Inversion Principle.

We'll begin with the role of type awareness in Python's dynamic environment, then delve into practical aspects of Python's typing system. Finally, we'll explore automated static type-checking tools for early issue detection.

By the chapter's end, you'll understand how to effectively use type hints in Python projects, writing code that's more robust, maintainable, and aligned with Clean Architecture principles. This knowledge will be crucial as we progress to building complex, scalable systems in later chapters.

In this chapter, we're going to cover the following main topics:

- Understanding type awareness in Python's dynamic environment
- Leveraging Python's typing system
- Leveraging automated static type-checking tools

Let's begin our exploration of Python type hinting and its role in strengthening Clean Architecture implementations.

Technical requirements

The code examples presented in this chapter and throughout the rest of the book are tested with Python 3.13. All examples can be found in the book's accompanying GitHub repository at `https://github.com/PacktPublishing/Clean-Architecture-with-Python`. This chapter does refer to **Visual Studio Code (VS Code)**. VS Code can be downloaded from `https://code.visualstudio.com/download`.

Understanding type awareness in Python's dynamic environment

To fully appreciate Python's type system, it's important to distinguish between dynamically typed languages like Python and statically typed languages like Java or C++. In statically typed languages, variables have a fixed type that's determined at compile time. Python, as a dynamically typed language, allows variables to change types during runtime, offering great flexibility but also introducing potential challenges. This dynamic typing is both a blessing and a challenge when implementing Clean Architecture. While it offers flexibility and rapid development, it can also lead to unclear interfaces and hidden dependencies, issues that Clean Architecture aims to address. In this section, we'll explore how type awareness can enhance our Clean Architecture implementations without sacrificing Python's dynamic nature.

Evolution of typing in Python

Python's approach to typing has evolved significantly over time. While originally a purely dynamically typed language, Python introduced optional static typing with the addition of type hinting syntax in Python 3.5 (2015) via PEP 484. This introduction was motivated by the growing complexity of Python applications, particularly in large-scale projects where Clean Architecture principles are most beneficial.

This standardization of type hints through PEP 484 marked a significant milestone in Python's evolution, providing a unified approach to adding type information to Python code. It paved the way for the broader adoption of static type checking in the Python ecosystem and the development of various tools and IDEs that leverage this type hinting information.

Python's approach to type hinting is part of a broader trend in dynamic languages. JavaScript, for instance, has seen the rise of TypeScript, a typed superset of JavaScript that compiles to plain JavaScript. While both Python and TypeScript aim to bring the benefits of static typing to dynamic languages, their approaches differ:

- **Integration**: Python's type hints are built into the language itself, whereas TypeScript is a separate language that compiles to JavaScript
- **Optionality**: Python's type hints are entirely optional and can be gradually adopted, while TypeScript enforces type-checking more strictly

The success of TypeScript in the JavaScript ecosystem further validates the value of adding type information to dynamic languages. Both Python's type hints and TypeScript demonstrate how combining the flexibility of dynamic typing with the robustness of static typing can lead to more maintainable and scalable codebases.

The evolution of type hinting in Python was driven by several important factors. It significantly improves code readability and serves as a form of self-documentation, making it easier for developers to understand the intended use of variables and functions. This enhanced clarity is particularly valuable in maintaining Clean Architecture's separation of concerns. Type hints also enable better **integrated development environment (IDE)** and tool support, facilitating more accurate code completion and error detection. This improved tooling support is crucial when working with complex architectures, helping developers navigate between different layers and components more efficiently.

Furthermore, type hinting makes refactoring and maintaining large codebases considerably easier. In the context of Clean Architecture, where we strive to create systems that are adaptable to change, this benefit is particularly significant.

Type hints act as a safety net during large-scale refactoring efforts, helping to ensure that changes in one part of the system don't inadvertently break interfaces or expectations in another part.

Perhaps most importantly for our Clean Architecture implementations, type hints allow us to catch certain types of errors earlier in the development process. By making our intentions explicit through type annotations, we can identify potential issues at design time or during static analysis, rather than encountering them at runtime. This early error detection aligns perfectly with Clean Architecture's goal of creating robust, maintainable systems.

As we delve deeper into the specifics of type hinting in the following sections, keep in mind that these features are tools to enhance our Python implementations of Clean Architecture. They offer a way to make our architectural boundaries more explicit and our code more self-documenting, all while retaining the flexibility and expressiveness that make Python such a powerful language for software development.

Dynamic typing versus type hinting

To understand the significance of type hints in Python, it's crucial to distinguish between Python's fundamental dynamic typing and the role of type hints. These two concepts serve different purposes and operate at different stages of the development process.

Dynamic typing

In a dynamically typed language such as Python, variables can hold values of any type, and these types can change during runtime. This flexibility is a core feature of Python. Let's look at an example:

```python
x = 5          # x is an integer
x = "hello"    # Now x is a string
```

This flexibility allows for rapid development and expressive code but can lead to runtime errors if not managed carefully. Consider the following example:

```python
def add_numbers(a, b):
    return a + b


# Works fine, result is 8:
result = add_numbers(5, 3)
# Raises TypeError: unsupported operand type(s) for +: 'int' and 'str':
result = add_numbers(5, "3")
```

In this case, the `add_numbers` function works as expected when given two integers, but raises a `TypeError` when given an integer and a string. This error only occurs at runtime, which can be problematic if it's in a critical part of your application or if it's not caught by your testing process.

Type hinting

Type hints allow developers to annotate variables and function parameters in addition to re-turning values with their expected types. Regarding type hints, let's revisit our simple function to add numbers:

```python
def add_numbers(a: int, b: int) -> int:
    return a + b


# Works fine, result is 8:
result = add_numbers(5, 3)
# IDE or type checker would flag this as an error:
result = add_numbers(5, "3")
```

Let's break down the type hinting syntax used in this function:

- `a: int` and `b: int`: These annotations indicate that both a and b are expected to be integers. The colon (`:`) is used to separate the parameter name from its type.
- `-> int`: This arrow notation after the function's parameter list specifies the return type. In this case, it indicates that add_numbers is expected to return an integer.

These type annotations provide clear information about the function's expected inputs and output, making the code more self-documenting and easier to understand.

Key points about type hints include the following:

- They don't affect Python's runtime behavior. Python remains dynamically typed.
- They serve as documentation, making code intentions clearer.
- They enable static analysis tools to catch potential type-related errors before runtime.
- They improve IDE support for code completion and refactoring.

Type hints unlock the power of static analysis tools to catch potential errors before runtime. While Python itself provides the syntax for type hints, it doesn't enforce them at runtime. The Python interpreter treats type hints as decorative metadata. It's third-party tools such as *mypy* or *pyright* that perform the actual static type checking. These tools analyze your code without executing it, using the type hints to infer and check types across your entire codebase. They can be run as standalone commands, integrated into IDEs for real-time feedback, or incorporated into continuous integration pipelines, allowing for type-checking at various stages of development.

In the *Leveraging automated static type checking tools* section of this chapter, we'll dive deeper into how to use these tools, to perform static type checking across your entire codebase at key points in the developer workflow.

Type awareness in Clean Architecture

The introduction of type hints is particularly relevant to Clean Architecture. In the previous chapter, we discussed the importance of clear interfaces and dependency inversion. Type hints can play a crucial role in achieving these goals, making our architectural boundaries more explicit and easier to maintain.

Consider how type hints can enhance the Shape example we introduced in *Chapter 2*, here with a more complete utilization of type hints:

```python
from abc import ABC, abstractmethod
import math


class Shape(ABC):
    @abstractmethod
    def area(self) -> float:
        pass


class Rectangle(Shape):
    def __init__(self, width: float, height: float) -> None:
        self.width = width
        self.height = height

    def area(self) -> float:
        return self.width * self.height


class Circle(Shape):
    def __init__(self, radius: float) -> None:
        self.radius = radius

    def area(self) -> float:
        return math.pi * self.radius ** 2


class AreaCalculator:
```

```python
def calculate_area(self, shape: Shape) -> float:
    return shape.area()
```

Let's take a closer look at this example:

- The area method in the Shape class is annotated to return a float, clearly communicating the expected return type for all shape implementations.
- The Rectangle and Circle classes specify that their constructors expect float parameters and return None. This -> None annotation explicitly indicates that constructors don't return a value, which is implicit in Python but made clear through type hinting.
- The concrete area methods in Rectangle and Circle are annotated to return float, adhering to the contract defined in the Shape abstract base class.
- The AreaCalculator class explicitly states that its calculate_area method expects a Shape object as an argument and returns a float.

These type hints make the interfaces more explicit, helping to maintain Clean Architecture's boundaries between components. It's important to note that these type hints don't enforce anything at runtime. Rather, they serve as documentation and enable static analysis tools to catch potential type errors before execution.

They provide several benefits in a Clean Architecture context:

- **Clear interfaces**: Type hints make the contracts between different layers of your architecture explicit. In our example, it's clear that any Shape must have an area method that returns a float.
- **Dependency inversion**: They help enforce the Dependency Rule by clearly defining the abstract interfaces that higher-level modules depend on. The AreaCalculator depends on the abstract Shape, not on concrete implementations.
- **Testability**: Type hints make it easier to create and use mock objects that conform to expected interfaces. For testing, we could easily create a mock Shape that adheres to the documented interface requirements.
- **Maintainability**: As your project grows, type hints serve as living documentation, making it easier for developers to understand and modify the code. They provide immediate insight into the expected types of method parameters and return values

By leveraging type hints in this way, we create a more robust implementation of Clean Architecture. The explicitly documented interfaces and clear dependencies make our code more self-documenting and help catch type-related issues early through static analysis. As we build more complex systems, these benefits compound, resulting in a codebase that's easier to understand, modify, and extend. In the next section, we'll explore some challenges and considerations to keep in mind when integrating type hints into your Clean Architecture designs.

Challenges and considerations

When leveraging type hints in your Python projects, it's important to be aware of several key considerations:

- They don't replace the need for proper testing and error handling
- There's a learning curve for developers new to static typing concepts
- Planned incorporation into your team's development workflow and **continuous integration, continuous deployment (CI/CD)** pipeline is essential for successful adoption

As we delve deeper into Python's typing system in the following sections and the remainder of the book, we'll explore how to leverage these features to create more robust, maintainable, and self-documenting Clean Architecture implementations. We'll see how type awareness can help us create clearer boundaries between architectural layers, make our dependencies more explicit, and catch potential issues earlier in the development process.

Remember, the goal is not to turn Python into a statically typed language but to use type awareness as a tool to enhance our Clean Architecture designs. By the end of this chapter, you'll have a solid understanding of how to balance Python's dynamic nature with the benefits of type awareness in your Clean Architecture implementations.

Leveraging Python's typing system

In the realm of Clean Architecture, the role of a robust type system extends far beyond simple error prevention. It serves as a powerful tool for expressing and enforcing architectural boundaries, supporting key principles such as abstraction, polymorphism, and dependency inversion. Python's typing system, when leveraged effectively, becomes an invaluable asset in implementing these crucial concepts.

As we start to consider more advanced features of Python's typing system, we'll see how they can significantly enhance our Clean Architecture implementations. These features allow us to create more expressive and precise interfaces between different layers of our application, leading to code that is not only more robust but also more self-documenting and maintainable.

In this section, we'll explore a range of typing features, from type aliases and union types to literal and `TypedDict` types. We'll then see how these can be applied to support SOLID principles in our Clean Architecture designs. By the end of this section, you'll have a comprehensive understanding of how to use Python's type system to create cleaner, more maintainable architectural boundaries.

We'll start with a review of basic type hinting, then delve into more advanced features, and finally see how these features support SOLID principles in the context of Clean Architecture.

Basic type hinting: from simple types to containers

We've already seen how to use basic type hints for simple types. Let's quickly recap the syntax:

- For integers: `count: int`

- For floating-point numbers: `price: float`

- For strings: `name: str`

- For booleans: `is_active: bool`

- For function annotations: follow the `def function_name(parameter: type) -> return_type: pattern`

Now, let's look at how we can use type hints with container types such as lists and dictionaries:

```python
def process_order(items: list[str],
                  quantities: list[int]) -> dict[str, int]:
    return {item: quantity for item,
            quantity in zip(items, quantities)}


# Usage
order = process_order(['apple', 'banana', 'orange'], [2, 3, 1])
print(order)
# Output: {'apple': 2, 'banana': 3, 'orange': 1}
```

Let's take a closer look at this example.

- `list[str]` indicates that items should be a list of strings

- `list[int]` specifies that quantities should be a list of integers

- `-> dict[str, int]` tells us that the function returns a dictionary with string keys and integer values

These type hints provide clear information about the expected structure of the input and output data, which is particularly valuable in Clean Architecture, where we often deal with complex data structures passing between different layers of the application.

Why do I sometimes see `list` and other times `List` in Python code?

You might notice that some Python code uses `list` (lowercase) while other code uses `List` (capitalized) for type annotations. This is because support for built-in generic types was introduced in Python 3.9. Before that, you needed to import the `List` stand-in type from the typing package. For code in Python 3.9+, you can simply use built-in collection names such as `list` and `dict`.

In Clean Architecture, such type hints are especially useful when defining interfaces between different layers of the application. They provide a clear contract for data passing between the Domain layer, use cases, and external interfaces, helping to maintain clean boundaries and reduce the risk of data inconsistencies.

As we move forward, we'll see how more advanced typing features can further enhance our ability to express complex relationships and constraints, supporting robust Clean Architecture implementations in Python.

Sequence: flexibility in collection types

The **Sequence** type hint from the typing module is a powerful tool for expressing collections in a way that aligns well with the SOLID principles, particularly the Liskov Substitution Principle and the Open–Closed Principle.

Here's an example demonstrating its use:

```python
from typing import Sequence


def calculate_total(items: Sequence[float]) -> float:
    return sum(items)


# Usage
print(calculate_total([1.0, 2.0, 3.0]))  # Works with list
print(calculate_total((4.0, 5.0, 6.0)))  # Also works with tuple
```

Using Sequence instead of a specific type such as List or Tuple offers several advantages:

- **Liskov Substitution Principle**: Sequence allows the function to work with any sequence type (lists, tuples, and custom sequence classes) without breaking the contract

- **Open–Closed Principle**: The calculate_total function is open for extension (it can work with new sequence types) but closed for modification (we don't need to change the function to support new types)

- **Interface Segregation Principle**: By using Sequence, we're only requiring the minimal interface needed (iteration over elements), rather than committing to a specific collection type with potentially unnecessary methods

In Clean Architecture, the Sequence type hint proves valuable across various layers. In the Use Case layer, it facilitates processing collections of entities or value objects. In the Interface Adapters layer, it enables flexible APIs that work with various collection types. In the Domain layer, Sequence expresses the need for a collection without specifying its implementation, maintaining separation of concerns. This versatility makes Sequence a powerful tool for creating adaptable and maintainable Clean Architecture implementations in Python.

Union and Optional types

In Clean Architecture, we often need to handle multiple possible types or optional values, especially at the boundaries between layers. **Union types** and **Optional types** are perfect for these scenarios:

```python
from typing import Union, Optional


def process_input(data: Union[str, int]) -> str:
    return str(data)


def find_user(user_id: Optional[int] = None) -> Optional[str]:
    if user_id is None:
        return None
    # ... logic to find user ...
    return "User found"


# Usage
result1 = process_input("Hello")  # Works with str
result2 = process_input(42)       # Works with int
user = find_user()                # Optional parameter
```

Union types allow a value to be one of several types, while `Optional` is a shorthand for `Union[Some_Type, None]`. These constructs are particularly useful in Clean Architecture for creating flexible interfaces between layers while maintaining type safety.

It should be noted that in Python 3.10+, the union syntax was simplified to a concise literal use of the pipe character (`|`):

```python
def process_input(data: Union[str, int]) -> str:
```

The preceding line would be simplified to the following:

```python
def process_input(data: str | int) -> str:
```

Literal types

Literal types allow us to specify exact values that a variable can take. This is especially useful in Clean Architecture for enforcing specific values at interface boundaries:

```python
from typing import Literal


LogLevel = Literal["DEBUG", "INFO", "WARNING", "ERROR"]


def set_log_level(level: LogLevel) -> None:
    print(f"Setting log level to {level}")


# Usage
set_log_level("DEBUG")  # Valid
set_log_level("CRITICAL")  # Type checker would flag this as an error
```

Literal types help in creating more precise interfaces, reducing the chance of invalid data propagating through the system. This aligns well with Clean Architecture's emphasis on clear boundaries and contracts between layers.

Type aliases

Type aliases help in simplifying complex type annotations, making our code more readable and maintainable. This is particularly useful in Clean Architecture when dealing with complex domain models or data transfer objects.

Consider the following example:

```python
# Type aliases
UserDict = dict[str, str]
```

```python
UserList = list[UserDict]


def process_users(users: UserList) -> None:
    for user in users:
        print(f"Processing user: {user['name']}")


# Usage
users: UserList = [{"name": "Alice"}, {"name": "Bob"}]
process_users(users)
```

Let's take a closer look at this code:

- UserDict is a type alias for dict[str, str], representing a user object with string keys and values
- UserList is a type alias for list[UserDict], representing a list of user dictionaries

Type aliases provide more readable names for complex types, improving code clarity without creating new types. They enable us to write code that is both expressive and aligned with the principles of Clean Architecture, promoting separation of concerns, maintainability, and clarity.

NewType

NewType creates distinct types, providing additional type safety. This is valuable in Clean Architecture for defining clear domain concepts:

```python
from typing import NewType


UserId = NewType('UserId', int)
ProductId = NewType('ProductId', int)


def process_order(user_id: UserId,
                  product id: ProductId) -> None:
    print(f"Processing order for User {user_id} and Product {product_id}")


# Usage
user_id = UserId(1)
product_id = ProductId(1)  # Same underlying int, but distinct type


process_order(user_id, product_id)
```

```python
# This would raise a type error:
# process_order(product_id, user_id)
```

NewType creates distinct types that are recognized by static type checkers, preventing accidental mixing of similar but conceptually different values. This helps catch potential errors early in the development process and enhances the overall type safety of your Clean Architecture implementation.

Both type aliases and NewType align well with Clean Architecture principles by improving code readability, ensuring type safety across layer boundaries, and clearly defining domain concepts. This leads to more expressive, type-safe, and maintainable Clean Architecture implementations in Python.

The Any type

The **Any type** is a special type hint that essentially tells the type checker to allow any type. It's used when you want to indicate that a variable can be of any type, or when you're dealing with code where the type is genuinely not known or could vary widely. We can see its use in this general logging example:

```python
from typing import Any


def log_data(data: Any) -> None:
    print(f"Logged: {data}")


# Usage
log_data("A string")
log_data(42)
log_data({"key": "value"})
```

In Clean Architecture, we generally aim to be as specific as possible about types, especially at layer boundaries. The Any type should be seen as a last resort, often indicating a need for refactoring or a more specific type definition. It's most appropriate when interfacing with external systems where the type is truly unknown or highly variable. Within your own code, see the use of Any as a signal to refactor the code to the use of specific types versus the use of the catch-all Any type.

These advanced typing features provide powerful tools for implementing Clean Architecture in Python. They allow us to create more expressive, precise, and self-documenting interfaces between different layers of our application. As we move forward, we'll explore how these features can be applied to support SOLID principles in our Clean Architecture designs.

Leveraging automated static type-checking tools

As we've explored Python's typing system and its benefits for Clean Architecture, it's crucial to understand how to effectively apply these type hints in practice. Python, being a dynamically typed language, doesn't enforce type-checking at runtime. This is where automated static type-checking tools come into play, bridging the gap between Python's dynamic nature and the benefits of static typing. This approach offers several key benefits:

- **Early error detection**: Catch type-related issues before runtime, reducing the likelihood of bugs in production

- **Improved code quality**: Enforce consistent use of types across your project, leading to more robust and self-documenting code

- **Enhanced refactoring**: Make large-scale code changes with more confidence, as the type checker can identify many of the places that need to be updated

- **Better IDE support**: Enable more accurate code completion, navigation, and refactoring tools in your development environment

These benefits are particularly valuable in Clean Architecture implementations, where maintaining clear boundaries between layers and ensuring the correctness of data flow is paramount.

In this section, we'll focus on how to leverage these automated tools to enforce type consistency, catch errors early, and improve the overall development experience. We'll use mypy's command line interface (CLI) but then use another tool as an extension to the VS Code IDE.

The mypy CLI

Mypy is a powerful static type checker that can be run directly from the command line. This makes it easy to integrate into your development workflow and deployment pipelines. Let's walk through how to use mypy and interpret its output.

First, you'll need to install mypy. Since it's a Python module, you can easily install it using pip:

```
$ pip install mypy
```

Once installed, you can use mypy to check your Python files for type errors. Let's look at a simple example. Assume you have a Python file named user_service.py with the following content:

```python
def get_user(user_id: int) -> dict:
    # Simulating user retrieval
    return {"id": user_id,
            "name": "John Doe",
```

```python
                "email": "john@example.com"}

def send_email(user: dict, subject: str) -> None:
    print(f"Sending email to {user['email']} with subject: {subject}")


# Usage
user = get_user("123")
send_email(user, "Welcome!")
```

To check this file with mypy, run the following:

```
$ mypy user_service.py
user_service.py:9: error: Argument 1 to "get_user" has incompatible type
"str"; expected "int"  [arg-type]
Found 1 error in 1 file (checked 1 source file)
```

Let's break down what mypy is telling us:

- It identifies the file (user_service.py) and the line number (9) where the error occurs

- It describes the error: we're passing a string ("123") to get_user, but the function expects an integer

- It categorizes the error as an [arg-type] issue, indicating a problem with argument types

This output is incredibly valuable. It catches a type mismatch that could lead to runtime errors, allowing us to fix it before the code is even executed.

We can correct the error by changing user = get_user("123") to user = get_user(123) and then rerun mypy:

```
$ mypy user_service.py
Success: no issues found in 1 source file
```

Now, mypy reports no issues, confirming that our type annotations are consistent with how we're using the functions.

Configuring mypy

While mypy works well out of the box, you can customize its behavior using a configuration file. This is particularly useful for large projects or when you want to gradually adopt type checking.

Create a file named `mypy.ini` in your project root:

```ini
[mypy]
ignore_missing_imports = True
strict_optional = True
warn_redundant_casts = True
warn_unused_ignores = True
warn_return_any = True
warn_unreachable = True
```

This configuration does the following:

- Ignores missing imports, which is useful when working with third-party libraries without type stubs
- Enables strict checking of `Optional` types
- Warns about redundant type casts and unused `type: ignore` comments
- Warns when a function returns Any implicitly
- Alerts you to unreachable code

With this configuration, mypy will provide more comprehensive checking, helping you catch a wider range of potential issues in your Clean Architecture implementation.

By regularly running mypy as part of your development process, you can catch type-related issues early, ensuring that your Clean Architecture layers interact correctly and maintain their intended boundaries.

The configuration options for mypy are vast and can be tailored to fit the needs of your specific project. For a complete list of available options and their descriptions, refer to the official mypy documentation at `https://mypy.readthedocs.io/en/stable/config_file.html`.

Mypy in deployment pipelines

Integrating mypy into your deployment pipeline is a crucial step in ensuring type consistency across your project, especially in a Clean Architecture context where maintaining clear boundaries between layers is paramount.

While the specific implementation details may vary depending on your chosen CI/CD tool, the fundamental concept remains the same: run mypy as part of your automated checks before deploying your code. Given that mypy operates via a straightforward CLI, incorporating it into most deployment pipelines is relatively straightforward.

For instance, you might run mypy checks in the following instances:

- After each commit push
- As part of pull request validation
- Before merging into the main branch
- Prior to deploying to staging or production environments

This approach helps catch type-related issues early in the development process, reducing the likelihood of type errors making their way into production.

As an example, here's a simple GitHub Actions workflow that runs mypy followed by unit tests:

```yaml
name: Python Type Check and Test

on: [push, pull_request]

jobs:
  build:
    runs-on: ubuntu-latest
    steps:
    - uses: actions/checkout@v2
    - name: Set up Python
      uses: actions/setup-python@v2
      with:
        python-version: '3.13'
    - name: Install dependencies
      run: |
        python -m pip install --upgrade pip
        pip install mypy pytest
    - name: Run mypy
      run: mypy .
    - name: Run tests
      run: pytest
```

This workflow does the following:

- Triggers on push or pull request events
- Sets up a Python environment
- Installs necessary dependencies (including mypy and pytest)

- Runs mypy on the entire project
- Runs the project's unit tests

By including mypy in your deployment pipeline, you ensure that all code changes are type-checked before they're integrated, helping maintain the integrity of your Clean Architecture implementation.

Remember, while this example uses GitHub Actions, the principle applies to any CI/CD tool. The key is to run mypy as part of your automated checks, leveraging its CLI to integrate smoothly into your existing deployment processes.

Leveraging type hints in IDEs for improved development experience

While having a deployment pipeline with type checking is essential for maintaining code quality, the most effective approach involves catching type issues in real time as the code is being written. This immediate feedback allows developers to address type inconsistencies instantly, reducing the time and effort spent on fixing issues later in the development process.

Modern IDEs have embraced this approach, leveraging type hints to provide an enhanced coding experience with immediate type-checking feedback. While this functionality is available in most popular Python IDEs, we'll focus on VS Code as our primary example due to its widespread use and robust Python support.

In VS Code, the **Pylance** extension has become the preferred tool for Python type checking. Pylance, which uses `pyright` as its type-checking engine, integrates seamlessly into VS Code, offering real-time type-checking along with other advanced features that significantly improve the Python development experience.

With Pylance installed in VS Code, developers receive instant visual cues regarding any type issues:

```python
1   def get_user(user_id: int) -> dict:
2       # Simulating user retrieval
3       return {"id": user_id, "name": "John Doe", "email": "john@example.com"}
4
5   def send_email(user: dict, subject: str) -> None:
6       print(f"Sending email to {user['email']} with subject: {subject}")
7
8   # Usage
9   user = get_user("123")  # Type error: "123" is a string, not an int
```

```
⊗ main.py 1 of 1 problem                                                    ↓ ↑ ×

Argument of type "Literal['123']" cannot be assigned to parameter "user_id" of type "int" in function "get_user"
    "Literal['123']" is not assignable to "int" Pylance(reportArgumentType)
```

```python
10   send_email(user, "Welcome!")
```

Figure 3.1: VS Code with the Pylance extension installed

In *Figure 3.1*, we see that the use of a string where an integer is expected is decorated in the IDE editor with a precise explanation of what the issue is.

This real-time feedback creates a powerful synergy with the type hints we've incorporated into our Clean Architecture implementation. It allows developers to maintain strict type consistency across architectural boundaries as they code, rather than relying solely on post-development checks.

You can install the Pylance extension from the VS Code marketplace (`https://marketplace.visualstudio.com/items?itemName=ms-python.vscode-pylance`), in addition to reading more about its features and configuration.

Additional type-checking features

While real-time feedback and deployment pipeline checks are crucial, there are additional features that can enhance your type-checking workflow.

The Problems tab in VS Code

VS Code offers a **Problems** tab that aggregates all issues in your code, including type errors detected by Pylance. This tab provides a comprehensive overview of type inconsistencies across your project.

```
user_service.py > ...
 8    # Usage
 9    user = get_user("123")  # Type error: "123" is a string, not an int
10    send_email(user, "Welcome!")
```

```
PROBLEMS  1    OUTPUT  ···        Filter (e.g. text, **/*.ts, !**/node_modules/**)

∨  user_service.py  1
      ⊗ Argument of type "Literal['123']" cannot be assigned to parameter "us...  Pylance(reportArgumentType) [Ln 9, Col 17]  ∧
        "Literal['123']" is not assignable to "int"
```

Figure 3.2: VS Code Problems tab

In *Figure 3.2*, we see the aggregation of the types checks we saw inline earlier. Developers can use this tab as a final check before committing code, ensuring no type issues are overlooked.

Git pre-commit hooks

Git supports pre-commit hooks, allowing you to run checks automatically before each commit. You can configure these hooks to run mypy and unit tests, preventing commits that introduce type errors or break existing functionality.

For more information on setting up Git hooks, refer to the official Git documentation: `https://git-scm.com/book/en/v2/Customizing-Git-Git-Hooks`

By incorporating these additional features into your workflow, you create multiple layers of type-checking in your development process. This comprehensive approach helps maintain the integrity of your Clean Architecture implementation, catching type inconsistencies at every stage from writing code to committing changes.

Gradual adoption strategy

Introducing static type checking in Python projects can sometimes face resistance, particularly from developers accustomed to Python's dynamic nature. To ensure a smooth transition, it's crucial to work collaboratively with your team, clearly communicating the rationale and benefits of type hinting.

Here's a strategy for gradual adoption:

1. Conduct a team meeting to discuss and formulate a plan for incorporating type checking.
2. Implement a policy requiring type hints for all new code.
3. Minimize initial disruption by configuring mypy to ignore specific modules or packages. This can be done in the mypy configuration file:

    ```
    [mypy.unwanted_module]
    ignore_errors = True
    [mypy.some_package.*]
    ignore_errors = True
    ```

4. Create scheduled maintenance tasks to progressively add type hints to existing code, prioritizing critical paths.

By employing these tools and strategies, you can substantially improve the robustness and maintainability of your Clean Architecture implementations. The most effective approach combines checks at various stages: real-time feedback in the IDE, pre-commit hooks, and validation in the deployment pipeline. This multi-layered strategy ensures early error detection, enhances code navigation, and maintains consistent type checking throughout the development life cycle. Ultimately, this comprehensive approach leads to more reliable, maintainable, and scalable Python applications, fully leveraging the power of Python's type system in your Clean Architecture projects.

Summary

In this chapter, we explored type awareness in Python's dynamic environment and its role in strengthening Clean Architecture implementations. We learned how to leverage Python's typing system and type hints to create more robust, self-documenting code and discovered the value of automated static type-checking tools in catching errors early.

You gained skills in implementing type hints in functions, classes, and variables, improving code clarity and reliability. You also learned how to set up and use static type-checking tools such as mypy to verify type consistency in your projects. These skills are fundamental to creating maintainable and scalable Clean Architecture implementations in Python, enhancing code quality and alignment with Clean Architecture principles.

In the next chapter, *Domain-Driven Design: Crafting the Core Business Logic*, we'll build upon type-enhanced Python and the SOLID principles from *Chapter 2*. We'll explore the Domain layer of Clean Architecture, learning how to model and implement core business logic that's independent of external concerns. Using a personal task management application as an example, we'll apply type awareness techniques and SOLID principles to create a robust, well-structured domain model, setting the stage for a truly clean and maintainable architecture.

Further reading

- *Python Type Checking (Guide)* (`https://realpython.com/python-type-checking/`)
- *Type Hints Cheat Sheet* (`https://mypy.readthedocs.io/en/stable/cheat_sheet_py3.html`)
- *Continuous Integration with Python: An Introduction* (`https://realpython.com/python-continuous-integration/`)

Part 2

Implementing Clean Architecture in Python

In this part, we move from theoretical understanding to practical implementation, exploring the core layers of Clean Architecture and how they work together in a complete system. You'll learn how to craft domain models that encapsulate business logic, implement application use cases that orchestrate domain operations, create interface adapters that translate between layers, integrate with external frameworks, and build comprehensive testing strategies. Through our task management system example, you'll see how these components form a cohesive, maintainable architecture.

This part of the book includes the following chapters:

- *Chapter 4, Domain-Driven Design: Crafting the Core Business Logic*
- *Chapter 5, The Application Layer: Orchestrating Use Cases*
- *Chapter 6, The Interface Adapters Layer: Controllers and Presenters*
- *Chapter 7, The Frameworks and Drivers Layer: External Interfaces*
- *Chapter 8, Implementing Test Patterns with Clean Architecture*

4

Domain-Driven Design: Crafting the Core Business Logic

In the previous chapters, we laid the groundwork for understanding Clean Architecture and its principles. We explored the SOLID principles that guide robust software design and learned how to leverage Python's type system to create more maintainable code. Now, we turn our attention to the innermost layer of Clean Architecture: the **Entity layer**, also commonly known as the **Domain layer**.

The Entity layer represents the core of our application, encapsulating the essential business concepts and rules. This layer is independent of external concerns and forms the foundation upon which the rest of our Clean Architecture is built. By focusing on this core, we ensure that our application remains true to its fundamental purpose, regardless of the technologies or frameworks used in outer layers.

In this chapter, we'll dive deep into the implementation of the Entity layer, using **Domain-Driven Design (DDD) principles**. We'll use a personal task management application as our ongoing example, demonstrating how to model and implement core business concepts in Python. You'll learn how to identify and model domain entities, maintain a clear separation of concerns, and create a robust foundation for our Clean Architecture implementation. By the end, you'll understand how to create entities that embody core concepts and business rules, setting the stage for the layers that will build upon this solid core.

In this chapter, we'll cover the following main topics:

- Identifying and modeling core entities using DDD principles
- Implementing entities in Python
- Advanced domain concepts
- Ensuring the independence of the Entity layer

Technical requirements

The code examples presented in this chapter and throughout the rest of the book are tested with Python 3.13. All examples can be found in the book's accompanying GitHub repository at `https://github.com/PacktPublishing/Clean-Architecture-with-Python`.

Identifying and modeling the Domain layer using DDD

In *Chapter 1*, we emphasized the critical importance of the Entity layer in Clean Architecture. This layer forms the heart of your software, encapsulating the core business logic and rules. DDD provides a systematic approach to effectively model this crucial component.

DDD offers tools and techniques to identify, model, and implement the essential components of our Entity layer, bridging the gap between business realities and software design. By applying DDD principles within our Clean Architecture framework, we create a domain model that not only accurately reflects business needs but also serves as a solid foundation for a flexible, maintainable software system.

Key benefits of integrating DDD with Clean Architecture include the following:

- Alignment with business needs
- Improved communication between developers and domain experts
- Enhanced flexibility and maintainability
- Natural scalability through clear boundaries and interfaces

Throughout this chapter, we'll use a personal task management system as our running example to illustrate these concepts. This practical example will help us ground the abstract concepts of DDD in a relatable, real-world scenario.

Understanding DDD

Having established the importance of the Domain layer in Clean Architecture, we now turn to DDD's specific techniques for implementing this layer effectively. Introduced by Eric Evans in 2003 (`https://en.wikipedia.org/wiki/Domain-driven_design`), DDD provides concrete practices that help us translate business requirements into robust domain models.

While Clean Architecture tells us that domain entities should be at our system's core, DDD provides the how: specific modeling techniques like **entities**, **value objects**, and **domain services** that we'll explore in this chapter. These practices help us create domain models that not only enforce business rules but also communicate their intent clearly through code. Where Clean Architecture provides the structural blueprint for organizing code layers, DDD offers the tactical patterns for implementing that core business logic effectively.

At its core, DDD emphasizes a close collaboration between technical and domain experts. This collaboration aims to:

1. Develop a shared understanding of the domain

2. Create a model that accurately represents the domain's complexities

3. Implement this model in code, preserving its integrity and expressiveness

By adopting DDD principles in our Clean Architecture approach, we gain several key benefits:

- **Alignment with business needs**: Our software becomes a true reflection of the business domain, making it more valuable and easier to adapt as business needs evolve

- **Improved communication**: DDD establishes a common language between developers and domain experts, reducing misunderstandings and improving overall project cohesion

- **Flexibility and maintainability**: A well-designed domain model is inherently more flexible and easier to maintain, as it's built around core business concepts rather than technical constraints

- **Scalability**: DDD's focus on bounded contexts (covered in the *Core concepts of domain modeling* section) and clear interfaces between different parts of the system naturally leads to more scalable architectures

By integrating DDD principles with Clean Architecture, we forge a powerful methodology for developing software that aligns closely with business needs while maintaining technical flexibility. DDD provides the tools and techniques to effectively model the core of our system—the Entity layer—which is central in Clean Architecture and independent of external concerns. This synergy ensures that our Domain layer truly encapsulates essential business concepts and rules, supporting the creation of systems that are flexible, maintainable, and resilient to technological changes. As we delve into DDD concepts and apply them to our task management system, we'll begin with the crucial step of analyzing our business requirements.

Analyzing business requirements

The first step in applying DDD principles is to thoroughly analyze the business requirements. This process involves more than just listing features; it requires a deep dive into the core concepts, workflows, and rules that govern the domain.

For our task management system, we need to consider questions such as the following:

- What defines a task's uniqueness?
- How does the priority of a task affect its behavior in the system?
- What rules govern the transition of a task between different statuses?
- How do task lists or projects relate to individual tasks?
- What happens to a task when its deadline passes?

These types of question help us understand the fundamental aspects of our domain. For instance, we might determine that a task is uniquely identified by a globally unique ID and that its priority can influence its position in a task list. We might define rules such as "a completed task cannot be moved back to *In Progress* without first being reopened."

It's crucial to note that, at this stage of DDD, we're not writing any code. As a developer, you might feel an urge to start implementing these concepts immediately. However, resist this temptation. The power of DDD lies in thoroughly understanding and modeling the domain before writing a single line of code. This upfront investment in domain analysis will pay dividends in the form of a more robust, flexible, and accurate software model down the line.

Core concepts of domain modeling

DDD provides several key concepts for modeling our domain effectively. Central to these is the idea of a **ubiquitous language**, which is a common, rigorous vocabulary shared by both developers and domain experts. This language is used consistently in code, tests, and conversations, helping to prevent misunderstandings and keep the model aligned with the business domain.

In our task management system, this language includes terms such as the following:

- **Task**: A unit of work to be completed
- **Project**: A collection of related tasks

- **Due Date**: The deadline for task completion

- **Priority**: The task's importance level (e.g. *Low*, *Medium*, or *High*)

- **Status**: The task's current state (e.g. *To Do*, *In Progress*, or *Done*)

With this ubiquitous language established, let's explore the fundamental structural concepts of DDD that will help us implement our domain model:

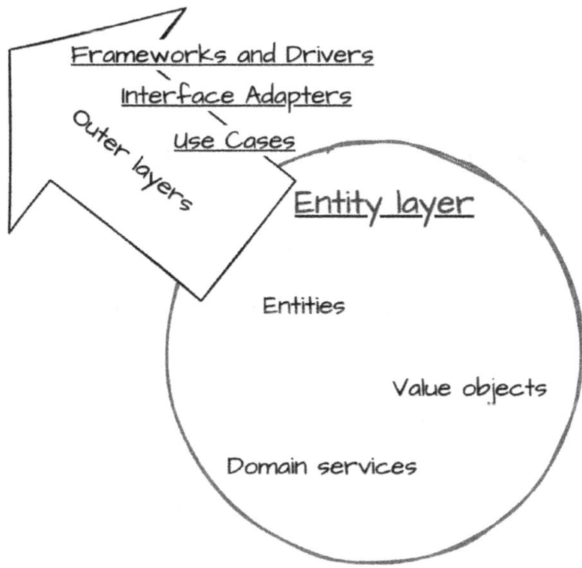

Figure 4.1: Clean Architecture layers and DDD concepts

As shown in *Figure 4.1*, Clean Architecture places the Entity layer at the core of our system, while DDD provides the specific components (entities, value objects, and domain services) that populate this layer. Let's review them now:

- **Entities**: These are objects defined by their identity that persists even when their attributes change. An Order remains the same Order even if its status changes from pending to shipped. In Clean Architecture, these core business objects embody the most stable rules at the system's center.

- **Value objects**: These are immutable objects defined by their attributes rather than identity. Two Money objects with the same currency and amount are considered equal. They encapsulate cohesive behaviors without needing unique identification, increasing domain expressiveness while reducing complexity.

- **Domain services**: These represent stateless operations that don't naturally belong to a single entity or value object. They handle domain logic that spans multiple objects, like calculating shipping costs based on an order's items and a customer's location.

These modeling components form the foundation of our Entity layer in Clean Architecture. While DDD gives us the vocabulary and techniques to identify and model these components based on business realities, Clean Architecture provides the framework for organizing them within our codebase, ensuring they remain independent from external concerns. This complementary relationship will become even clearer as we implement these concepts in Python.

Modeling the task management domain

Let's apply the core concepts of DDD to our task management system, translating theoretical concepts into practical components of our domain model.

Task management application entities and value objects

Our system has two primary entities:

- **Task**: The core entity representing a unit of work, with a persistent identity despite changing attributes (e.g., status transitions)
- **User**: Represents a system user who manages tasks, also with a persistent identity

We also have several important value objects:

- **Task status**: An enumeration (e.g., *To Do*, *In Progress*, or *Done*) representing a task's state
- **Priority**: Indicates task importance (e.g., *Low*, *Medium*, or *High*)
- **Deadline**: Represents due date and time, encapsulating related behaviors such as overdue checking

These value objects enhance our model's expressiveness. For instance, a task has a task status rather than a simple string, carrying more semantic meaning and potential behavior.

Task management application domain services

Complex operations that don't belong to a single entity or value object are implemented as domain services:

- **Task priority calculator**: Calculates a task's priority based on various factors
- **Reminder service**: Manages the creation and sending of task reminders

These services keep our entities and value objects focused and cohesive.

Leveraging bounded contexts

Bounded contexts are conceptual boundaries that define where specific domain models apply. They encapsulate domain details, ensure model consistency, and interact through well-defined interfaces. This aligns with Clean Architecture's emphasis on clear component boundaries, facilitating modular and maintainable system design.

We can identify three distinct bounded contexts in our system:

- **Task management**: The core context, handling task-related operations
- **User account management**: Handles user-related operations
- **Notification**: Manages generating and sending notifications to users

These contexts create clear boundaries within our system, allowing independent development while enabling necessary interactions.

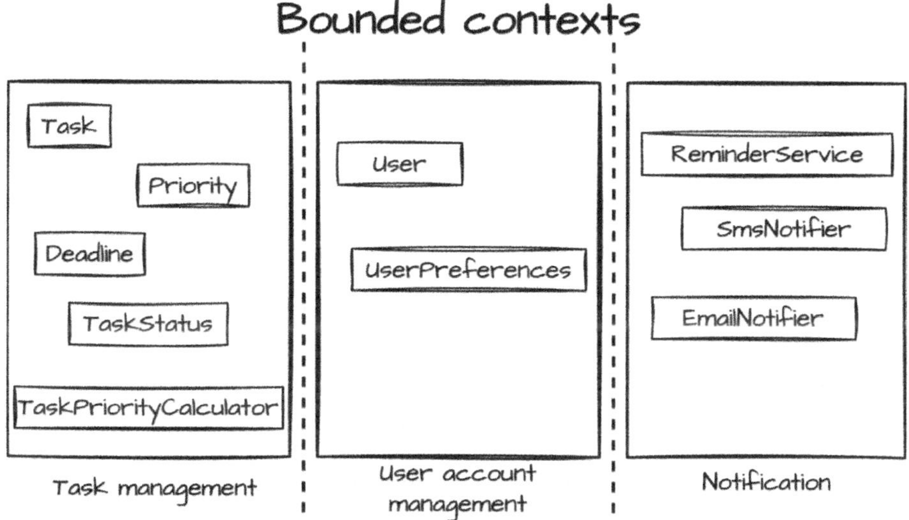

Figure 4.2: Three potential bounded contexts for our task management application

This model forms the core of our Clean Architecture design, with entities and value objects at the center of our Entity layer. Our ubiquitous language ensures code reflects domain concepts accurately; domain services house complex multi-object logic, and bounded contexts manage system complexity at a higher level.

In the next section, we'll implement this conceptual model in Python, creating rich domain entities that encapsulate fundamental business rules.

Implementing entities in Python

With our domain model conceptualized using DDD principles, we now turn to the practical implementation of these concepts in Python. This section will focus on creating rich domain entities that encapsulate fundamental business rules, laying the groundwork for our Clean Architecture implementation.

Introduction to Python entities

Having established our understanding of entities in DDD, let's explore how to implement them effectively in Python. Our implementation will focus on creating classes with unique identifiers and methods that encapsulate business logic, translating DDD concepts into practical Python code.

Key implementation considerations include the following:

- **Identity**: Implementing unique identifiers using Python's Universally Unique Identifier (UUID) system

- **Mutability**: Leveraging Python's object-oriented features to manage state changes

- **Life cycle**: Managing object creation, modification, and deletion through Python class methods

- **Business rules**: Using Python's type system and class methods to enforce business rules

An introduction to data classes in Python

In our implementation, we'll be using Python's data classes, introduced in Python 3.7. **Data classes** are a concise way to create classes that mainly store data but can also have behavior. They automatically generate several special methods, such as `__init__()`, `__repr__()`, and `__eq__()`, reducing boilerplate code.

Key advantages of data classes include the following:

- **Reduced boilerplate**: Automatically generates common methods

- **Clarity**: Clearly expresses the structure of the data

- **Immutability option**: Can create immutable objects, aligning with DDD principles for value objects

- **Default values**: Easily specifies default values for attributes

Data classes align well with Clean Architecture principles by promoting clear, focused entities that encapsulate data and behavior. They help us create entities that are easy to understand, maintain, and test.

For more information on data classes, refer to the official Python documentation: `https://docs.python.org/3/library/dataclasses.html`.

Now, let's examine how we can use data classes to implement our `Entity` base class:

```python
from dataclasses import dataclass, field
from uuid import UUID, uuid4


@dataclass
class Entity:
    # Automatically generates a unique UUID for the 'id' field;
    # excluded from the __init__ method
    id: UUID = field(default_factory=uuid4, init=False)

    def __eq__(self, other: object) -> bool:
        if not isinstance(other, type(self)):
            return NotImplemented
        return self.id == other.id

    def __hash__(self) -> int:
        return hash(self.id)
```

This `Entity` base class provides a foundation for all our entities, ensuring they have a unique identifier and appropriate equality and hashing behavior.

Ensuring proper class equality in Python

As we've seen in our Entity base class, we've implemented the __eq__ and __hash__ methods to ensure proper identity and equality checks. This is crucial for entities, as two tasks with the same attributes but different IDs should be considered different entities.

Creating domain entities

Now, let's implement our core domain entity: the `Task` entity. This entity will encapsulate the fundamental concepts and rules related to tasks in our task management system.

Implementing the Task entity

First, let's look at the basic structure of our Task entity:

```python
from dataclasses import dataclass, field
from typing import Optional
```

```python
@dataclass
class Task(Entity):
    title: str
    description: str
    due_date: Optional[Deadline] = None
    priority: Priority = Priority.MEDIUM
    status: TaskStatus = field(default=TaskStatus.TODO, init=False)
```

This `Task` entity encapsulates the core attributes of a task in our system. Let's break down each attribute:

- `title`: A string representing the name or brief description of the task
- `description`: A more detailed explanation of what the task entails
- `due_date`: An optional `Deadline` object indicating when the task should be completed
- `priority`: Represents the importance of the task, defaulting to `MEDIUM`
- `status`: Indicates the current state of the task, defaulting to `TODO`

Now, let's implement our value objects:

```python
from enum import Enum
from dataclasses import dataclass
from datetime import datetime, timedelta


class TaskStatus(Enum):
    TODO = "TODO"
    IN_PROGRESS = "IN_PROGRESS"
    DONE = "DONE"


class Priority(Enum):
    LOW = 1
    MEDIUM = 2
    HIGH = 3


# frozen=True makes this immutable as it should be for a Value Object
@dataclass(frozen=True)
class Deadline:
    due_date: datetime
```

```python
    def __post_init__(self):
        if self.due_date < datetime.now(timezone.utc):
            raise ValueError("Deadline cannot be in the past")

    def is_overdue(self) -> bool:
        return datetime.now(timezone.utc) > self.due_date

    def time_remaining(self) -> timedelta:
        return max(
            timedelta(0),
            self.due_date - datetime.now(timezone.utc)
        )

    def is_approaching(
        self, warning_threshold: timedelta = timedelta(days=1)
    ) -> bool:
        return timedelta(0) < self.time_remaining() <= warning_threshold
```

These value objects help to constrain the possible values for task status, priority, and deadline, ensuring data integrity and providing semantic meaning to these attributes.

Here are some usage examples of the Task entity with these value objects:

```python
# Create a new task
task = Task(
    title="Complete project proposal",
    description="Draft and review the proposal for the
                new client project",
    priority=Priority.HIGH
)

# Check task properties
print(task.title)      # "Complete project proposal"
print(task.priority)   # Priority.HIGH
print(task.status)     # TaskStatus.TODO
```

After establishing our core Task entity structure and its supporting value objects, let's explore how to enhance these foundations by incorporating business rules that govern task behavior and maintain data consistency.

Encapsulating business rules in entities

When implementing domain entities, it's crucial to enforce business rules to ensure the entity always remains in a valid state. **Business rules**, often called **invariants**, are fundamental to the entity's definition in the domain. Entities should encapsulate the business rules that apply directly to them.

Let's add some basic business rules to our `Task` entity:

```python
@dataclass
class Task(Entity):
    # ... previous attributes ...

    def start(self) -> None:
        if self.status != TaskStatus.TODO:
            raise ValueError(
                "Only tasks with 'TODO' status can be started")
        self.status = TaskStatus.IN_PROGRESS

    def complete(self) -> None:
        if self.status == TaskStatus.DONE:
            raise ValueError("Task is already completed")
        self.status = TaskStatus.DONE

    def is_overdue(self) -> bool:
        return self.due_date is not None and self.due_date.is_overdue()
```

Now, let's explore how these business rules work in practice. The following examples demonstrate how the `Task` entity enforces its invariants and maintains its internal consistency:

```python
from datetime import datetime, timedelta

# Create a task
task = Task(
    title="Complete project proposal",
    description="Draft and review the proposal for the
                new client project",
    due_date=Deadline(datetime.now(timezone.utc) + timedelta(days=7)),
    priority=Priority.HIGH
)
```

```python
# Start the task
task.start()
print(task.status)  # TaskStatus.IN_PROGRESS

# Complete the task
task.complete()
print(task.status)  # TaskStatus.DONE

# Try to start a completed task
try:
    task.start()  # This will raise a ValueError
except ValueError as e:
    print(str(e))  # "Only tasks with 'TODO' status can be started"

# Check if the task is overdue
print(task.is_overdue())  # False
```

These methods enforce business rules such as the following:

- A task can only be started if it's in the TODO status

- A completed task cannot be completed again

- The task knows if it's overdue based on its deadline

By encapsulating these rules within the entity, we ensure that the Task entity always adheres to the core business rules of our domain, regardless of how it's used in the application.

Distinguishing entity-level rules from domain-level rules

While the rules we've implemented are appropriate for the Task entity, not all business rules belong at the entity level. For example, consider a rule such as *"A user can't have more than five high-priority tasks at one time."* This rule involves multiple tasks and possibly user settings, so it doesn't belong in the Task entity.

Such rules are more appropriately implemented in domain services or application-layer use cases. We'll explore how to implement these higher-level rules in the *Implementing domain services* section later in this chapter.

By structuring our entities this way, we maintain a clear separation between entity-specific rules and broader domain rules, adhering to Clean Architecture principles and keeping our entities focused and maintainable.

Value objects in Clean Architecture

Having introduced value objects conceptually, let's examine their specific implementation in our task management system. We've created several key value objects:

- `TaskStatus`: Represents the current state of a task (e.g., *To Do*, *In Progress*, or *Done*)

- `Priority`: Indicates the importance of a task (e.g., *Low*, *Medium*, or *High*)

- `Deadline`: Represents the due date and time for a task, with additional behavior such as checking whether it's overdue

Beyond the conceptual benefits already discussed, our implementation demonstrates specific advantages in Clean Architecture:

- **Immutability**: Once created, their state cannot be changed. This helps prevent bugs and makes our code easier to reason about.

- **Equality based on attributes**: Two value objects with the same attributes are considered equal, unlike entities that have a unique identity.

- **Encapsulation of domain concepts**: They represent domain ideas as first-class citizens in our code, improving expressiveness.

- **Prevention of primitive obsession**: They replace the use of primitive types to represent domain concepts, adding semantic meaning and type safety.

- **Simplified testing**: Value objects are easy to create and use in tests, improving the test-ability of our system.

Consider the difference between using a string for task status versus a `TaskStatus` enum:

```python
# Using string (problematic)
task = Task("Complete project", "The important project")
task.status = "Finished"  # Allowed, but invalid
print(task.status == "done")  # False, case-sensitive

# Using TaskStatus enum (robust)
task = Task("Complete project", "The important project")
task.status = TaskStatus.DONE  # Type-safe
print(task.status == TaskStatus.DONE)  # True, no case issues
```

Python's support for lightweight value objects (such as enums) and modern IDE features enhances the developer experience, making it easier to implement a Clean Architecture that truly reflects the domain model.

Implementing domain services

While many business rules can be encapsulated within entities and value objects, some rules or operations involve multiple entities or complex logic that doesn't naturally fit within a single entity. For these cases, we can encapsulate the needed logic into domain services. Let's implement a simple `TaskPriorityCalculator` service:

```python
class TaskPriorityCalculator:
    @staticmethod
    def calculate_priority(task: Task) -> Priority:
        if task.is_overdue():
            return Priority.HIGH
        elif (
            task.due_date and task.due_date.time_remaining() <=
            timedelta(days=2)
        ):
            return Priority.MEDIUM
        else:
            return Priority.LOW
```

This domain service encapsulates the logic for calculating a task's priority based on its due date. It's a stateless operation that doesn't belong to any specific entity but is still an important part of our domain logic.

By implementing our domain model in this way, we create a rich, expressive set of Python classes that accurately represent our task management domain. These classes encapsulate fundamental business rules, ensuring that our core domain logic remains consistent and well-organized.

At its current state, our application might be organized thusly (the full code is available on GitHub at `https://github.com/PacktPublishing/Clean-Architecture-with-Python`):

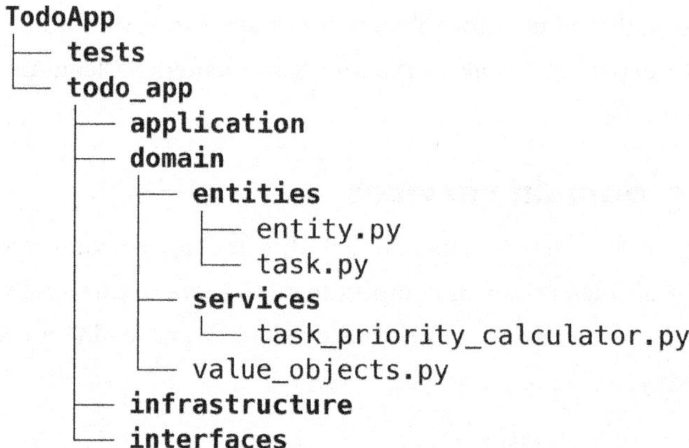

Figure 4.3: Todo app structure with domain components implemented

In the next section, we'll explore more advanced domain concepts, building upon this foundation to create a comprehensive domain model that fully leverages the power of DDD in our Clean Architecture implementation.

Enhancing the domain model with aggregates and factories

Having established our core entities, value objects, and domain services, we now turn our attention to more advanced domain concepts. These concepts will help us create a more robust and flexible domain model, further enhancing our Clean Architecture implementation.

DDD patterns

DDD offers several advanced patterns that can help us manage complexity and maintain consistency in our domain model. Let's explore some of these patterns and how they apply to our task management system.

Aggregates

Aggregates are a crucial pattern in DDD for maintaining consistency and defining transactional boundaries within the domain. An aggregate is a cluster of domain objects that we treat as a single unit for data changes. Each aggregate has a root and a boundary. The root is a single, specific entity contained in the aggregate, and the boundary defines what is inside the aggregate.

In our task management system, a natural aggregate would be a project containing multiple tasks. Let's implement this:

```python
# TodoApp/todo_app/domain/entities/project.py

from dataclasses import dataclass, field
from typing import Optional
from uuid import UUID


@dataclass
class Project(Entity):
    name: str
    description: str = ""
    _tasks: dict[UUID, Task] = field(default_factory=dict, init=False)

    def add_task(self, task: Task) -> None:
        self._tasks[task.id] = task

    def remove_task(self, task_id: UUID) -> None:
        self._tasks.pop(task_id, None)

    def get_task(self, task_id: UUID) -> Optional[Task]:
        return self._tasks.get(task_id)

    @property
    def tasks(self) -> list[Task]:
        return list(self._tasks.values())
```

In this implementation, `Project` serves as the aggregate root. It encapsulates operations that maintain the consistency of the aggregate, such as adding, removing, or getting tasks.

The usage of `Project` would look like this:

```python
from datetime import datetime

# Project usage
project = Project("Website Redesign")
task1 = Task(
    title="Design homepage",
```

```python
    description="Create new homepage layout",
    due_date=Deadline(datetime(2023, 12, 31)),
    priority=Priority.HIGH,
)
task2 = Task(
    title="Implement login",
    description="Add user authentication",
    due_date=Deadline(datetime(2023, 11, 30)),
    priority=Priority.MEDIUM,
)
project.add_task(task1)
project.add_task(task2)

print(f"Project: {project.name}")
print(f"Number of tasks: {len(project.tasks)}")
print(f"First task: {project.tasks[0].title}")
```

Key points about this aggregate are as follows:

- **Encapsulation**: Project controls access to its tasks. External code can't directly modify the task collection.

- **Consistency**: Methods such as `add_task` and `remove_task` ensure that the aggregate remains in a consistent state.

- **Identity**: While individual `Task` entities have their own global identities (UUIDs), within the context of `Project`, they are also identified by their relationship to the project. This means that `Project` can manage tasks using project-specific concepts (such as order or position) in addition to their global IDs.

- **Transactional boundary**: Any operation that affects multiple tasks within a list (such as marking all as complete) should be done through `Project` to ensure consistency.

- **Invariants**: `Project` can enforce invariants that apply to the collection as a whole. For example, we could add a method to ensure that no two tasks in the list have the same title.

Using aggregates like this helps us manage complex domains by grouping related entities and value objects into cohesive units. This not only simplifies our domain model but also helps in maintaining data integrity and consistency.

When designing aggregates, it's important to consider performance implications. Aggregates should be designed to be as small as possible while still maintaining consistency. In our case, if a project grows too large, we might need to consider pagination or lazy loading strategies when accessing tasks.

By implementing a project as an aggregate, we've created a powerful abstraction that encapsulates the complexities of managing multiple tasks. This aligns perfectly with Clean Architecture principles, as it allows us to express complex domain rules and relationships in a clear, encapsulated manner.

The factory pattern

In traditional object-oriented programming, the **factory pattern** is often used to encapsulate object creation logic. However, modern Python features have reduced the need for standalone factories in many cases. Let's explore how Python's language features address object creation and when factories might still be useful.

Data classes and object creation

Our Task entity, implemented as a `dataclass` type, already provides a clean and efficient way to create objects:

```python
@dataclass
class Task(Entity):
    title: str
    description: str
    due_date: Optional[Deadline] = None
    priority: Priority = Priority.MEDIUM
    status: TaskStatus = field(default=TaskStatus.TODO, init=False)
```

This `dataclass` definition automatically generates an `__init__` method, handling much of what a traditional factory might do. It sets default values, manages optional parameters, and ensures type consistency (when using type checkers).

Extending object creation with Python features

For more complex initialization scenarios, Python offers a couple of idiomatic approaches:

- **Class methods as alternative constructors:**

```python
@dataclass
class Task(Entity):
    # ... existing attributes ...

    @classmethod
```

```python
    def create_urgent_task(cls, title: str, description: str,
                           due_date: Deadline):
        return cls(title, description, due_date, Priority.HIGH)
```

- **Using the __post_init__ feature from** `dataclass` **for complex initialization:**

```python
@dataclass
class Task(Entity):
    # ... existing attributes ...

    def __post_init__(self):
        if not self.title.strip():
            raise ValueError("Task title cannot be empty")
        if len(self.description) > 500:
            raise ValueError(
                "Task description cannot exceed 500 characters")
```

These methods allow for more complex object creation logic while maintaining the benefits of data classes.

When traditional factories might still be appropriate

Despite these Python features, there are scenarios where a standalone factory might still be beneficial:

- **Complex object graphs**: When creating an object requires setting up relationships with other objects or performing complex calculations
- **Dependency injection**: When the creation process requires external dependencies that you want to keep separate from the entity itself
- **Polymorphic creation**: When you need to create different subclasses based on runtime conditions

Here's an example where a factory might be appropriate:

```python
class TaskFactory:
    def __init__(self, user_service, project_repository):
        self.user_service = user_service
        self.project_repository = project_repository

    def create_task_in_project(self, title: str, description: str,
                               project_id: UUID, assignee_id: UUID):
```

```python
        project = self.project_repository.get_by_id(project_id)
        assignee = self.user_service.get_user(assignee_id)

        task = Task(title, description)
        task.project = project
        task.assignee = assignee

        if project.is_high_priority() and assignee.is_manager():
            task.priority = Priority.HIGH

        project.add_task(task)
        return task
```

In this case, the factory encapsulates the complex logic of creating a task within the context of a project and an assignee, including business rules that depend on the project and user status.

By understanding these patterns and when to apply them, we can create a more expressive and maintainable domain model that aligns with Clean Architecture principles while leveraging Python's strengths.

Ensuring domain independence

The independence of the Domain layer is a cornerstone of Clean Architecture, directly tied to the Dependency Rule we first introduced in *Chapter 1*. This rule, stating that dependencies should only point inward toward the Domain layer, is crucial for maintaining the purity and flexibility of our core business logic. In this section, we'll explore practical applications of this rule and strategies to ensure domain independence.

The Dependency Rule in practice

Let's examine how the Dependency Rule applies to our task management system, using examples that highlight common violations and their corrections.

Example 1

Task entity with database dependency:

```python
@dataclass
class TaskWithDatabase:
    title: str
    description: str
```

```python
        db: DbConnection  # This violates the Dependency Rule
        due_date: Optional[Deadline] = None
        priority: Priority = Priority.MEDIUM
        status: TaskStatus = field(default=TaskStatus.TODO, init=False)


        def mark_as_complete(self):
            self.status = TaskStatus.DONE
            self.db.update(self) # This violates the Dependency Rule
```

In this example, the `TaskWithDatabase` class violates the Dependency Rule by directly depending on a database connection. The `db` attribute and the `update` call in `mark_as_complete` introduce external concerns into our domain entity.

Example 2

Project aggregate with UI dependency:

```python
@dataclass
class ProjectWithUI(Entity):
    name: str
    ui: UiComponent  # Violates the Dependency Rule
    description: str = ""
    _tasks: dict[UUID, Task] = field(default_factory=dict, init=False)


    def add_task(self, task: Task):
        self._tasks[task.id] = task
        self.ui.refresh()  # Violates the Dependency Rule
```

Here, `ProjectWithUI` incorrectly depends on a UI component, mixing presentation concerns with domain logic.

These examples not only violate the Dependency Rule but also break the **Single Responsibility Principle (SRP)** from SOLID. The `TaskWithDatabase` class is responsible for both task management and database operations, while `ProjectWithUI` handles both project management and UI updates. These violations compromise the independence and focus of our Domain layer, making it less flexible, harder to test, and more challenging to maintain.

By removing these external dependencies and adhering to the SRP, we create pure domain entities that focus solely on core business concepts and rules. This approach ensures that our Domain layer remains the stable core of our application, unaffected by changes in external systems, databases, or user interfaces.

In the next section, we'll explore strategies for avoiding external dependencies and maintaining the purity of our Domain layer.

Avoiding external dependencies

To maintain the purity and independence of our Domain layer, we need to be vigilant about avoiding dependencies on external frameworks, databases, or UI components. One key strategy is to use abstractions for external concerns. Let's see how this works in practice with our task management system.

First, let's define an abstract `TaskRepository` in the Domain layer:

```python
# In the Domain layer :
# (e.g., todo_app/domain/repositories/task_repository.py)
from abc import ABC, abstractmethod
from todo_app.domain.entities.task import Task


class TaskRepository(ABC):
    @abstractmethod
    def save(self, task: Task):
        pass


    @abstractmethod
    def get(self, task_id: str) -> Task:
        pass
```

This abstract class defines the contract for task persistence without specifying any implementation details. It belongs to the Domain layer and represents the interface that any task storage mechanism must fulfill.

Now, let's see how a domain service might use this repository:

```python
# In the Domain layer (e.g., todo_app/domain/services/task_service.py)
from todo_app.domain.entities.task import Task
from todo_app.domain.repositories.task_repository import TaskRepository


class TaskService:
    def __init__(self, task_repository: TaskRepository):
        self.task_repository = task_repository


    def create_task(self, title: str, description: str) -> Task:
```

```python
        task = Task(title, description)
        self.task_repository.save(task)
        return task

    def mark_task_as_complete(self, task_id: str) -> Task:
        task = self.task_repository.get(task_id)
        task.complete()
        self.task_repository.save(task)
        return task
```

This `TaskService` demonstrates how domain logic can interact with the persistence abstraction without knowing anything about the actual storage mechanism.

The concrete implementation of the `TaskRepository` would reside in an outer layer, such as the Infrastructure layer:

```python
# In an outer layer
# .../infrastructure/persistence/sqlite_task_repository.py
from todo_app.domain.entities.task import Task
from todo_app.domain.repositories.task_repository import TaskRepository


class SQLiteTaskRepository(TaskRepository):
    def __init__(self, db_connection):
        self.db = db_connection

    def save(self, task: Task):
        # Implementation details...
        pass

    def get(self, task_id: str) -> Task:
        # Implementation details...
        pass
```

This structure demonstrates the Dependency Rule in action:

- The Domain layer (`TaskRepository` and `TaskService`) defines and uses abstractions without knowledge of concrete implementations
- The Infrastructure layer (`SQLiteTaskRepository`) implements the abstractions defined by the Domain layer

- The flow of dependency points inward; the Infrastructure layer depends on the Domain layer's abstraction, not vice versa
- Our Domain layer remains independent of specific database technologies or other external concerns
- We can easily swap out SQLite for another database or storage mechanism without modifying the Domain layer

By adhering to the Dependency Rule, we ensure that our Domain layer remains the stable core of our application, unaffected by changes in external systems or technologies. This separation allows us to evolve different parts of our system independently, facilitating easier testing, maintenance, and adaptation to changing requirements.

For instance, if we decided to switch from SQLite to PostgreSQL, we would only need to create a new `PostgreSQLTaskRepository` in the Infrastructure layer, implementing the `TaskRepository` interface. The Domain layer, including our `TaskService`, would remain unchanged.

This approach to structuring our code not only maintains the purity of our Domain layer but also provides flexibility for future changes and ease of testing, which are key benefits of Clean Architecture.

Domain layer independence and testability

The independence of the Domain layer significantly enhances testability. By keeping domain logic separate from infrastructure concerns, we can easily unit test our core business rules without the need for complex setup or external dependencies.

When our Domain layer is independent, we can do the following:

- Write unit tests that run quickly, without the need for database setup or network connections
- Test our business logic in isolation, without worrying about the complexities of UI or persistence layers
- Use simple stubs or mocks for any external dependencies, focusing our tests on the business logic itself

This independence makes our tests more reliable, faster to run, and easier to maintain. We'll dive deeper into testing in *Chapter 8*.

Refactoring toward a purer domain model

Maintaining a pure domain model is an ongoing process that requires vigilance and regular refactoring. As our understanding of the domain evolves and as we face practical constraints in development, our initial implementations may drift from the ideal. This is a natural part of the software development process. What's crucial is that we remain diligent in reviewing and refining our domain models, recognizing their foundational importance to our application.

Two key factors drive the need for refactoring:

- **Evolving domain understanding**: As we work with stakeholders and gain deeper insights into the business domain, we often discover that our initial models need adjustment to better reflect reality.

- **Practical compromises**: Sometimes, to meet deadlines or work within existing constraints, we may make compromises that introduce non-domain concerns into our model. While these compromises can be necessary in the short term, it's important to revisit and address them to maintain the long-term health of our application.

Let's explore some strategies for maintaining and refactoring toward a purer domain model:

- **Conduct regular code reviews**: Focus on identifying any violations of the Dependency Rule or introductions of non-domain concerns.

- **Refactor continuously**: As your understanding of the domain evolves, continually refactor your domain model to better reflect this understanding.

- **Be wary of frameworks**: Resist the temptation to use convenient framework features in your Domain layer. The short-term gain in development speed often leads to long-term pain in maintainability and flexibility.

- **Use DDD patterns**: Patterns such as entities, value objects, and aggregates help keep your domain model focused and pure.

- **Favor explicitness over implicitness**: Avoid *magic* behaviors that implicitly call external services. Make dependencies and behaviors explicit.

Here's an example of refactoring to maintain domain purity:

```python
from dataclasses import dataclass, field
from typing import Optional


# Before refactoring
@dataclass
```

```python
class Task(Entity):
    title: str
    description: str
    due_date: Optional[Deadline] = None
    priority: Priority = Priority.MEDIUM
    status: TaskStatus = field(default=TaskStatus.TODO, init=False)

    def mark_as_complete(self):
        self.status = TaskStatus.DONE
        # Sending an email notification - this violates domain purity
        self.send_completion_email()

    def send_completion_email(self):
        # Code to send an email notification
        print(f"Sending email: Task '{self.title}' has been completed.")
```

In the preceding version, there are indications that the `Task` entity may be implementing an excessive amount of behavior, violating the SRP of SOLID.

Here is the refactored version:

```python
# After refactoring
from abc import ABC, abstractmethod
from dataclasses import dataclass, field
from typing import Optional

@dataclass
class Task(Entity):
    title: str
    description: str
    due_date: Optional[Deadline] = None
    priority: Priority = Priority.MEDIUM
    status: TaskStatus = field(default=TaskStatus.TODO, init=False)

    def mark_as_complete(self):
        self.status = TaskStatus.DONE
        # No email sending here;
        # this is now the responsibility of an outer layer
```

```python
class TaskCompleteNotifier(ABC):
    @abstractmethod
    def notify_completion(self, task):
        pass


# This would be implemented in an outer layer
class EmailTaskCompleteNotifier(TaskCompleteNotifier):
    def notify_completion(self, task):
        print(f"Sending email: Task '{task.title}' has been completed.")
```

In the refactored version, we have done the following:

- We've removed the `send_completion_email` method from the `Task` entity. Sending notifications is not a core responsibility of a task and should be handled in an outer layer.

- We've introduced an abstract `TaskCompleteNotifier` class. The actual implementation of this (e.g., sending an email) would be done in an outer layer. This allows us to keep the notion of *notifying about task completion* in our domain model without including the details of how that notification happens.

These changes keep our domain model pure and focused on core business concepts and rules. The `Task` entity now only concerns itself with what a task is and its basic behaviors, not with how to send emails or interact with the system clock.

This example demonstrates how we can refactor our domain model to remove non-domain concerns and make it more testable and maintainable. It also shows how we can use abstractions (such as `TaskCompleteNotifier`) to represent domain concepts without including implementation details in our Domain layer.

By regularly reviewing and refactoring our domain model, we ensure that it remains a true representation of our business domain, free from external concerns. This ongoing process is crucial for maintaining the integrity of our Clean Architecture implementation and the long-term maintainability of our application.

Remember, the goal isn't perfection from the start but, rather, continuous improvement. Each refactoring step moves us closer to a cleaner, more expressive domain model that serves as a solid foundation for our entire application.

In conclusion, maintaining the independence of domain concepts from external frameworks and systems is crucial for effective Clean Architecture. By using abstractions such as the `TaskRepository` interface and adhering to the Dependency Rule, we ensure our Domain layer remains focused on core business logic. This approach creates clear boundaries between the domain and external concerns, allowing infrastructure changes without affecting central business rules. Through dependency inversion and careful interface design, we create a robust, flexible foundation that can adapt to changing requirements while preserving the integrity of our core domain model.

Summary

In this chapter, we delved into the heart of Clean Architecture: the Entity layer, also known as the Domain layer. We explored how to identify, model, and implement core business concepts using DDD principles.

We began by analyzing business requirements and defining a ubiquitous language for our task management system. We then examined key DDD concepts such as entities, value objects, and bounded contexts, seeing how they align with Clean Architecture principles.

Next, we implemented these concepts in Python, creating rich domain entities such as `Task` and value objects such as `Priority` and `Deadline`. We encapsulated business rules within these entities, ensuring they maintain their integrity regardless of how they're used in the broader application.

Finally, we focused on ensuring the independence of the Entity layer, exploring strategies to avoid external dependencies and maintain clear boundaries between our core domain logic and infrastructure concerns.

By applying these principles, we've created a robust foundation for our Clean Architecture implementation. This Entity layer (focused purely on business logic and free from external concerns) will serve as the stable core around which the rest of our application will be built.

In the next chapter, we'll explore the Application layer, where we'll see how to orchestrate our domain objects to fulfill specific use cases while maintaining the separation of concerns established in our Entity layer.

Further reading

- *Domain-Driven Design: Tackling Complexity in the Heart of Software* by Eric Evans (`https://www.informit.com/store/domain-driven-design-tackling-complexity-in-the-heart-9780321125217`). This book provides a systematic approach to DDD, offering best practices and techniques to develop software projects facing complex domains.

- *Implementing Domain-Driven Design* by Vaughn Vernon (`https://www.oreilly.com/library/view/implementing-domain-driven-design/9780133039900/`). This book presents a top-down approach to understanding DDD, connecting strategic patterns with fundamental tactical programming tools.

- *Building Evolutionary Architectures: Support Constant Change* by Rebecca Parsons, Neal Ford and Patrick Kua (`https://www.thoughtworks.com/en-us/insights/books/building-evolutionary-architectures`). This book offers guidance on enabling incremental architectural change over time to support constant evolution in software development.

Get this book's PDF version and more

Scan the QR code (or go to `packtpub.com/unlock`). Search for this book by name, confirm the edition, and then follow the steps on the page.

Note: Keep your invoice handy. Purchases made directly from Packt don't require an invoice.

5

The Application Layer: Orchestrating Use Cases

In *Chapter 4*, we developed the Domain layer of our task management system and implemented entities, value objects, and domain services that encapsulate our core business rules. While this gives us a solid foundation, business rules alone don't make a usable application. We need a way to coordinate these domain objects to fulfill user needs such as creating tasks, managing projects, and handling notifications. This is where the **Application layer** comes in.

The Application layer acts as the conductor in our Clean Architecture orchestra. It coordinates domain objects and external services to accomplish specific use cases while maintaining the strict boundary between our business rules and the outside world. By implementing this layer correctly, we create applications that are not only functional but also maintainable and adaptable to change.

In this chapter, we'll explore how to implement an effective Application layer using our task management system as an example. We'll see how to create use cases that orchestrate domain objects while maintaining clean architectural boundaries. You'll learn how to implement request and response models that clearly define use case boundaries, and how to manage dependencies on external services without compromising architectural integrity.

In this chapter, we're going to cover the following main topics:

- Understanding the role of the Application layer
- Implementing use case interactors
- Defining request and response models
- Maintaining separation from external concerns

Technical requirements

The code examples presented in this chapter and throughout the rest of the book are tested with Python 3.13. For brevity, in addition to the lack of logging statements, some code examples in the chapter are only partially implemented. Complete versions of all examples can be found in the book's accompanying GitHub repository at `https://github.com/PacktPublishing/Clean-Architecture-with-Python`.

Understanding the role of the Application layer

The Application layer serves as a thin layer that coordinates our domain objects and services to accomplish meaningful user tasks. While our domain model provides the building blocks, tasks, projects, deadlines, it's the Application layer that assembles these pieces into useful features.

The Application layer serves another critical function: information hiding. In *Chapter 4*, we saw how domain entities hide their internal state and implementation details. The Application layer extends this principle across architectural boundaries, hiding infrastructure details from the domain and domain complexities from external interfaces. This deliberate hiding of information is what makes the additional effort of creating ports, adapters, and request/response models worthwhile. By exposing only what's necessary through carefully designed interfaces, we create a system where components can evolve independently yet work together seamlessly.

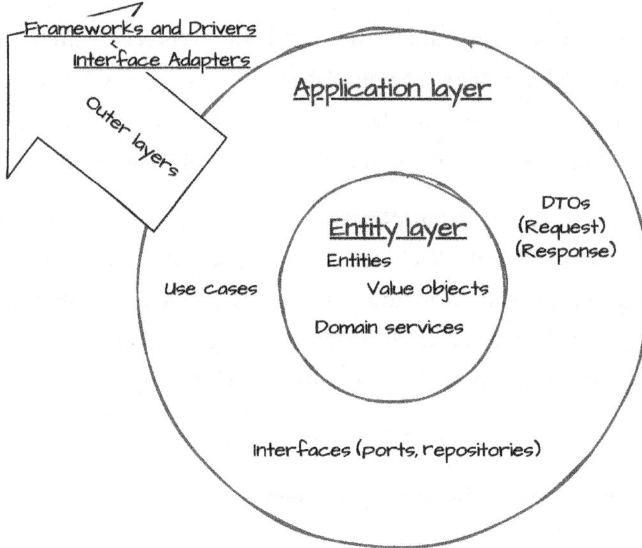

Figure 5.1: Application layer and task management

In *Figure 5.1*, we illustrate how the Application layer fits within Clean Architecture's concentric layers. It acts as a mediator between the Domain layer, where our core business entities such as Task and Project reside, and the outer layers of our system. By encapsulating use cases that orchestrate domain entities, the Application layer maintains the Dependency Rule: outer layers depend inward, and inner layers remain unaffected by changes in outer layers.

The Application layer has several distinct responsibilities:

- **Use case orchestration:**

    - Coordinating domain objects to accomplish user tasks

    - Managing the sequence of operations

    - Ensuring business rules are properly applied

- **Error handling and validation:**

    - Validating input before it reaches domain objects

    - Catching and translating domain errors

    - Providing consistent error responses

- **Transaction management:**

    - Ensuring operations are atomic when needed

    - Maintaining data consistency

    - Managing rollbacks on failures

- **Boundary translation:**

    - Converting external data formats to domain formats

    - Transforming domain objects for external presentation

    - Managing cross-boundary communication

These responsibilities work together to create a robust orchestration layer that maintains clean boundaries while ensuring reliable application behavior.

Error handling with result types

Before diving into our implementation patterns, it's essential to understand a fundamental concept in our Application layer: the use of the **result type**. This pattern forms the backbone of our error-handling strategy, providing explicit handling of success and failure rather than relying solely on exceptions. This approach provides several benefits:

- Makes success/failure paths explicit in function signatures
- Provides consistent error handling across the application
- Maintains clean architectural boundaries by translating domain errors
- Improves testability and error handling predictability

First, we define a standardized `Error` class to represent all application-level errors:

```python
class ErrorCode(Enum):
    NOT_FOUND = "NOT_FOUND"
    VALIDATION_ERROR = "VALIDATION_ERROR"
    # Add other error codes as needed


@dataclass(frozen=True)
class Error:
    """Standardized error information"""
    code: ErrorCode
    message: str
    details: Optional[dict[str, Any]] = None

    @classmethod
    def not_found(cls, entity: str, entity_id: str) -> Self:
        return cls(
            code=ErrorCode.NOT_FOUND,
            message=f"{entity} with id {entity_id} not found"
        )

    @classmethod
    def validation_error(cls, message: str) -> Self:
        return cls(
            code=ErrorCode.VALIDATION_ERROR,
            message=message
        )
```

Next, we define a `Result` class that encapsulates either a successful value or an error:

```python
@dataclass(frozen=True)
class Result:
    """Represents success or failure of a use case execution"""
    value: Any = None
    error: Optional[Error] = None

    @property
    def is_success(self) -> bool:
        return self.error is None

    @classmethod
    def success(cls, value: Any) -> Self:
        return cls(value=value)

    @classmethod
    def failure(cls, error: Error) -> Self:
        return cls(error=error)
```

The use of result types enables clean orchestration of domain operations, as demonstrated in this usage example:

```python
try:
    project = find_project(project_id)
    task = create_task(task_details)
    project.add_task(task)
    notify_stakeholders(task)
    return Result.success(TaskResponse.from_entity(task))
except ProjectNotFoundError:
    return Result.failure(Error.not_found("Project", str(project_id)))
except ValidationError as e:
    return Result.failure(Error.validation_error(str(e)))
```

The usage example above demonstrates several key advantages of the result pattern:

- **Clean error paths**: Notice how the error cases are handled uniformly through `Result.failure()`, providing a consistent interface regardless of the underlying error type

- **Explicit domain translation**: The conversion from domain-specific errors (`ProjectNotFoundError`) to application-level errors happens cleanly at the boundary

- **Self-contained context**: The `Result` object packages both the outcome and any error context, making the function's behavior completely clear from its return value
- **Testing clarity**: The example makes it easy to test both success and failure cases by checking the result's state rather than trying to catch exceptions

Error handling boundaries in Clean Architecture

When implementing error handling in the Application layer, we explicitly catch and transform only expected domain and business errors into results. Thus, we don't have an `except Exception:` clause paired with the expected errors. This separation maintains clean architectural boundaries. Concerns such as global error handling remain in the outer layers.

Application layer patterns

To understand how the Application layer manages its responsibilities, let's examine how data flows through our architecture:

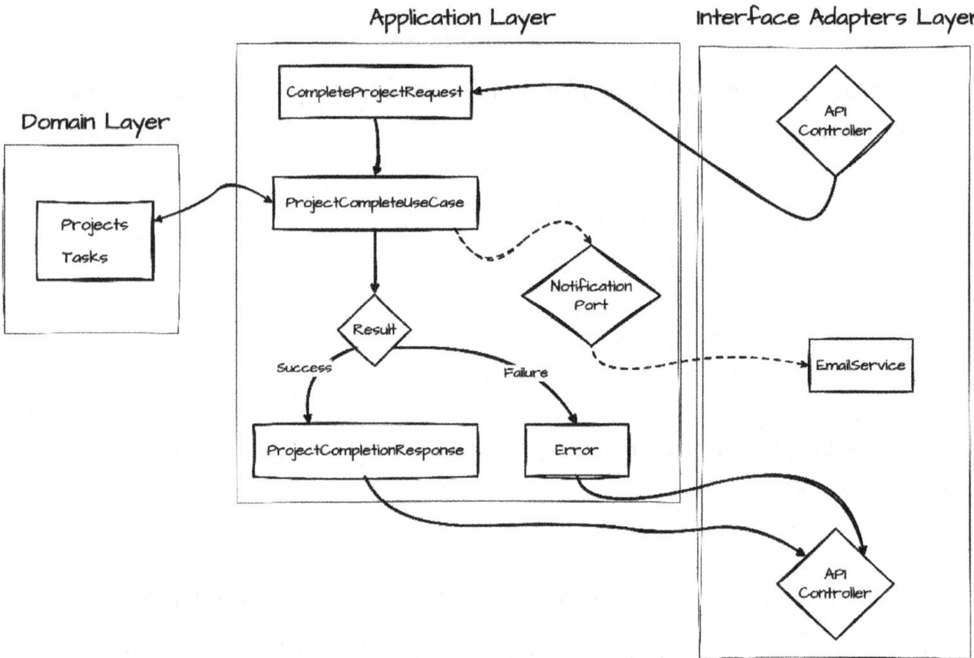

Figure 5.2: Request/Response flow in Clean Architecture

The flow shown in *Figure 5.2* demonstrates several key patterns working together. A request enters through the Interface Adapters layer and is handled by our Application layer's **data transfer objects (DTOs)**, which validate and transform the input into formats our domain can process. Use cases then orchestrate domain operations, working with these validated inputs to interact with domain objects and coordinate with external services through ports. The use cases return results that encapsulate either success (with a response DTO) or failure (with an error), which the Interface Adapters layer can then map directly to appropriate HTTP responses. Don't worry about understanding all the discrete components in *Figure 5.2* now; we'll cover them in more detail throughout the chapter.

This choreographed interaction relies on three foundational patterns that work together to maintain clean architectural boundaries:

- **Use case interactors**: These serve as the primary orchestrators, implementing specific business operations while managing transactions and coordinating domain objects. They ensure each operation is focused and its execution is consistent.

- **Interface boundaries**: Establish clear contracts between our Application layer and the services it depends on.

- **Dependency inversion**: Enables flexible implementation and straightforward testing through these boundaries, ensuring our core business logic remains decoupled from external concerns.

Initially, our use cases will work with simple parameters and return basic data structures. As our application grows, we'll introduce more sophisticated patterns for handling data that cross our architectural boundaries. This evolution helps us maintain a clean separation between layers while keeping our code adaptable to change.

These patterns align naturally with the SOLID principles we explored in *Chapter 2*. Use cases embody the Single Responsibility Principle by focusing each operation on a specific goal. Interface definitions support interface segregation by defining focused, client-specific contracts.

Planning for evolution

Applications rarely remain static—successful ones inevitably grow in scope and complexity. What starts as a simple task management system might need to evolve to support multiple teams, integrate with various external services, or handle complex workflow automation. The Application layer patterns we've explored enable this evolution with minimal friction.

Let's examine how our task management system can grow through real-world scenarios:

- **Use case extensibility:**

  - Expanding task notifications from email to include Slack or similar communication platforms

  - Composing individual use cases, such as *assign task* and *set deadline,* into higher-level operations such as *sprint planning*

- **Clean dependencies:**

  - Starting with local file storage for attachments, then seamlessly adding S3 support through the same interface

  - Switching database engines from SQLite to PostgreSQL without modifying use case code

- **Consistent boundaries:**

  - Handling data transformation in Request objects across new API versions (v1 versus v2) while reusing the same underlying use case code

  - Implementing distinct Response transformers for different clients (mobile, web, CLI) while sharing identical core business logic

This architectural foundation lets us confidently evolve our system. When the marketing team requests Salesforce integration, or when compliance requires audit logging, these capabilities can be added without disrupting existing functionality or compromising architectural integrity.

In the next section, we'll explore how to implement these concepts in Python, creating robust use case interactors that uphold the principles of Clean Architecture.

Implementing use case interactors

Having explored the theoretical foundations of the Application layer, we now turn to practical implementation. Use case interactors are the concrete classes that implement application-specific business rules. The term *interactors* emphasizes their role in interacting with and coordinating various parts of the system. While the Domain layer defines what the business rules are, interactors define how and when these rules are applied in response to specific application needs. In Python, we can implement these interactors in a way that's both clean and expressive.

Structuring a use case

A well-designed use case interactor orchestrates domain objects while maintaining clean architectural boundaries. Let's examine how this is achieved:

```python
@dataclass(frozen=True)
class CompleteTaskUseCase:
    """Use case for marking a task as complete and notifying
    stakeholders"""
    task_repository: TaskRepository

    def execute(
            self,
            task_id: UUID,
            completion_notes: Optional[str] = None
    ) -> Result:
    ...
```

First, looking at the outer structure of a use case, we see some key components. Dependency interfaces are injected, and the class has a public execute method that returns a Result object.

Next, let's examine the execute method:

```python
    def execute(
            self,
            task_id: UUID,
            completion_notes: Optional[str] = None
    ) -> Result:

        try:
            # Input validation
            task = self.task_repository.get(task_id)
            task.complete(
                notes=completion_notes
            )
            self.task_repository.save(task)

            # Return simplified task data
            return Result.success({
                "id": str(task.id),
```

```python
                "status": "completed",
                "completion_date": task.completed_at.isoformat()
            })

        except TaskNotFoundError:
            return Result.failure(Error.not_found("Task", str(task_id)))
        except ValidationError as e:
            return Result.failure(Error.validation_error(str(e)))
```

Here, we can see the orchestration of business rules upon the `Task` domain object to accomplish the discrete goal of the use case: completing the task.

This implementation embodies several key architectural principles:

- **Encapsulation**: The use case class provides a clear boundary around a specific business operation.
- **Interface definition**: The execute method provides a clean, focused interface using the result type. The result pattern ensures both success and failure paths are explicit in our interface, making error handling a first-class concern.
- **Error handling**: Domain errors are caught and translated into application-level errors.
- **Dependency injection**: Dependencies are passed in through the constructor, adhering to the Dependency Inversion Principle introduced in *Chapter 2*.

Of these principles, dependency injection deserves special attention as it enables much of our architectural flexibility.

Dependency injection

Earlier we saw how dependency injection helps maintain clean architectural boundaries in our use cases. Let's expand on this by examining how to structure our interfaces to maximize the benefits of dependency injection while ensuring our use cases remain flexible and testable. In Python, we can implement this elegantly using abstract base classes:

```python
class TaskRepository(ABC):
    """Repository interface defined by the Application Layer"""
    @abstractmethod
    def get(self, task_id: UUID) -> Task:
        """Retrieve a task by its ID"""
        pass
```

```python
    @abstractmethod
    def save(self, task: Task) -> None:
        """Save a task to the repository"""
        pass


    @abstractmethod
    def delete(self, task_id: UUID) -> None:
        """Delete a task from the repository"""
        pass


class NotificationService(ABC):
    """Service interface for sending notifications"""
    @abstractmethod
    def notify_task_assigned(self, task_id: UUID) -> None:
        """Notify when a task is assigned"""
        pass


    @abstractmethod
    def notify_task_completed(self, task: Task) -> None:
        """Notify when a task is completed"""
        Pass
```

By defining these interfaces in the Application layer, we strengthen our architectural boundaries while providing clear contracts for outer layers to implement. This approach provides several advanced benefits beyond basic dependency injection:

- Interface definitions express exactly what the Application layer needs, no more and no less
- Abstract methods document the expected behavior through clear method signatures and docstrings
- The Application layer maintains control over its dependencies while remaining independent of their implementations
- Test implementations can focus on exactly what each use case requires

A concrete implementation adhering to this contract might take a form such as this:

```python
class MongoDbTaskRepository(TaskRepository):
    """MongoDB implementation of the TaskRepository interface"""
    def __init__(self, client: MongoClient):
```

```python
        self.client = client
        self.db = client.task_management
        self.tasks = self.db.tasks

    def get(self, task_id: UUID) -> Task:
        """Retrieve a task by its ID"""
        document = self.tasks.find_one({"_id": str(task_id)})
        if not document:
            raise TaskNotFoundError(task_id)
        # ... remainder of method implementation


    # Other interface methods implemented ...
```

This example demonstrates how outer layers can implement the interfaces defined by our Application layer, handling the specifics of data persistence while adhering to the contract our business logic expects.

Handling complex operations

Real-world use cases often involve multiple steps and potential failure points. Let's examine how to manage this complexity while maintaining Clean Architecture principles. Consider a project completion scenario that requires the coordination of multiple tasks.

The `CompleteProjectUseCase` follows our established pattern:

```python
@dataclass(frozen=True)
class CompleteProjectUseCase:
    project_repository: ProjectRepository
    task_repository: TaskRepository
    notification_service: NotificationService

    def execute(
        self,
        project_id: UUID,
        completion_notes: Optional[str] = None
    ) -> Result:
        ...
```

Now, let's examine its execute method:

```python
def execute(
        self,
        project_id: UUID,
        completion_notes: Optional[str] = None
    ) -> Result:
        try:
            # Validate project exists
            project = self.project_repository.get(project_id)

            # Complete all outstanding tasks
            for task in project.incomplete_tasks:
                task.complete()
                self.task_repository.save(task)
                self.notification_service.notify_task_completed(task)

            # Complete the project itself
            project.mark_completed(
                notes=completion_notes
            )
            self.project_repository.save(project)

            return Result.success({
                "id": str(project.id),
                "status": project.status,
                "completion_date": project.completed_at,
                "task_count": len(project.tasks),
                "completion_notes": project.completion_notes,
            })

        except ProjectNotFoundError:
            return Result.failure(Error.not_found(
                "Project", str(project_id)))
        except ValidationError as e:
            return Result.failure(Error.validation_error(str(e)))
```

This implementation demonstrates several patterns for managing complexity:

- **Coordinated operations**: The use case manages multiple related operations as a single logical unit:

    - Completing all outstanding tasks

    - Updating the project status

    - Notifying stakeholders

- **Error management**: The use case provides comprehensive error handling:

    - Domain-specific errors are caught and translated.

    - Each operation's potential failures are considered. In a more involved example, you might see a rollback of the `Task` saves if the `Project` update or save failed.

    - Error responses are consistent and informative.

- **Clear dependencies**: Required services are explicitly defined:

    - Defining repositories for data access

    - Providing notification services for external communication

    - Injecting dependencies for flexibility and testing

- **Input validation**: Parameters are validated before processing:

    - Required IDs are checked for existence

    - Optional parameters are handled appropriately

    - Domain rules are enforced

- **Transactional integrity**: Changes to both tasks and projects are handled as a cohesive operation:

    - The code example could be extended to support true transactionality by just capturing the starting state and then rolling back if one of our statements fails. See the code for `CompleteProjectUseCase` in the book's accompanying GitHub repository for an example of this.

By applying these patterns consistently across our Application layer, we create a robust system that handles complex operations gracefully while maintaining clean architectural boundaries and clear separation of concerns.

Defining request and response models

In the previous section, our use cases worked directly with primitive types and dictionaries. While this approach can work for simple cases, as our application grows, we need more structured ways to handle data crossing our architectural boundaries. Request and response models serve this purpose, providing specialized DTOs that handle data transformation between the outer layers and our application core. Building on the information hiding principles we introduced earlier, these models extend this concept to architectural boundaries, specifically protecting our domain logic from external format details while shielding external interfaces from domain implementation specifics. This reciprocal boundary protection is particularly important as different interfaces evolve at different rates.

Request models

Request models capture and validate incoming data before it reaches our Application layer's use cases. They provide a clear structure for input data and perform preliminary validation:

```python
@dataclass(frozen=True)
class CompleteProjectRequest:
    """Data structure for project completion requests"""
    project_id: str  # From API (will be converted to UUID)
    completion_notes: Optional[str] = None

    def __post_init__(self) -> None:
        """Validate request data"""
        if not self.project_id.strip():
            raise ValidationError("Project ID is required")

        if self.completion_notes and len(self.completion_notes) > 1000:
            raise ValidationError(
                "Completion notes cannot exceed 1000 characters")

    def to_execution_params(self) -> dict:
        """Convert validated request data to use case parameters"""
        return {
            'project_id': UUID(self.project_id),
            'completion_notes': self.completion_notes
        }
```

Request models serve multiple architectural purposes by establishing a clear boundary between outer and inner layers. Through input validation and the to_execution_params method, they ensure that use cases remain focused purely on business logic. The validation step catches malformed data early, while to_execution_params transforms API-friendly formats (such as string IDs) into proper domain types (such as UUIDs) that our business logic expects.

This transformation capability is particularly powerful as it:

- Keeps use cases clean and focused, working only with domain types
- Centralizes data conversion logic in a single, predictable location
- Allows API formats to evolve without impacting core business logic
- Improves testability by providing clear format boundaries

By the time data flows through a request model to reach our use cases, it has been both validated and transformed into the precise format our domain logic expects. This maintains Clean Architecture's separation of concerns, ensuring that outer layer implementation details (such as how IDs are formatted in HTTP requests) never leak into our core business rules.

Response models

Response models handle the transformation of domain objects into structures suitable for external consumption. They maintain our clean architectural boundaries by explicitly controlling what domain data is exposed and how it's formatted:

```python
@dataclass(frozen=True)
class CompleteProjectResponse:
    """Data structure for project completion responses"""
    id: str
    status: str
    completion_date: str
    task_count: int
    completion_notes: Optional[str]

    @classmethod
    def from_entity(cls,
                    project: Project,
                    user_service: UserService
    ) -> 'CompleteProjectResponse':
        """Create response from domain entities"""
```

```
        return cls(
            id=str(project.id),
            status=project.status,
            completion_date=project.completed_at,
            task_count=len(project.tasks),
            completion_notes=project.completion_notes,
        )
```

While `to_execution_params` of the request model transforms inbound data to match domain expectations, `from_entity` handles the outbound journey by converting domain objects into formats suitable to traverse the boundary to the Adapters layer. This symmetrical pattern means our use cases can work purely with domain objects while both input and output are automatically adapted to external needs.

The `from_entity` method serves several key purposes:

- Protects domain objects from exposure to external layers
- Controls exactly what data is exposed and in what format (e.g., converting UUIDs back to strings)
- Provides a consistent serialization point for all external interfaces
- Allows computed or derived fields (such as `task_count`) without modifying domain objects
- Includes computed or aggregate data not present in the base entity
- Optimizes performance by omitting large amounts of irrelevant data
- Includes operation-specific metadata

Let's revisit an evolved version of the `CompleteProjectUseCase` to show how request models, domain logic, and response models work together:

```
@dataclass(frozen=True)
class CompleteProjectUseCase:
    project_repository: ProjectRepository
    task_repository: TaskRepository
    notification_service: NotificationService

    # Using CompleteProjectRequest vs discreet parameters
    def execute(self, request: CompleteProjectRequest) -> Result:
        try:
            params = request.to_execution_params()
```

```python
        project = self.project_repository.get(params["project_id"])
        project.mark_completed(notes=params["completion_notes"])

        # Complete all outstanding tasks
        # ... Truncated for brevity

        self.project_repository.save(project)
        # using CompleteProjectResponse vs handbuilt dict
        response = CompleteProjectResponse.from_entity(project)
        return Result.success(response)

    except ProjectNotFoundError:
        return Result.failure(
            Error.not_found("Project", str(params["project_id"]))
        )
    except ValidationError as e:
        return Result.failure(Error.validation_error(str(e)))
```

This example demonstrates how our use case remains focused purely on orchestrating domain logic while request and response models handle the necessary transformations at our architectural boundaries. The use case receives an already-validated request, works with proper domain types throughout its execution, and returns a response model wrapped in a `Result` object that can be consumed by any outer layer implementation.

In the Interface Adapters layer, these response models can be consumed by a variety of components including controllers handling HTTP requests, command-line interface command processors, or message queue handlers. Each adapter can transform the response data appropriately for its specific transport mechanism, converting it to JSON over HTTP, console output, or message payloads as needed.

Maintaining separation from external services

While request and response models handle data transformation at our API surface, our application must also interact with external services like email systems, file storage, and third-party APIs. The Application layer maintains separation from these services through **ports**— interfaces that define exactly what capabilities our application requires without specifying implementation details. In our task management system, external services might include:

- Email services for sending notifications (such as SendGrid or AWS SES)

- File storage systems for attachments (such as AWS S3 or Google Cloud Storage)

- Authentication services (such as Auth0 or Okta)
- Calendar integration services (such as Google Calendar or Microsoft Outlook)
- External messaging systems (such as Slack or Microsoft Teams)

While request/response models and ports both serve to maintain clean architectural boundaries, they address different aspects of the system's interaction with the outside world. Request/response models handle data transformation at our API boundaries, following consistent interfaces across all use cases (for example, `from_entity` and `to_execution_params`) to ensure uniform data handling.

Ports, in contrast, define interfaces for the services our Application layer depends on with each port being specifically crafted to represent a particular external service's capabilities. This dual approach ensures our core business logic remains independent of both data format details and external implementation specifics.

Interface boundaries

Ports allow the Application layer to specify exactly what capabilities it needs from external services without being coupled to specific implementations. Let's examine how these boundary mechanisms work together:

```python
# Port: Defines capability needed by Application Layer
class NotificationPort(ABC):

    @abstractmethod
    def notify_task_completed(self, task: Task) -> None:
        """Notify when a task is completed"""
        pass

    # other capabilities as needed
```

This interface exemplifies information hiding at architectural boundaries. It reveals only the operations our Application layer needs while concealing all implementation details—whether notifications are sent via email, SMS, or another mechanism remains completely hidden from our core business logic.

Then, in each use case, we might leverage the defined port like this:

```python
@dataclass
class SetTaskPriorityUseCase:
    task_repository: TaskRepository
```

```python
    notification_service: NotificationPort # Depends on
                                           # capability interface

def execute(self, request: SetTaskPriorityRequest) -> Result:
    try:
        params = request.to_execution_params()

        task = self.task_repository.get(params['task_id'])
        task.priority = params['priority']

        self.task_repository.save(task)

        if task.priority == Priority.HIGH:
            self.notification_service.notify_task_high_priority(task)

        return Result.success(TaskResponse.from_entity(task))
    except ValidationError as e:
        return Result.failure(Error.validation_error(str(e)))
```

This approach demonstrates the distinct roles of our boundary mechanisms:

- Request/response models handle the transformation of data at API boundaries
- Ports define the service capabilities our use cases need
- The Application layer uses both to maintain clean separation while coordinating the overall flow

You might recall in our previous example in the *Handling complex operations* section that we referenced a concrete `NotificationService`; here, we've matured our design by defining an abstract interface or port (`NotificationPort`). This shift from implementation to interface better aligns with the Dependency Rule and provides clearer architectural boundaries.

By depending only on the abstract capability interface rather than concrete implementations, our use case maintains information hiding in both directions: the use case knows nothing about notification implementation details, while notification services know nothing about use case internals beyond the parameters provided through the interface.

We can now explore how to effectively manage the external dependencies these boundaries help us control.

Supporting evolving service requirements

As systems evolve, we need patterns that allow us to add new capabilities and adapt to changing service implementations. Let's examine two key patterns for managing this evolution.

Supporting optional integration

As applications grow, we often want to make certain service integrations optional or environment-specific. The optional services pattern helps manage this:

```python
@dataclass(frozen=True)
class TaskManagementUseCase:
    task_repository: TaskRepository
    notification_service: NotificationPort
    _optional_services: dict[str, Any] = field(default_factory=dict)

    def register_service(self, name: str, service: Any) -> None:
        """Register an optional service"""
        self._optional_services[name] = service

    def complete_task(self, task_id: UUID) -> Result:
        try:
            task = self.task_repository.get(task_id)
            task.complete()
            self.task_repository.save(task)

            # Required notification
            self.notification_service.notify_task_completed(task)

            # Optional integrations
            if analytics := self._optional_services.get('analytics'):
                analytics.track_task_completion(task.id)
            if audit := self._optional_services.get('audit'):
                audit.log_task_completion(task.id)

            return Result.success(TaskResponse.from_entity(task))
        except ValidationError as e:
            return Result.failure(Error.validation_error(str(e)))
```

This approach provides several advantages:

- Core business operations remain focused and stable through the primary `task_repository` and `notification_service` dependencies
- New capabilities can be added without modifying existing code using the flexible `_optional_services` dictionary
- Optional services can be configured based on deployment needs via the `register_service` method
- Testing remains straightforward as dependencies are explicit in the constructor, with optional services clearly separated from the core requirements

The use of a dictionary to store optional services combined with conditional execution (e.g., `if analytics := self._optional_services.get('analytics')`) provides a clean pattern for gracefully handling features that may or may not be present in any given deployment.

Adapting to service changes

When integrating with third-party services or managing system upgrades, we often need to switch between different interfaces. The adapter pattern helps us manage this:

```python
class ModernNotificationService:
    """Third-party service with a different interface"""
    def send_notification(self, payload: dict) -> None:
        # Modern service implementation
        pass


class ModernNotificationAdapter(NotificationPort):
    """Adapts modern notification service to work with our interface"""
    def __init__(self, modern_service: ModernNotificationService):
        self._service = modern_service

    def notify_task_completed(self, task: Task) -> None:
        self._service.send_notification({
            "type": "TASK_COMPLETED",
            "taskId": str(task.id)
        })
```

The adapter pattern is particularly valuable in several scenarios:

- **Integrating with third-party services**: The `ModernNotificationService` can be wrapped without modifying its interface
- **Managing system upgrades**: The adapter's translation layer (`send_notification` to specific notification methods) isolates changes in service implementations
- **Supporting multiple implementations**: Different services can be adapted to the same `NotificationPort` interface
- **Transitioning between service versions**: The mapping of structured payloads in `notify_task_completed` allows protocol evolution while maintaining backward compatibility

By using these patterns together, we can create systems that gracefully handle both optional features and changing service implementations while maintaining clean architectural boundaries.

Summary

In this chapter, we explored the Application layer of Clean Architecture, focusing on how it orchestrates domain objects and coordinates with external services to fulfill user needs. We learned how to implement use cases that maintain clean architectural boundaries while providing meaningful functionality.

Through our task management system example, we discovered how to create use case interactors that coordinate domain objects while respecting the Dependency Rule introduced in *Chapter 1*. We built upon the SOLID principles from *Chapter 2* and the type-awareness patterns from *Chapter 3* to create robust, maintainable implementations. Our use cases effectively orchestrate the domain objects and services we developed in *Chapter 4*, showing how Clean Architecture layers work together harmoniously.

We implemented several key patterns and concepts:

- Use case interactors that orchestrate domain operations
- Request and response models that create clear boundaries
- Error handling patterns that maintain architectural separation
- Interface definitions that keep external concerns isolated

These implementations demonstrated how to maintain the integrity of our architecture while handling real-world requirements. We saw how proper boundaries allow our application to evolve and adapt to changing needs without compromising its core design.

In *Chapter 6*, we'll explore how our clean boundaries enable the creation of effective adapters that translate between our Application layer and the outside world. We'll see how the patterns we've established with request/response models and ports naturally extend to implementing controllers, gateways, and presenters.

Further reading

- *Building Microservices: Designing Fine-Grained Systems* by Sam Newman. Although focused on microservices, this book's chapters on service boundaries, inter-service communication, and data handling provide valuable insights for creating well-defined boundaries in application layers and can be applied to monolithic applications as well.

- *Hexagonal Architecture* by Alistair Cockburn (`https://alistair.cockburn.us/hexagonal-architecture/`). This article explains the ports and adapters (or hexagonal architecture) pattern, which is highly complementary to Clean Architecture principles. It provides a clear understanding of managing dependencies and boundary translation, which are central to implementing the Application layer.

Get this book's PDF version and more

Scan the QR code (or go to `packtpub.com/unlock`). Search for this book by name, confirm the edition, and then follow the steps on the page.

Note: Keep your invoice handy. Purchases made directly from Packt don't require an invoice.

6

The Interface Adapters Layer: Controllers and Presenters

In *Chapters 4 and 5*, we built the core of our task management system—the domain entities that represent our business concepts and the use cases that orchestrate them. The Application layer's request/response models handle translation between use cases and domain objects, ensuring our core business rules remain pure and focused. However, there's still a gap between these use cases and the outside world such as web interfaces or command-line tools. This is where the **Interface Adapters layer** comes in.

The Interface Adapters layer serves as the translator between our application's core and external concerns. It converts data between formats convenient for external agencies and those expected by our use cases. Through carefully designed controllers and presenters, this layer maintains the architectural boundaries that keep our core business rules isolated and maintainable.

In this chapter, we'll explore how to implement the Interface Adapters layer in Python, seeing how it upholds Clean Architecture's Dependency Rule. We'll learn how controllers coordinate external input with our use cases, and how presenters transform domain data for various output needs.

By the end of this chapter, you'll understand how to create a flexible Interface Adapters layer that protects your core business logic while supporting multiple interfaces. You'll implement clean architectural boundaries that make your system more maintainable and adaptable to change.

In this chapter, we're going to cover the following main topics:

- Designing the Interface Adapters layer
- Implementing controllers in Python

- Enforcing boundaries through Interface Adapters
- Building presenters for data formatting

Technical requirements

The code examples presented in this chapter and throughout the rest of the book are tested with Python 3.13. For brevity, code examples in the chapter may be partially implemented. Complete versions of all examples can be found in the book's accompanying GitHub repository at `https://github.com/PacktPublishing/Clean-Architecture-with-Python`.

Designing the Interface Adapters layer

In Clean Architecture, each layer serves a specific purpose in maintaining separation of concerns. As we've seen in previous chapters, the Domain layer encapsulates our core business rules, while the Application layer orchestrates use cases. But how do we connect these pure business-focused layers with the practical needs of user interfaces, databases, and external services? This is the role of the Interface Adapters layer.

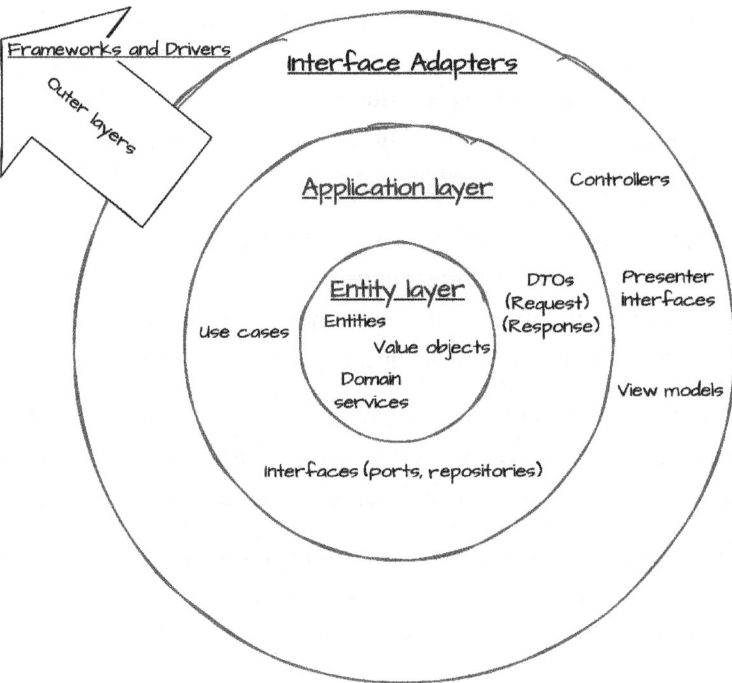

Figure 6.1: Interface Adapters layer with the primary components

In the next section we will dive into the details of the Interface Adapters layer's role and see examples of this layer in our tasks management application.

Interface Adapters layer's role in Clean Architecture

The Interface Adapters layer acts as a set of translators between our application's core and external details such as a web framework or a command-line interface. This layer is crucial because it allows us to maintain clean architectural boundaries while enabling practical interaction with external concerns. By sitting between the Application layer and external interfaces, it ensures that:

- Our core business logic remains pure and focused
- External concerns can't leak into inner layers
- Changes to external interfaces don't affect our core logic
- Multiple interfaces can interact with our system consistently

The key principle governing this layer is the Dependency Rule: dependencies must point inward toward the core business rules. The Interface Adapters layer rigidly enforces this rule by ensuring all translations maintain proper architectural boundaries.

Responsibilities of the Interface Adapters layer

As we delve deeper into Clean Architecture's Interface Adapters layer, it's essential to understand its core responsibilities. Just as a translator must be fluent in both languages they work with, this layer must understand both the precise language of our application core and the varied dialects of external interfaces. These responsibilities form two distinct but complementary flows of data through our system, each requiring careful handling to maintain our architectural boundaries.

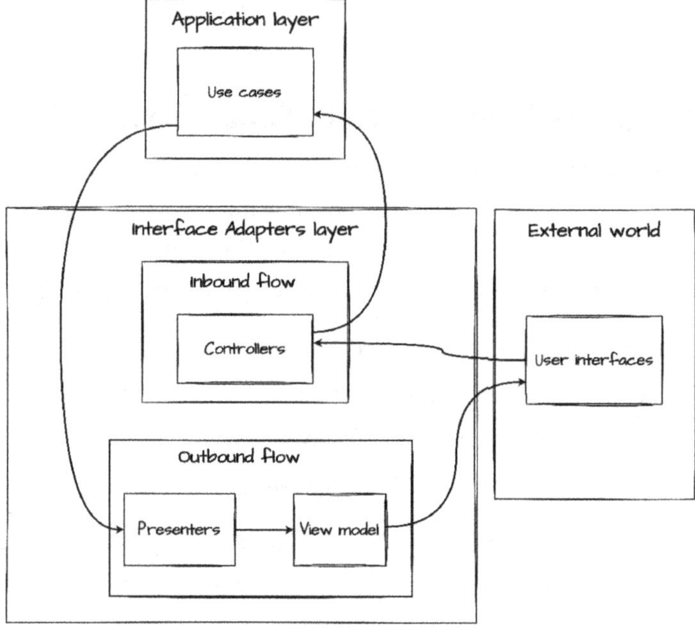

Figure 6.2: Bidirectional data flow through the Interface Adapters layer

In *Figure 6.2*, we see the Interface Adapters layer manages the bidirectional flow of data between our application core and external concerns:

- **Inbound data flow**:

  - Converting external requests into application-specific formats

  - Ensuring data meets application requirements

  - Coordinating with use cases to execute operations

- **Outbound data flow**:

  - Transforming application results for external consumption

  - Providing interface-appropriate data formats

  - Maintaining separation between core logic and external interfaces

These responsibilities form the foundation for the specific components we'll examine next.

Interface Adapters layer versus Application layer boundaries

When first working with Clean Architecture, it's common to wonder about the distinction between data transformation in the Interface Adapters layer versus the Application layer. After all, both layers appear to handle data conversion. However, these layers serve fundamentally different purposes in our architecture, and understanding these differences is crucial for maintaining clean boundaries in our system.

While both the Interface Adapters layer and Application layer handle data transformation, they serve different purposes and maintain different boundaries:

- **Application layer:**

    - Transforms between domain entities and use case-specific formats

    - Focuses on business rule coordination

    - Works with domain-specific types and structures

- **Interface Adapters layer:**

    - Transforms between use case formats and external interface needs

    - Focuses on external interface coordination

    - Works with interface-specific formats and primitive types

This clear separation ensures that our system maintains strong boundaries between its core business logic and external interfaces.

Key components and their relationships

With an understanding of the Interface Adapters layer's responsibilities and boundaries, we can now examine the specific components that implement these concepts. These components work together like a well-orchestrated team, each playing a specific role in maintaining our architectural boundaries while enabling practical system interaction. While we'll explore detailed implementations later in this chapter, understanding how these components collaborate provides essential context for our Clean Architecture design.

The Interface Adapters layer implements its responsibilities through three key components:

- **Controllers** handle inbound flow, serving as entry points for external requests into our system. They ensure that data crossing into our application core meets our system's requirements while protecting our use cases from external concerns.

- **Presenters** manage outbound flow, transforming use case results into formats suitable for external consumption. The Interface Adapters layer defines the presenter interfaces, establishing the contract that both use cases and concrete presenter implementations must follow.

- **View models** serve as data carriers between presenters and views, containing only primitive types and simple data structures. This simplicity ensures that views can easily consume the formatted data while maintaining clean architectural boundaries.

These components interact in a carefully orchestrated flow that always respects the Dependency Rule:

1. External requests flow through controllers

2. Controllers coordinate with use cases

3. Use cases return results through defined interfaces

4. Presenters format results into view models

5. Views consume the formatted data

This carefully orchestrated interaction ensures that our system maintains clean boundaries while remaining practical and maintainable.

Interface design principles

When designing interfaces in the Interface Adapters layer, we must balance clean architectural boundaries with practical implementation concerns. As we saw in *Chapter 5* with request/response models, careful interface design enables smooth data flow while maintaining proper separation between layers. The principles guiding interface design in this layer help us achieve this balance while adhering to Clean Architecture's core tenets.

Three key principles shape our interface design:

- The **Dependency Rule** takes precedence in all design decisions. All dependencies must point inward toward use cases and entities. This means our interface adapters depend on application interfaces (like the `CreateTaskUseCase` we saw in *Chapter 5*), but the application never depends on our adapters. This rule ensures that changes to external interfaces can't affect our core business logic.

- The **Single Responsibility Principle** guides component boundaries. Each adapter handles one specific type of transformation: controllers handle input validation and conversion, while presenters manage output formatting. This separation makes our system easier to maintain and modify. For example, a `TaskController` focuses solely on validating and converting task-related input, while a `TaskPresenter` handles only the formatting of task data for display.

- The **Interface Segregation Principle** ensures our interfaces remain focused and cohesive. Rather than creating large, monolithic interfaces, we design small, purpose-specific interfaces that serve distinct client needs. For instance, instead of a single large `TaskOperations` interface, we might have separate interfaces for task creation, completion, and querying. This granularity provides flexibility and makes our system more adaptable to change.

By following these principles, we create interfaces that effectively bridge the gap between our clean, focused core business logic and the practical needs of external interfaces. As we explore specific implementations in the following sections, we'll see how these principles guide our design decisions and lead to more maintainable code.

Implementing controllers in Python

Having established the theoretical foundations of the Interface Adapters layer, we turn now to practical implementation using Python. Python's language features offer several elegant mechanisms for implementing Clean Architecture's controller patterns. Through data classes, abstract base classes (ABCs), and type hints, we can create clear and maintainable interface boundaries while keeping our code Pythonic.

While Clean Architecture provides a set of principles and patterns, it does not prescribe a rigid implementation approach. As we proceed, remember that this represents one possible implementation of Clean Architecture's principles; the key is maintaining clean boundaries and separation of concerns, regardless of specific implementation details.

Controller responsibilities and patterns

As we saw in our examination of Interface Adapters layer components, controllers in Clean Architecture have a focused set of responsibilities: they accept input from external sources, validate and transform that input into the format our use cases expect, coordinate use case execution, and handle the results appropriately.

Let's examine a concrete implementation that demonstrates these principles:

```python
@dataclass
class TaskController:
    create_use_case: CreateTaskUseCase
    # ... additional use cases as needed
    presenter: TaskPresenter

    def handle_create(
        self,
        title: str,
        description: str
    ) -> OperationResult[TaskViewModel]:
        try:
            request = CreateTaskRequest(
                title=title,
                description=description
            )
            result = self.create_use_case.execute(request)

            if result.is_success:
                view_model = self.presenter.present_task(result.value)
                return OperationResult.succeed(view_model)

            error_vm = self.presenter.present_error(
                result.error.message,
                str(result.error.code.name)
            )
            return OperationResult.fail(error_vm.message, error_vm.code)

        except ValueError as e:
            error_vm = self.presenter.present_error(
                str(e), "VALIDATION_ERROR")
            return OperationResult.fail(error_vm.message, error_vm.code)
```

This controller demonstrates several key Clean Architecture principles. First, notice how it depends only on injected dependencies: both the use case and presenter are constructed elsewhere and brought into the controller via constructor injection.

To understand why this **dependency injection pattern** is so important, consider this counter example:

```python
# Anti-example: Tightly coupled controller
class TightlyCoupledTaskController:
    def __init__(self):
        # Direct instantiation creates tight coupling
        self.use_case = TaskUseCase(SqliteTaskRepository())
        self.presenter = CliTaskPresenter()

    def handle_create(self, title: str, description: str):
        # Implementation details...
        pass
```

This counter or anti-example demonstrates several problems:

- Direct instantiation of concrete classes creates tight coupling
- The controller knows too much about implementation details
- Testing becomes difficult as dependencies can't be replaced
- Changes to implementations force changes to the controller

Returning to our clean implementation, the `handle_create` method shows the controller's core responsibilities in action. It begins by accepting primitive types (`title` and `description` strings) from the external world—keeping the interface simple and framework-agnostic. These inputs are then transformed into a proper request object, validating and formatting the data before it reaches our use case.

For brevity, we're showing only the `handle_create` implementation, but in practice, this controller would have additional use cases injected (like `complete_use_case`, `set_priority_use_case`, etc.) and corresponding handler methods implemented. This pattern of dependency injection and handler implementation remains consistent across all controller operations.

The controller's error-handling strategy is particularly noteworthy. It catches validation errors before they reach the use case and handles both successful and failed results from the use case execution. In all cases, it uses the presenter to format responses appropriately for external consumption, returning them wrapped in an `OperationResult` that makes success and failure cases explicit. This pattern builds on the result type we introduced in *Chapter 5*, adding view model support for interface-specific formatting. We'll discuss the use of `OperationResult` in more detail in *Building Presenters for Data Formatting*.

This clean separation of concerns ensures that our business logic remains unaware of how it's being called while providing a robust and maintainable interface for external clients.

Working with request models in controllers

We saw `CreateTaskRequest` earlier in our examination of the `TaskController`, and in *Chapter 5*'s coverage of the Application layer. Now let's examine more closely how controllers work with these request models to maintain clean boundaries between external input and our use cases:

```python
@dataclass(frozen=True)
class CreateTaskRequest:
    """Request data for creating a new task."""
    title: str
    description: str
    due_date: Optional[str] = None
    priority: Optional[str] = None

    def to_execution_params(self) -> dict:
        """Convert request data to use case parameters."""
        params = {
            "title": self.title.strip(),
            "description": self.description.strip(),
        }
        if self.priority:
            params["priority"] = Priority[self.priority.upper()]
        return params
```

While the Application layer defines these request models, controllers are responsible for their proper instantiation and use. The controller ensures input validation occurs before use case execution:

```python
# In TaskController
try:
    request = CreateTaskRequest(title=title, description=description)
    # Request is now validated and properly formatted
    result = self.create_use_case.execute(request)
except ValueError as e:
    # Handle validation errors before they reach use cases
    return OperationResult.fail(str(e), "VALIDATION_ERROR")
```

This separation ensures that our use cases only ever receive properly validated and formatted data, maintaining clean architectural boundaries while providing robust input handling.

Maintaining controller independence

The effectiveness of our Interface Adapters layer depends heavily on maintaining proper isolation between our controllers and both external and internal concerns.

Let's look more closely into how our `TaskController` achieves this independence:

```python
@dataclass
class TaskController:
    create_use_case: CreateTaskUseCase  # Application Layer interface
    presenter: TaskPresenter            # Interface Layer abstraction
```

This simple dependency structure demonstrates several key principles. First, the controller depends only on abstractions; it knows nothing about concrete implementations of either the use case or presenter.

Let's take a moment to clarify what we mean by *abstractions* in Python. As we'll soon see, the `TaskPresenter` follows a classical interface pattern using Python's ABC, establishing a formal interface contract. For use cases like `CreateTaskUseCase`, we take advantage of Python's duck typing, since each use case needs only an `execute` method with defined parameters and return types, any class providing this method fulfills the interface contract without needing ABC formality.

This flexibility in defining interfaces is one of Python's strengths. We can choose formal ABC interfaces when we need to enforce complex contracts or rely on duck typing for simpler interfaces. It's the developer's choice of the style they prefer. Both approaches maintain Clean Architecture's dependency principles while staying idiomatic to Python.

Taking a mental inventory, notice what's missing from our controller:

- No web framework imports or decorators
- No database or storage concerns
- No direct instantiation of dependencies
- No knowledge of concrete view implementations

This careful isolation means our controller can be used by any delivery mechanism—whether it's a web API, command-line interface (CLI), or message queue consumer. Consider what happens when we violate this isolation:

```python
# Anti-example: Controller with framework coupling
class WebTaskController:
    def __init__(self, app: FastAPI):
        self.app = app
        self.use_case = CreateTaskUseCase()  # Direct instantiation too!

    async def handle_create(self, request: Request):
        try:
            data = await request.json()
            # Controller now tightly coupled to FastAPI
            return JSONResponse(status_code=201, content={"task": result})
        except ValidationError as e:
            raise HTTPException(status_code=400, detail=str(e))
```

This counter example violates our isolation principles by:

- Importing and depending on a specific web framework
- Handling HTTP-specific concerns
- Mixing framework error handling with business logic

The decision about how to expose our controller's functionality belongs in the Frameworks layer. In *Chapter 7*, we'll see how to create proper framework-specific adapters that wrap our clean controller implementation. This allows us to maintain clean architectural boundaries while still leveraging the full capabilities of frameworks like FastAPI, Click for command-line, or message queue libraries.

The interfaces our controller depends on demonstrate Clean Architecture's careful attention to boundaries: use case interfaces defined by the Application layer establish our inward dependencies, while presenter interfaces defined in our Interface Adapters layer give us control over outward data flow. This careful arrangement of interfaces ensures we maintain the Dependency Rule while keeping our system flexible and adaptable.

Enforcing boundaries through interface adapters

While our examination of controllers demonstrated how to handle incoming requests, Clean Architecture's interface boundaries require careful attention to data flow in both directions. In this section, we'll explore patterns for maintaining clean boundaries throughout our system, particularly focusing on the explicit handling of success and failure cases. These patterns complement our controllers and presenters while ensuring that all cross-boundary communication remains clear and maintainable.

Explicit success/failure patterns at boundaries

At our architectural boundaries, we need clear, consistent ways to handle both successful operations and failures. Operations can fail for many reasons— invalid input, business rule violations, or system errors—and each type of failure might need different handling by the external interface. Similarly, successful operations need to provide their results in a format suitable for the interface that requested them. We've seen this mechanism in play in the controller examples shown earlier.

```python
class TaskController:

    def handle_create(
        self,
        title: str,
        description: str
    ) -> OperationResult[TaskViewModel]:
```

The `OperationResult` pattern addresses these needs by providing a standardized way to handle both success and failure cases. This pattern ensures that our interface adapters always communicate outcomes explicitly, making it impossible to overlook error cases and providing a clear structure for success scenarios:

```python
@dataclass
class OperationResult(Generic[T]):
    """Represents the outcome of controller operations."""
    _success: Optional[T] = None
    _error: Optional[ErrorViewModel] = None

    @classmethod
    def succeed(cls, value: T) -> 'OperationResult[T]':
        """Create a successful result with the given view model."""
```

```python
        return cls(_success=value)

    @classmethod
    def fail(cls, message: str,
             code: Optional[str] = None) -> 'OperationResult[T]':
        """Create a failed result with error details."""
        return cls(_error=ErrorViewModel(message, code))
```

Notice how the class is defined as `OperationResult(Generic[T])`. This means our class can work with any type T. When we instantiate the class, we replace T with a specific type—for example, when we write `OperationResult[TaskViewModel]`, we're saying: *this operation will either succeed with a* `TaskViewModel` *or fail with an error (*`ErrorViewModel`*)*. This type safety helps catch potential errors early while making our code's intent clearer.

This explicit handling of outcomes provides a foundation for clean boundary crossing that we'll see applied throughout our interface adapters. As we move into looking at data transformation patterns, we'll see how this clarity in success and failure handling helps maintain clean architectural boundaries while enabling practical functionality.

If we look at some application code (residing in the Frameworks layer) we see how this `OperationResult` can be utilized to drive application flow:

```python
# pseudo-code example of a CLI app working with a OperationResult
result = app.task_controller.handle_create(title, description)
if result.is_success:
    task = result.success
    print(f"{task.status_display} [{task.priority_display}] {task.title}")
    return 0
print(result.error.message, fg='red', err=True)
    return 1
```

Clean data transformation flows

As data moves through our architectural boundaries, it undergoes several transformations. Understanding these transformation flows helps us maintain clean boundaries while ensuring our system remains maintainable:

```python
# Example transformation flow in TaskController
def handle_create(
    self, title: str, description: str
```

```python
) -> OperationResult[TaskViewModel]:
    try:
        # 1. External input to request model
        request = CreateTaskRequest(title=title, description=description)

        # 2. Request model to domain operations
        result = self.use_case.execute(request)

        if result.is_success:
            # 3. Domain result to view model
            view_model = self.presenter.present_task(result.value)
            return OperationResult.succeed(view_model)

        # 4. Error handling and formatting
        error_vm = self.presenter.present_error(
            result.error.message,
            str(result.error.code.name)
        )
        return OperationResult.fail(error_vm.message, error_vm.code)

    except ValueError as e:
        # 5. Validation error handling
        error_vm = self.presenter.present_error(
            str(e), "VALIDATION_ERROR")
        return OperationResult.fail(error_vm.message, error_vm.code)
```

This example shows a complete transformation chain:

1. External input validation and conversion

2. Use case execution with domain types

3. Success case transformation to view model

4. Error case handling and formatting

5. Validation error handling

Each step in this chain maintains clean boundaries while ensuring data moves properly between layers.

Interface adapters and architectural boundaries

While we've focused on controllers and presenters as key interface adapters, not every interaction between layers requires an adapter. Understanding when adapters are needed helps maintain Clean Architecture without unnecessary complexity.

```python
# Defined in Application layer
class TaskRepository(ABC):
    @abstractmethod
    def get(self, task_id: UUID) -> Task:
        """Retrieve a task by its ID."""
        pass


# Implemented directly in Infrastructure Layer
class SqliteTaskRepository(TaskRepository):
    def get(self, task_id: UUID) -> Task:
        # Direct implementation of interface
        pass
```

No adapter is needed here because:

- The Application layer defines the exact interface needed
- Implementation can directly fulfill this interface
- No data format conversion is required
- The Dependency Rule is maintained without adaptation

This differs from controllers and presenters which must handle varying external formats and protocols. The key question when deciding if an adapter is needed is: *Does this interaction need format conversion between layers?* If the outer layer can work directly with the interface defined by the inner layer, an adapter in the Interface layer may not be necessary.

This distinction helps us maintain Clean Architecture principles while avoiding unnecessary abstraction. By understanding when adapters are needed, we can create more maintainable systems that respect architectural boundaries without overcomplicating our design.

Building presenters for data formatting

Throughout this chapter, we've referenced presenters as key components of our Interface Adapters layer. Now we'll examine them in detail, seeing how they maintain clean architectural boundaries while preparing domain data for external consumption.

Presenters complement our controllers, handling the outbound flow of data just as controllers manage inbound requests. By implementing the humble object pattern, presenters help us create more testable and maintainable systems while keeping our views simple and focused.

Understanding the humble object pattern

The **humble object pattern** addresses a common challenge in Clean Architecture: how to handle presentation logic, which often resists unit testing, while maintaining clean architectural boundaries.

The term *humble object* comes from the strategy of making a component as simple and devoid of complex logic as possible. In presentation contexts, this means creating an extremely basic view that does nothing more than display pre-formatted data. The view becomes *humble* by design, containing minimal intelligence.

For example, a humble view might be:

- A simple HTML template rendering pre-formatted data
- A React component that only displays passed props
- A CLI display function that prints formatted strings

The pattern splits responsibilities between two components:

- A *humble view* containing minimal logic that's hard to test
- A Presenter containing all presentation logic in an easily testable form

Consider how our task management system might display task information in a CLIs:

```python
# The "humble" view - simple, minimal logic, hard to test
def display_task(task_vm: TaskViewModel):
    print(f"{task_vm.status_display} [{task_vm.priority_display}]
        {task_vm.title}")
    if task_vm.due date display:
        print(f"Due: {task_vm.due_date_display}")
```

All formatting decisions—how to display status, priority levels, dates—live in our presenter, not the view model (`TaskViewModel`) itself. This separation brings several benefits:

- Views remain simple and focused on display
- Presentation logic stays testable

- Business rules remain isolated from display concerns
- Multiple interfaces can share formatting logic

It's worth noting that the emphasis on presenters can vary based on your specific needs. If you're building a Python API that serves data to a JavaScript frontend, you might need minimal presentation logic. However, in full-stack Python applications using frameworks like Django or Flask, robust presenters help maintain clean separation between business logic and display concerns. Understanding the pattern lets you make informed decisions based on your circumstances.

Defining presenter interfaces

Clean Architecture's success relies heavily on well-defined interfaces at architectural boundaries. For presenters, these interfaces establish clear contracts for transforming domain data into presentation-ready formats:

```python
class TaskPresenter(ABC):
    """Abstract base presenter for task-related output."""

    @abstractmethod
    def present_task(self, task_response: TaskResponse) -> TaskViewModel:
        """Convert task response to view model."""
        pass

    @abstractmethod
    def present_error(self, error_msg: str,
                      code: Optional[str] = None) -> ErrorViewModel:
        """Format error message for display."""
        pass
```

This interface, defined in our Interface Adapters layer, serves several key purposes:

- Establishes a clear contract for task presentation
- Enables multiple interface implementations
- Maintains the Dependency Rule by keeping domain logic unaware of presentation details
- Makes testing easier through clear abstraction

Notice how the interface uses domain-specific types (`TaskResponse`) as input but returns view-specific types (`TaskViewModel`). This boundary crossing is where we transform domain concepts into presentation-friendly formats.

Working with view models

View models serve as data carriers between presenters and views, ensuring clean separation between presentation logic and display concerns. They encapsulate formatted data in a way that any view implementation can easily consume:

```python
@dataclass(frozen=True)
class TaskViewModel:
    """View-specific representation of a task."""
    id: str
    title: str
    description: str
    status_display: str      # Pre-formatted for display
    priority_display: str    # Pre-formatted for display
    due_date_display: Optional[str]  # Pre-formatted for display
    project_display: Optional[str]   # Pre-formatted project context
    completion_info: Optional[str]   # Pre-formatted completion details
```

Several key principles guide our view model design:

- Use only primitive types (strings, numbers, booleans)
- Pre-format all display text
- Make no assumptions about the display mechanism
- Remain immutable (notice the `frozen=True`)
- Include only data needed for display

This simplicity ensures that our views remain truly *humble*—they need only read and display these pre-formatted values, with no knowledge of domain concepts or formatting rules.

Implementing concrete presenters

With our presenter interfaces and view models defined, we can implement concrete presenters for specific interface needs. These concrete presenters are implemented in the Frameworks and Drivers layer, but we give you a sneak peek here for context. Let's examine a CLI-specific presenter implementation:

```python
class CliTaskPresenter(TaskPresenter):
    """CLI-specific task presenter."""

    def present_task(self, task_response: TaskResponse) -> TaskViewModel:
```

```python
            """Format task for CLI display."""
            return TaskViewModel(
                id=str(task_response.id),
                title=task_response.title,
                description=task_response.description,
                status_display=self._format_status(task_response.status),
                priority_display=self._format_priority(
                    task_response.priority),
                due_date_display=self._format_due_date(
                    task_response.due_date),
                project_display=self._format_project(
                    task_response.project_id),
                completion_info=self._format_completion_info(
                    task_response.completion_date,
                    task_response.completion_notes
                )
            )
```

The `present_task` method transforms our domain-specific `TaskResponse` into a view-friendly `TaskViewModel`. To support this transformation, the presenter implements several private formatting methods that handle specific aspects of the data:

```python
class CliTaskPresenter(TaskPresenter):  # continuing from above
    def _format_due_date(self, due_date: Optional[datetime]) -> str:
        """Format due date, indicating if task is overdue."""
        if not due_date:
            return "No due date"

        is_overdue = due_date < datetime.now(timezone.utc)
        date_str = due_date.strftime("%Y-%m-%d")
        return (
            f"OVERDUE - Due: {date_str}"
            if is_overdue else f"Due: {date_str}"
        )

    def present_error(self, error_msg: str,
                      code: Optional[str] = None) -> ErrorViewModel:
        """Format error message for CLI display."""
        return ErrorViewModel(message=error_msg, code=code)
```

This implementation demonstrates several key Clean Architecture principles:

- All formatting logic lives in the presenter, not views

- Domain concepts (like `TaskStatus`) are converted to display strings

- Error handling remains consistent with success cases

- Interface-specific formatting (CLI in this case) stays isolated

The presenter's formatting methods remain highly testable: we can verify that overdue tasks are properly marked, dates are correctly formatted, and error messages maintain consistency. This testability stands in stark contrast to testing UI components directly, demonstrating a key benefit of the humble object pattern.

> **Implementation flexibility**
>
> If you're building an API that primarily serves JSON to a JavaScript frontend, you might need minimal presentation logic. The presenter pattern becomes most valuable when you need complex formatting or support multiple interface types.

In *Chapter 7*, we'll see how different interfaces (CLI, web, or APIs) can implement their own presenters while sharing this common architecture. This flexibility demonstrates how Clean Architecture's careful attention to boundaries enables system evolution without compromising core business logic.

Through our exploration of controllers and presenters, we've now implemented a complete Interface Adapters layer for our task management system. Let's take a moment to review our architectural progress by examining the structure we've built across *Chapters 4–6*:

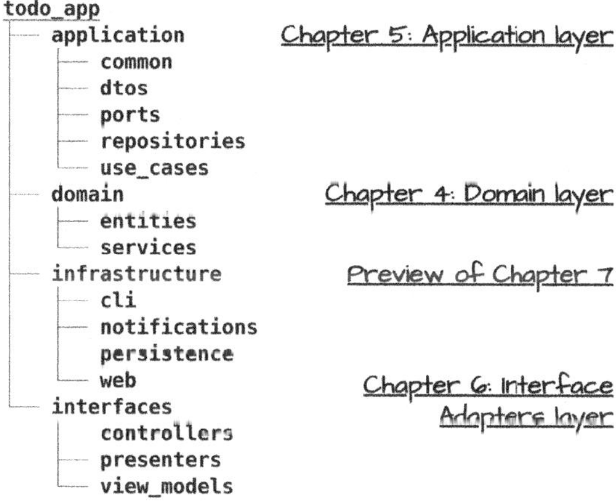

Figure 6.3: Folder structure with all layers in place

This structure reflects Clean Architecture's concentric layers. Our Domain layer, established in *Chapter 4*, remains pure and focused on business rules. The Application layer, added in *Chapter 5*, orchestrates these domain objects to accomplish specific use cases. Now, with our Interface Adapters layer, we've implemented the controllers and presenters that translate between our core business logic and external concerns, maintaining clean boundaries while enabling practical interaction with our system. See the accompanying GitHub repository (`https://github.com/PacktPublishing/Clean-Architecture-with-Python`) for a more extensive code example of the task management application example being used throughout the book.

Summary

In this chapter, we explored the Interface Adapters layer of Clean Architecture, implementing controllers and presenters that maintain clean boundaries while enabling practical interaction with external systems. We learned how controllers handle incoming requests, converting external input into formats our use cases can process, while presenters transform domain data into view-friendly formats.

Using our task management system as an example, we saw how to implement controllers that remain independent of specific input sources and presenters that separate formatting logic from view implementation details. We built on the result pattern from *Chapter 5*, introducing `OperationResult` for explicit success and failure handling at our architectural boundaries. The humble object pattern showed us how to maintain clean separation between presentation logic and views, improving both testability and maintainability.

In *Chapter 7* we'll explore how to implement specific interfaces that consume our controllers and presenters. You'll learn how to create command-line and web interfaces that interact with our system while maintaining the clean boundaries we've established.

Further reading

- *Clean DDD Lessons: Presenters* (`https://medium.com/unil-ci-software-engineering/clean-ddd-lessons-presenters-6f092308b75e`). A discussion of approaches to Presenters in Clean Architecture.

- *Implementing Clean Architecture—Are Asp.Net Controllers "Clean"?* (`https://www.plainionist.net/Implementing-Clean-Architecture-AspNet/`). An in-depth article discussing the pros and cons of multiple approaches to implementing views in Clean Architecture.

7

The Frameworks and Drivers Layer: External Interfaces

The **Frameworks and Drivers layer** represents the outermost ring of Clean Architecture, where our application meets the real world. In previous chapters, we built the core of our task management system from domain entities to use cases, and the Interface Adapters that coordinate between them. Now we'll see how Clean Architecture helps us integrate with external frameworks, databases, and services while keeping our core business logic pristine and protected.

Through practical implementation, we'll explore how Clean Architecture's careful attention to boundaries enables our application to work with various frameworks and external services without becoming dependent on them. We'll see how our task management system can leverage external capabilities—from user interfaces to data storage and notifications. This chapter demonstrates how Clean Architecture's principles translate into real-world implementations. Through hands-on examples, you'll see how Clean Architecture helps manage the complexities of external integrations while keeping your core business logic focused and maintainable.

By the end of this chapter, you'll understand how to implement the Frameworks and Drivers layer effectively, integrating external dependencies while maintaining architectural integrity. You'll be able to adapt these patterns to your own projects, ensuring your applications remain flexible and maintainable as external requirements evolve.

In this chapter, we're going to cover the following main topics:

- Understanding the Frameworks and Drivers layer
- Creating UI framework adapters
- Component organization and boundaries

- Implementing database adapters
- Integrating external services

Technical requirements

The code examples presented in this chapter and throughout the rest of the book are tested with Python 3.13. For brevity, code examples in the chapter may be partially implemented. Complete versions of all examples can be found in the book's accompanying GitHub repository at `https://github.com/PacktPublishing/Clean-Architecture-with-Python`. If you choose to run the email driver example in the Integrating external services section, you will need to register for a free SendGrid developer account at `https://app.sendgrid.com`.

Understanding the Frameworks and Drivers layer

Every significant software application must eventually interact with the real world. Databases need querying, files need reading, and users need interfaces. In Clean Architecture, these essential but volatile interactions are managed through the Frameworks and Drivers layer. This layer's unique position and responsibilities make it both powerful and potentially dangerous to our architectural goals.

Position in Clean Architecture

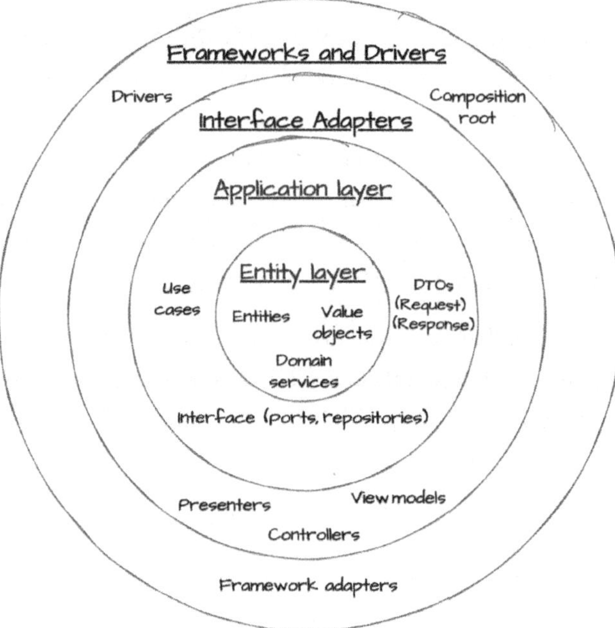

Figure 7.1: Frameworks and Drivers layer with the primary components

The Frameworks and Drivers layer's position at the architecture's edge is no accident; it represents what Clean Architecture calls the details of our system. These details, while essential for a functioning application, should remain disconnected from our core business logic. This separation creates a protective boundary that typically contains changes to just the outer layer. However, when new requirements do necessitate modifications to core business rules, Clean Architecture provides clear paths for implementing these changes systematically through each layer, ensuring our system evolves gracefully without compromising its architectural integrity.

Let's examine several key principles about the Frameworks and Drivers layer position in Clean Architecture:

External boundary: As the outermost layer, it handles all interactions with the outside world:

- User interfaces (command line interface (CLI), web, API endpoints)
- Database systems (drivers such as SQLite, or frameworks such as SQLAlchemy)
- External services and APIs
- File systems and device interactions

Dependency direction: Following Clean Architecture's fundamental rule, all dependencies point inward. Our frameworks and drivers depend on inner layer interfaces but never the reverse:

- A database adapter implements a repository interface defined by the Application layer
- A web controller uses interfaces from the Interface Adapters layer
- External service clients adapt to our internal abstractions from the Application layer

Implementation details: This layer contains what Clean Architecture considers details, specific technical choices that should be interchangeable:

- The choice between SQLite or PostgreSQL
- Using Click versus Typer for CLI implementation
- Selecting SendGrid or AWS SES for email notifications

This strategic positioning provides several key benefits:

- **Framework independence**: Core business logic remains unaware of specific framework choices
- **Easy testing**: External dependencies can be replaced with test doubles
- **Flexible evolution**: Implementation details can change without affecting inner layers
- **Clear boundaries**: Explicit interfaces define how external concerns interact with our system

For our task management system, this means that whether we're implementing a command-line interface, storing tasks in files, or sending notifications through email services, all these implementation details live in this outermost layer while respecting the interfaces defined by inner layers.

Next, we will explore the distinction between frameworks and drivers, helping us understand how to effectively implement each type of external dependency.

Frameworks versus drivers: understanding the distinction

While both frameworks and drivers reside in the outermost layer of Clean Architecture, they differ significantly in their integration complexity. This distinction stems from how they interact with the layers we explored in *Chapters 5 and 6*.

Frameworks are comprehensive software platforms that impose their own architecture and control flow:

- Web frameworks like Flask or FastAPI
- CLI frameworks like Click or Typer
- Object relational modeling (ORM) frameworks like SQLAlchemy

Frameworks like Click (which we'll implement for our CLI) require the full complement of Interface Adapters layer components to maintain clean architectural boundaries:

- Controllers that transform framework-specific requests into use case inputs
- Presenters that format domain data for framework consumption
- View models that structure data appropriately for framework display

Drivers, in contrast, are simpler components that provide low-level services without imposing their own structure or flow. Examples include database drivers, file system access components, and external API clients. Unlike frameworks, drivers don't dictate how your application works, they simply provide capabilities that you adapt to your needs.

These drivers interact with our application through ports—the abstract interfaces we first introduced in *Chapter 5*. We saw two key examples of ports in that chapter:

- Repository interfaces like `TaskRepository` for persistence operations
- Service interfaces like `NotificationPort` for external notifications

Following the patterns established in *Chapter 5*, drivers typically need only two components:

- A port defined in the Application layer (like `TaskRepository`)
- A concrete implementation in the Frameworks and Drivers layer

In the following examples we can see the distinction in code. First, we look at a framework example:

```python
# Framework example - requires multiple adapter components
@app.route("/tasks", methods=["POST"])
def create_task():
    """Framework requires full Interface Adapters stack"""
    result = task_controller.handle_create(  # Controller from Ch.6
        title=request.json["title"],
        description=request.json["description"]
    )
    return task_presenter.present(result)    # Presenter from Ch.6
```

Notice how the framework example requires both a controller to transform the request and a presenter to format the response.

Next, we look at a driver example:

```python
# Driver example - only needs interface and implementation
class SQLiteTaskRepository(TaskRepository):  # Interface from Ch.5
    """Driver needs only basic interface implementation"""
    def save(self, task: Task) -> None:
        self.connection.execute(
            "INSERT INTO tasks (id, title) VALUES (?, ?)",
            (str(task.id), task.title)
        )
```

Here we see that the SQLite driver simply implements the repository interface directly with a basic save operation.

This architectural distinction helps us implement appropriate integration strategies for each type of external dependency while maintaining Clean Architecture's Dependency Rule. These separations provide immediate practical benefits: when a security vulnerability emerges in your database driver, the fix involves only updating the outer layer implementation. When business requirements change how tasks are prioritized, those changes remain isolated in your domain logic. These aren't theoretical benefits, they're daily advantages that compound as systems grow.

Application composition

Having explored the distinction between frameworks and drivers, we now turn to a crucial question: how do these components come together into a cohesive application while maintaining clean architectural boundaries? This brings us to the concept of **application composition** which is the systematic assembly of our system's components.

In Clean Architecture, application composition serves as the orchestration point where our carefully separated components unite to form a working system. Think of it like assembling a complex machine. Each part must fit together precisely, but the assembly process itself shouldn't change how the individual components work.

The composition of a Clean Architecture application involves three key aspects working together:

Configuration management:

- Manages environment-specific settings
- Controls framework and driver selection
- Maintains separation between settings and business logic
- Enables different configurations for development, testing, and production

Component factories:

- Create properly configured implementations of interfaces
- Manage dependency lifecycles
- Handle initialization sequences
- Maintain Clean Architecture's Dependency Rule during object creation

Main application entry point:

- Orchestrates startup sequence
- Handles top-level error conditions
- Maintains clean separation between startup and business operations
- Serves as the composition root where dependencies are assembled

Let's see how these aspects work together in practice:

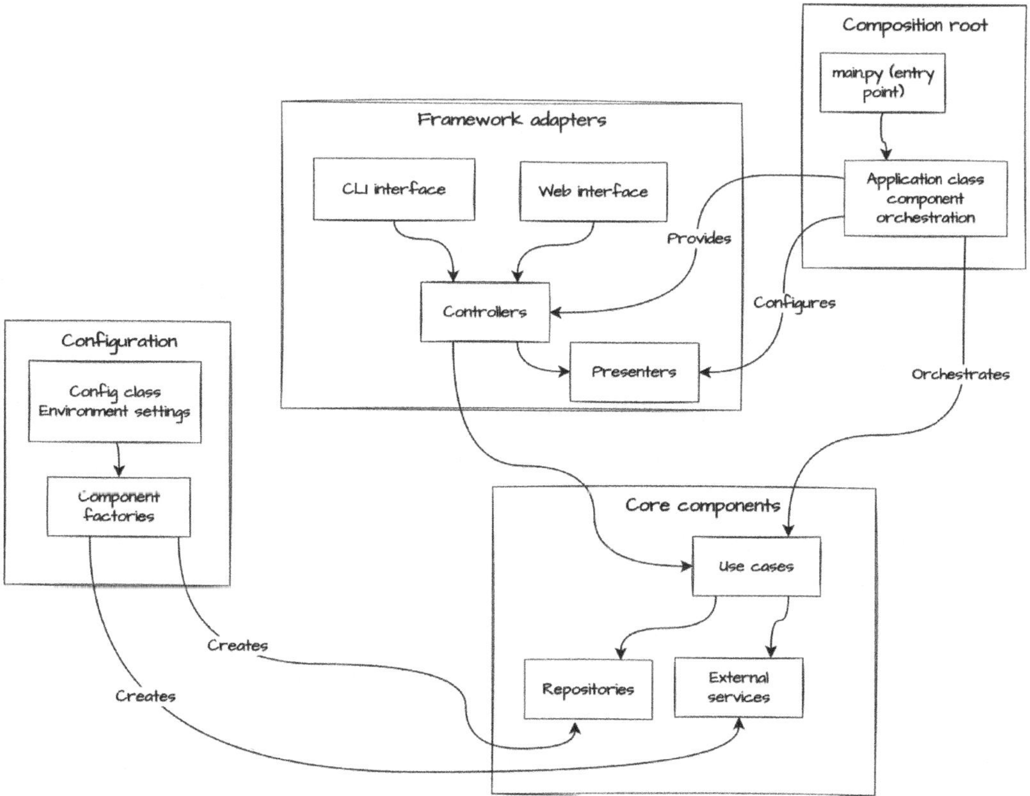

Figure 7.2: Clean Architecture composition flow showing configuration, composition root, and framework adapters

Our task management system implements these composition patterns in specific ways that demonstrate their practical value:

- The Configuration mechanism provides environment-aware settings that drive implementation choices, like selecting between in-memory or file-based storage

- The **Composition root**, through `main.py` and the `Application` class, coordinates the assembly of our components while maintaining clean architectural boundaries

- **Framework Adapters** connect our user interfaces to the core application through:

  - Controllers that translate UI requests into use case inputs

  - Presenters that format domain data for display

  - A clean separation that allows multiple interfaces to share core components

This architectural approach delivers several key benefits:

- Implementation flexibility through factory-based component creation
- Clean separation of concerns through well-defined boundaries
- Easy testing through component isolation
- Simple addition of new features without disrupting existing code

These benefits manifest throughout our implementation. In the following sections, we'll examine each infrastructure component from *Figure 7.2* in detail. We'll cover everything from configuration management to framework adapters, showing how they work together in practice through concrete patterns and code examples.

Clean Architecture patterns in the outer layer

The patterns we've explored establish clear strategies for integrating external concerns while protecting our core business logic. As we move into implementing specific components of our task management system, these patterns will work together in distinct ways to maintain architectural boundaries.

Consider how these patterns combine in practice: A web request arrives at our system's edge, triggering a cascade of clean architectural interactions. Framework adapters translate the request into our internal format, while ports enable database and notification operations without exposing their implementation details. All of this orchestration happens through our composition root, which ensures each component receives its properly configured dependencies.

As we dive deeper into these topics in the remainder of this chapter, we'll implement portions of our task management system to see these patterns in action—from CLI adapters translating user commands to repository implementations managing persistence. Each implementation will demonstrate not just the individual patterns, but how they cooperate to maintain Clean Architecture's core principles while delivering practical functionality.

Creating UI framework adapters

When integrating user interface frameworks, Clean Architecture's separation of concerns becomes particularly valuable. UI frameworks tend to be both volatile and opinionated, making it crucial to isolate their influence from our core business logic. In this section, we'll explore how to implement framework adapters that maintain clean boundaries while delivering practical user interfaces.

Framework adapters in practice

Let's begin by examining what we're building. Our task management system needs a user interface that allows users to manage projects and tasks effectively. *Figure 7.3* shows a typical interaction screen from our command-line interface:

```
TASK DETAILS
==============================
Title:        Buy groceries
Description:
Status:       [TODO]
Priority:     Normal
Completion:   Not completed

==============================

Actions:
[1] Edit title
[2] Edit description
[3] Edit priority
[4] Complete task
[5] Delete task
[Enter] Return to main menu
Choose an action []: 
```

Figure 7.3: Task editing interface in the CLI application

This interface demonstrates several key aspects of our system:

- Clear display of task details and status

- Simple, numbered menu for common operations

- Consistent formatting of domain concepts (status, priority)

- Intuitive navigation between different views

While this interface appears straightforward to users, its implementation requires careful orchestration across architectural boundaries. Each piece of information displayed and every action available represents data flowing through our Clean Architecture layers. *Figure 7.4* illustrates how a single operation—creating a project—flows through these boundaries:

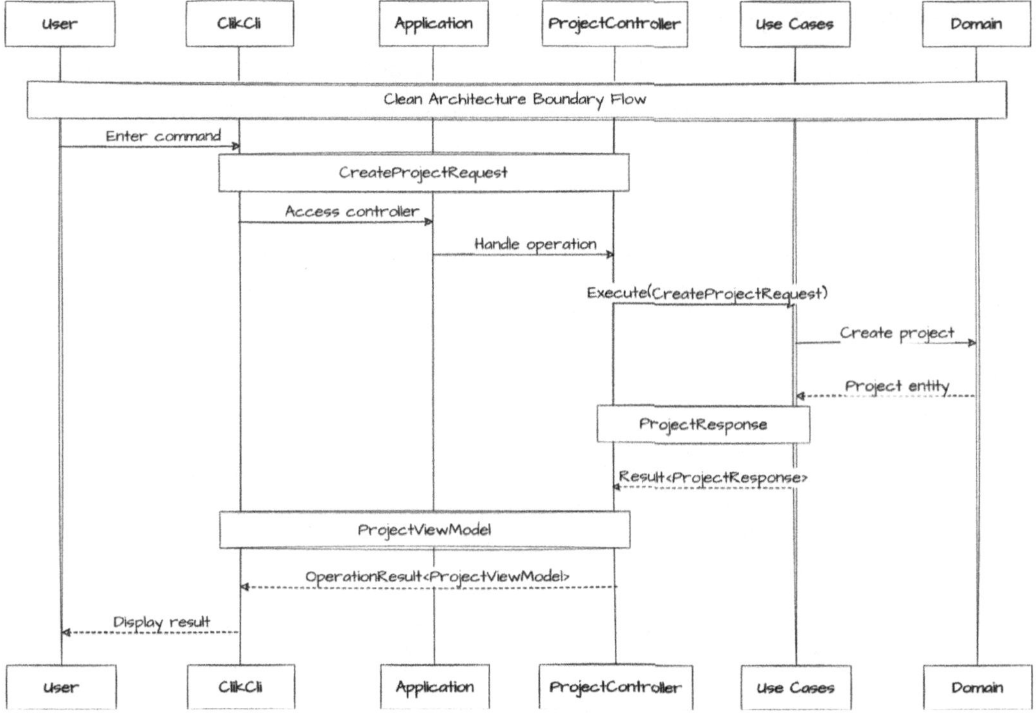

Figure 7.4: The entire request/response flow for creating a project

This sequence diagram reveals several important patterns:

- The CLI adapter translates user input into properly structured requests
- These requests flow through our architectural layers via well-defined boundaries
- Each layer performs its specific responsibilities (validation, business logic, etc.)
- Responses flow back through the layers, being transformed appropriately for display

With this understanding of how data flows through our architectural boundaries, let's examine how we organize the components that implement this flow.

Component organization and boundaries

As we saw in *Figure 7.2*, our application composition establishes a clear structure where each component has specific responsibilities. At the edges of this system, framework adapters must handle the transformation of data between external frameworks and our Clean Architecture while coordinating user interactions.

Looking at *Figure 7.4*, we can see that our CLI adapter sits at a crucial architectural boundary. We've chosen **Click**, a popular Python framework for building command-line interfaces, for our CLI implementation. The adapter must translate between Click's framework-specific patterns and our application's clean interfaces, managing both user input and the display of results.

Let's examine the core adapter structure:

```python
class ClickCli:
    def __init__(self, app: Application):
        self.app = app
        self.current_projects = []  # Cached list of projects for display

    def run(self) -> int:
        """Entry point for running the Click CLI application"""
        try:
            while True:
                self._display_projects()
                self._handle_selection()
        except KeyboardInterrupt:
            click.echo("\nGoodbye!", err=True)
            return 0

    # ... additional methods
```

This high-level structure demonstrates several key Clean Architecture principles:

Dependency injection:

- The adapter receives its Application instance through constructor injection
- This maintains the Dependency Rule by keeping the adapter dependent on inner layers
- No direct instantiation of application components occurs in the adapter

Framework isolation:

- Click-specific code remains contained within the adapter
- The Application instance provides a clean interface to our core business logic
- Framework concerns like user interaction and display caching stay at the edge

Let's examine a handler method of `ClickCli` to see how these components work together to create the interface shown in *Figure 7.3*:

```python
def _display_task_menu(self, task_id: str) -> None:
    """Display and handle task menu."""
    result = self.app.task_controller.handle_get(task_id)
    if not result.is_success:
        click.secho(result.error.message, fg="red", err=True)
        return

    task = result.success
    click.clear()
    click.echo("\nTASK DETAILS")
    click.echo("=" * 40)
    click.echo(f"Title:       {task.title}")
    click.echo(f"Description: {task.description}")
    click.echo(f"Status:      {task.status_display}")
    click.echo(f"Priority:    {task.priority_display}")
```

The `task` menu handler shows our architectural boundaries at work:

- Business operations flow through controllers as shown in *Figure 7.4*
- The Application instance shields our adapter from core business logic details
- Framework-specific code (Click commands) stays at the edges
- Error handling maintains clean separation between layers

Through this implementation style we maintain clear boundaries while delivering a practical user interface. This foundation enables us to implement specific functionality that handles both user interaction and business operations cleanly.

Now let's explore how the adapter processes specific user commands and interactions.

Implementing user interactions

As we build out the CLI, we need to translate user actions into business operations while maintaining clean architectural boundaries. This includes handling command input, displaying results, and managing the user's navigation through the system.

Let's examine how the `ClickCli` adapter class handles a typical interaction flow:

```python
def _handle_selection(self) -> None:
    """Handle project/task selection."""
    selection = click.prompt(
        "\nSelect a project or task (e.g., '1' or '1.a')",
        type=str,
        show_default=False
    ).strip().lower()

    if selection == "np":
        self._create_new_project()
        return
    try:
        if "." in selection:
            project_num, task_letter = selection.split(".")
            self._handle_task_selection(int(project_num),
                                        task_letter)
        else:  # Project selection
            self._handle_project_selection(int(selection))
    except (ValueError, IndexError):
        click.secho(
            "Invalid selection. Use '1' for project or '1.a' for task.",
            fg="red",
            err=True,
        )
```

This `selection` handler demonstrates several key patterns for managing user interaction while respecting clean architectural boundaries:

- **Input parsing:**

  - Validates and normalizes user input before processing
  - Provides clear feedback for invalid selections
  - Keeps input handling concerns at the framework boundary

- **Command routing:**

  - Maps user selections to appropriate handler methods

  - Maintains clean separation between input handling and business logic

  - Uses consistent patterns for different types of selection

If we follow the _create_new_project handle, we see interaction with the Application layer:

```python
def _create_new_project(self) -> None:
    """Create a new project."""
    name = click.prompt("Project name", type=str)
    description = click.prompt("Description (optional)",
                              type=str, default="")
    result = self.app.project_controller.handle_create(
        name, description)
    if not result.is_success:
        click.secho(result.error.message,
                    fg="red", err=True)
```

This implementation shows the clean transformation between the Framework and Drivers, and Application layers:

- Framework-specific input gathering using Click's prompt

- Direct delegation to application controllers for business operations

- Clean error handling that respects architectural boundaries

This careful attention to architectural boundaries helps us maintain a clean separation between our user interface and business logic while still delivering a cohesive user experience. Whether handling input or displaying output, each component maintains its specific responsibilities within Clean Architecture's concentric layering.

Domain insights through implementation

As we implement the CLI interface, we begin to discover insights about our domain model through actual user interaction patterns. Initially, our domain model treated project assignment as optional for tasks, providing flexibility in how users could organize their work. However, as we implemented the user interface, this flexibility revealed itself as a source of friction.

It should be called out that clean architectural boundaries protect us from implementation detail changes rippling through our system, such as swapping databases or UI frameworks. However, this discovery represents something different.

What we've uncovered is a fundamental insight about our domain model, requiring systematic change through our layers. This demonstrates how Clean Architecture guides us in handling both types of change appropriately—isolating technical implementations at the edges while providing clear paths for evolving our core domain model when needed.

The UI implementation showed that requiring users to choose between working with projects or standalone tasks created unnecessary complexity. Users had to make explicit decisions about project assignment for every task, and the interface needed special handling for both project-associated and independent tasks. This added cognitive load for users and implementation complexity for developers.

This realization leads us to an important domain insight: tasks inherently belong to projects in our users' mental model. Rather than treating project assignment as optional, we can simplify both our domain model and user interface by ensuring all tasks belong to a project, with an *Inbox* project serving as the default container for tasks that haven't been explicitly organized.

The development of user interfaces often serves as a crucial testing ground for our domain model, surfacing insights that might not be obvious during initial design. Let's take this opportunity to demonstrate how our clean architectural boundaries ensure we can implement these discoveries systematically while maintaining separation between framework concerns and core business logic.

Implementing domain insights: the task—project relationship

Let's examine the key code changes needed to reflect our refined understanding that tasks naturally belong to projects in our domain. We'll implement this insight starting from the Domain layer and working outward, using an *Inbox* project as a practical mechanism to support this natural organization:

```python
# 1. Domain Layer: Add ProjectType and update entities
class ProjectType(Enum):
    REGULAR = "REGULAR"
    INBOX = "INBOX"


@dataclass
class Project(Entity):
    name: str
```

```python
        description: str = ""
        project_type: ProjectType = field(default=ProjectType.REGULAR)


        @classmethod
        def create_inbox(cls) -> "Project":
            return cls(
                name="INBOX",
                description="Default project for unassigned tasks",
                project_type=ProjectType.INBOX
            )


@dataclass
class Task(Entity):
    title: str
    description: str
    project_id: UUID  # No longer optional
```

These Domain layer changes establish the foundation of our Inbox pattern. By introducing `ProjectType` and updating our entities, we enforce the business rule that all tasks must belong to a project, while the `create_inbox` factory method ensures consistent Inbox project creation. Note that the `Task` entity now requires a `project_id`, reflecting our refined domain model.

The changes then flow through to our Application layer:

```python
# 2. Application Layer: Update repository interface and use cases
class ProjectRepository(ABC):
    @abstractmethod
    def get_inbox(self) -> Project:
        """Get the INBOX project."""
        pass


@dataclass
class CreateTaskUseCase:
    task_repository: TaskRepository
    project_repository: ProjectRepository


    def execute(self, request: CreateTaskRequest) -> Result:
        try:
```

```python
        params = request.to_execution_params()
        project_id = params.get("project_id")
        if not project_id:
            project_id = self.project_repository.get_inbox().id
        # ... remainder of implementation
```

The Application layer changes demonstrate how Clean Architecture handles cross-layer requirements. The `ProjectRepository` interface gains Inbox-specific capabilities while the
`CreateTaskUseCase` enforces our new business rule by automatically assigning tasks to the inbox project when no explicit project is specified. This keeps our business rules centralized and
consistent. Additionally, the `ProjectResponse` model will have the `project_type` field added
and the `TaskResponse` model will make the `project_id` field required.

As a result of these changes our framework adapter simplifies:

```python
def  create task(self) -> None:
    """Handle task creation command."""
    title = click.prompt("Task title", type=str)
    description = click.prompt("Description", type=str)

    # Project selection is optional - defaults to Inbox
    if click.confirm("Assign to a specific project?", default=False):
        project_id = self._select_project()

    result = self.app.task_controller.handle_create(
        title=title,
        description=description,
        project_id=project_id  # Inbox handling in use case
    )
```

Rather than managing complex conditional logic for tasks with and without projects, the adapter
focuses purely on user interaction. The business rule of ensuring task–project association is handled by the use case, demonstrating how Clean Architecture's separation of concerns can lead to
simpler, more focused components. View models likewise simplify, no longer needing to handle
cases of tasks without projects.

This implementation demonstrates Clean Architecture's systematic approach to change:

- Domain changes establish new invariant business rules
- Application layer adapts to enforce these rules
- Framework adapters simplify to reflect the cleaner model
- Each layer maintains its specific responsibilities

By following Clean Architecture's boundaries, we implement our domain insight while maintaining separation of concerns and improving both user experience and code organization. In a less structured codebase, where business rules might be scattered across UI components and data access code, such a fundamental change would require hunting through multiple components to ensure consistent behavior. Clean Architecture's clear boundaries help us avoid these refactoring challenges. As we'll see in the next section, these same principles guide our implementation of database adapters, another crucial component of our Frameworks and Drivers layer.

Implementing database adapters

The implementation of database adapters in Clean Architecture provides a clear example of how driver integration differs from framework integration. As discussed earlier, drivers require simpler adaptation patterns than frameworks, typically needing only an interface in the Application layer and a concrete implementation in this outer layer.

Repository interface implementation

Recall from *Chapter 5* that our Application layer defines repository interfaces which establish clear contracts for any concrete implementation. These interfaces ensure our core business logic remains independent of storage details:

```python
class TaskRepository(ABC):
    """Repository interface for Task entity persistence."""

    @abstractmethod
    def get(self, task_id: UUID) -> Task:
        """Retrieve a task by its ID."""
        pass

    @abstractmethod
    def save(self, task: Task) -> None:
```

```
        """Save a task to the repository."""
        pass


    # ... remaining methods of interface
```

Let's implement this interface with an in-memory repository. While storing data in memory might seem impractical for a production system, this implementation offers several advantages. Most notably, it provides a lightweight, fast implementation ideal for testing—a benefit we'll explore more fully in *Chapter 8* when we discuss Clean Architecture's testing patterns.

```python
class InMemoryTaskRepository(TaskRepository):
    """In-memory implementation of TaskRepository."""

    def __init__(self) -> None:
        self._tasks: Dict[UUID, Task] = {}

    def get(self, task_id: UUID) -> Task:
        """Retrieve a task by ID."""
        if task := self._tasks.get(task_id):
            return task
        raise TaskNotFoundError(task_id)

    def save(self, task: Task) -> None:
        """Save a task."""
        self._tasks[task.id] = task


    # additional interface method implementations
```

This implementation demonstrates several key Clean Architecture principles. Note how it:

- Implements the interface defined by our Application layer
- Maintains clean separation between storage and business logic
- Handles domain-specific errors (`TaskNotFoundError`)
- Keeps implementation details (the dictionary storage) completely hidden from clients

While simple, this pattern provides the foundation for all our repository implementations. Whether storing data in memory, files, or a database, the core interaction patterns remain consistent thanks to our clean architectural boundaries.

For example, here's how we might implement file-based storage:

```python
class FileTaskRepository(TaskRepository):
    """JSON file-based implementation of TaskRepository."""

    def __init__(self, data_dir: Path):
        self.tasks_file = data_dir / "tasks.json"
        self._ensure_file_exists()

    def get(self, task_id: UUID) -> Task:
        """Retrieve a task by ID."""
        tasks = self._load_tasks()
        for task_data in tasks:
            if UUID(task_data["id"]) == task_id:
                return self._dict_to_task(task_data)
        raise TaskNotFoundError(task_id)

    def save(self, task: Task) -> None:
        """Save a task."""
        # ... remainder of implementation
```

This implementation demonstrates the power of Clean Architecture's interface-based approach:

- The same interface accommodates very different storage strategies
- Core business logic remains completely unaware of storage details
- Implementation complexity (like JSON serialization) stays isolated in the outer layer
- Error handling remains consistent across implementations

Our domain code can work with either implementation transparently:

```python
# Works identically with either repository
task = repository.get(task_id)
task.complete()
repository.save(task)
```

This flexibility extends beyond just these two implementations. Whether we later add SQLite, PostgreSQL, or cloud storage, our clean interfaces ensure that core business logic never changes.

Managing repository instantiation

As shown in *Figure 7.2*, configuration management plays a key role in our application composition. One of its primary responsibilities is directing the selection and creation of appropriate repository implementations. Our `Config` class provides a clean way to manage these decisions:

```python
class Config:
    @classmethod
    def get_repository_type(cls) -> RepositoryType:
        repo_type_str = os.getenv(
            "TODO_REPOSITORY_TYPE",
            cls.DEFAULT_REPOSITORY_TYPE.value
        )
        try:
            return RepositoryType(repo_type_str.lower())
        except ValueError:
            raise ValueError(f"Invalid repository type: {repo_type_str}")
```

We now utilize this configuration capability within the implementation of a factory that handles the actual instantiation of our repositories. This **factory pattern**, which we saw referenced in our application composition discussion, provides a clean way to create properly configured repository instances:

```python
def create_repositories() -> Tuple[TaskRepository, ProjectRepository]:
    repo_type = Config.get_repository_type()
    if repo_type == RepositoryType.FILE:
        data_dir = Config.get_data_directory()
        task_repo = FileTaskRepository(data_dir)
        project_repo = FileProjectRepository(data_dir)
        project_repo.set_task_repository(task_repo)
        return task_repo, project_repo
    elif repo_type == RepositoryType.MEMORY:
        task_repo = InMemoryTaskRepository()
        project_repo = InMemoryProjectRepository()
        project_repo.set_task_repository(task_repo)
        return task_repo, project_repo
    else:
        raise ValueError(f"Invalid repository type: {repo_type}")
```

This factory demonstrates several key Clean Architecture patterns in action. Configuration drives implementation choice through `Config.get_repository_type()`, while creation complexity is encapsulated in type-specific initialization blocks. Note how `project_repo.set_task_repository(task_repo)` handles dependency injection consistently across implementations. The factory returns abstract repository interfaces, keeping implementation details hidden from clients. These patterns come together to create a robust system for managing repository lifecycles while maintaining clean architectural boundaries.

With our repository creation patterns established, let's examine how these components orchestrate across our architectural boundaries to form a complete system.

Component orchestration overview

We've covered configuration classes, factory patterns, and composition principles—all working together to manage repository creation.

Let's step back and examine the complete picture. *Figure 7.5* focuses on our architectural overview from *Figure 7.2*, showing in detail how configuration and composition root components interact across our architectural boundaries:

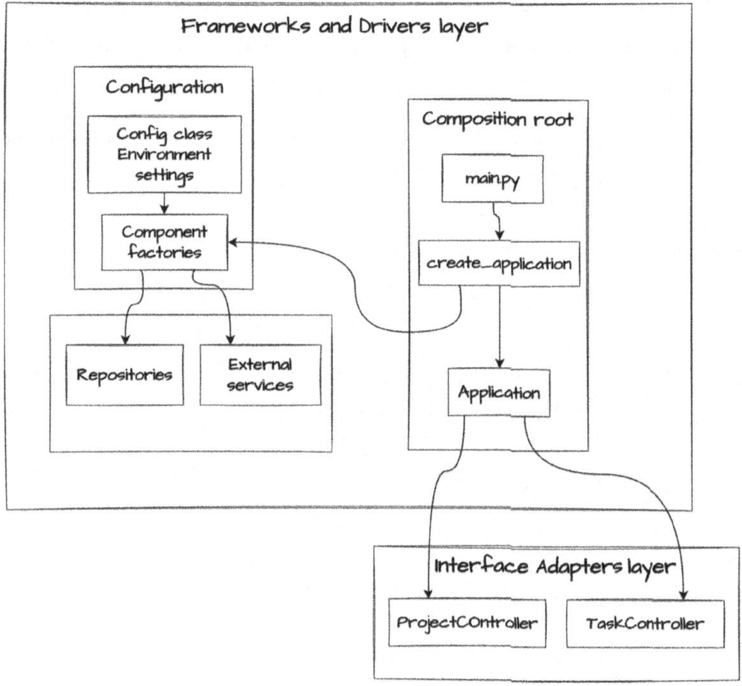

Figure 7.5: Component interactions between Frameworks and Drivers layer and the Interface Adapters layer

As shown in *Figure 7.5*, our composition flow starts with `main.py`, which initiates the application creation process. The `create_application` function serves as our primary factory, coordinating with configuration management and component factories to assemble a fully configured `Application` class instance. Each component maintains clean boundaries while working together to create a cohesive system:

- `Config` provides environment-aware settings that drive implementation choices
- Component factory methods (`create_repositories`) handle the complexities of ports instantiation and relationships
- `create_application` orchestrates the overall component assembly
- `Application` lives in our Frameworks and Drivers layer, coordinating with controllers in the Interface Adapters layer to provide framework adapters with access to our core business logic

This careful orchestration demonstrates Clean Architecture's power in managing complex system composition. While each component has clear, focused responsibilities, they work together to create a flexible, maintainable system that respects architectural boundaries. In the next section, we'll examine external service integration, taking a closer look at how the `Application` class and `main.py` bring these components together at runtime.

Integrating external services

While databases store our application state, external services enable our application to interact with the wider world by sending notifications, processing payments, or integrating with third-party APIs. Like databases, these services represent essential but volatile dependencies that must be managed carefully to maintain clean architectural boundaries.

External services in Clean Architecture

Recall from *Chapter 5* that our Application layer defines ports which are interfaces that specify how our core application interacts with external services. The `NotificationPort` interface exemplifies this approach:

```python
class NotificationPort(ABC):
    """Interface for sending notifications about task events."""

    @abstractmethod
    def notify_task_completed(self, task: Task) -> None:
        """Notify when a task is completed."""
```

```
        pass

    @abstractmethod
    def notify_task_high_priority(self, task: Task) -> None:
        """Notify when a task is set to high priority."""
        pass
```

This interface, defined in our Application layer, demonstrates several key Clean Architecture principles:

- The core application specifies exactly what notification capabilities it needs
- No implementation details leak into the interface
- The interface focuses purely on business operations
- Error handling remains abstract at this level

Let's examine how a task completion notification flows through our architectural boundaries:

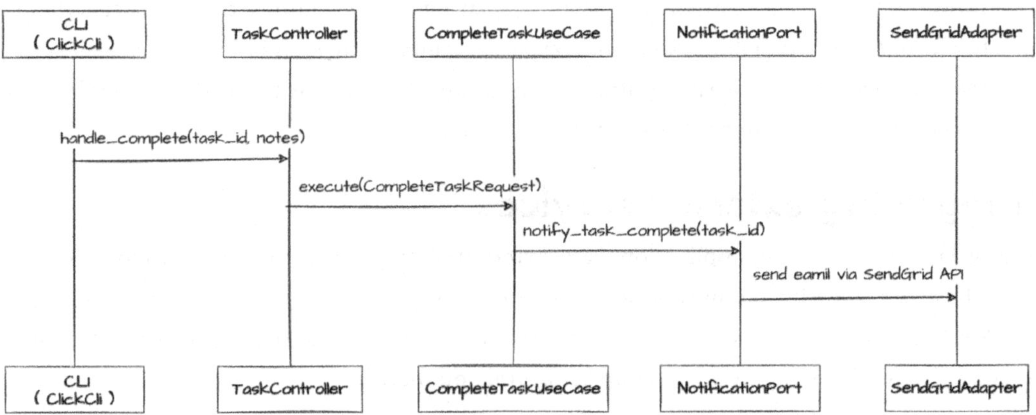

Figure 7.6: Notification flow through architectural layers

This sequence demonstrates Clean Architecture's careful management of dependencies:

- The use case knows only about the abstract `NotificationPort`
- The concrete SendGrid implementation lives at our system's edge
- Business logic remains completely unaware of email implementation details
- Specific service integration (SendGrid) happens cleanly at architectural boundaries

SendGrid integration

With our notification port interface defined, let's implement email notifications using **Send-Grid**—a cloud-based email service that provides APIs for sending transactional emails. By implementing our notification port with SendGrid, we'll demonstrate how Clean Architecture helps us integrate with third-party services while maintaining clean architectural boundaries:

```python
class SendGridNotifier(NotificationPort):

    def __init__(self) -> None:
        self.api_key = Config.get_sendgrid_api_key()
        self.notification_email = Config.get_notification_email()
        self._init_sg_client()

    def notify_task_completed(self, task: Task) -> None:
        """Send email notification for completed task if configured."""
        if not (self.client and self.notification_email):
            return
        try:
            message = Mail(
                from_email=self.notification_email,
                to_emails=self.notification_email,
                subject=f"Task Completed: {task.title}",
                plain_text_content=f"Task '{task.title}' has been
                                    completed."
            )
            self.client.send(message)
        except Exception as e:
            # Log error but don't disrupt business operations
            # ...
```

Our SendGrid implementation, like our repository implementations earlier, relies on configuration management to handle service-specific settings. Building on the patterns established in our repository configuration, our `Config` class grows to support notification settings:

```python
class Config:
    """Application configuration."""
    # Previous repository settings omitted...
```

```python
    @classmethod
    def get_sendgrid_api_key(cls) -> str:
        """Get the SendGrid API key."""
        return os.getenv("TODO_SENDGRID_API_KEY", "")


    @classmethod
    def get_notification_email(cls) -> str:
        """Get the notification recipient email."""
        return os.getenv("TODO_NOTIFICATION_EMAIL", "")
    # ... remainder of implementation
```

Let's see how this fits into our task completion workflow. Recall from *Chapter 5* our
`CompleteTaskUseCase` that coordinates task completion with notifications:

```python
@dataclass
class CompleteTaskUseCase:
    task_repository: TaskRepository
    notification_service: NotificationPort

    def execute(self, request: CompleteTaskRequest) -> Result:
        try:
            task = self.task_repository.get(request.task_id)
            task.complete(notes=request.completion_notes)
            self.task_repository.save(task)
            self.notification_service.notify_task_completed(task)
            # ... remainder of implementation
```

By implementing the `NotificationPort` with SendGrid, we demonstrate a key benefit of clean
architectural boundaries: adding email notifications requires changes only at the system's edge.
Since our Application layer defined the `NotificationPort` interface, and our use cases depend
only on this abstraction, implementing SendGrid notifications requires no changes to our core
business logic. Only the `SendGridNotifier` implementation and its associated composition root
wiring need to be added. This illustrates how Clean Architecture enables us to integrate powerful
external services while keeping our core application completely unchanged.

Application bootstrapping

As we saw in our discussion of component orchestration, the composition root brings together all our Frameworks and Drivers layer components while maintaining clean architectural boundaries. Let's further examine the implementation of this composition, starting with our `Application` container class.

The `Application` container class holds all the required application components as fields:

```python
@dataclass
class Application:
    """Container which wires together all components."""
    task_repository: TaskRepository
    project_repository: ProjectRepository
    notification_service: NotificationPort
    task_presenter: TaskPresenter
    project_presenter: ProjectPresenter
```

Then in our implementation we utilize the `__post_init__` method to construct these components:

```python
def __post_init__(self):
    """Wire up use cases and controllers."""
    # Configure task use cases
    self.create_task_use_case = CreateTaskUseCase(
      self.task_repository, self.project_repository)
    self.complete_task_use_case = CompleteTaskUseCase(
        self.task_repository, self.notification_service
    )
    self.get_task_use_case = GetTaskUseCase(self.task_repository)
    self.delete_task_use_case = DeleteTaskUseCase(self.task_repository)
    self.update_task_use_case = UpdateTaskUseCase(
        self.task_repository, self.notification_service
    )
    # Wire up task controller
    self.task_controller = TaskController(
        create_use_case=self.create_task_use_case,
        complete_use_case=self.complete_task_use_case,
        update_use_case=self.update_task_use_case,
        delete_use_case=self.delete_task_use_case,
```

```
        get_use_case=self.get_task_use_case,
        presenter=self.task_presenter,
    )
    # ... construction of Project use cases and controller
```

The Application class provides the structure for our component relationships, but we still need a way to create properly configured instances to inject into the `Application` container class. This is handled by our `create_application` factory method:

```python
def create_application(
    notification_service: NotificationPort,
    task_presenter: TaskPresenter,
    project_presenter: ProjectPresenter,
) -> "Application":
    """ Factory function for the Application container. """
    # Call the factory methods
    task_repository, project_repository = create_repositories()
    notification_service = create_notification_service()
    return Application(
        task_repository=task_repository,
        project_repository=project_repository,
        notification_service=notification_service,
        task_presenter=task_presenter,
        project_presenter=project_presenter,
    )
```

This factory function demonstrates Clean Architecture's dependency management in action:

- Method parameters (`notification_service`, `task_presenter`, `project_presenter`) accept abstract interfaces rather than concrete implementations
- The port components are created through factories: `create_repositories` and `create_notification_service` methods
- All these components come together in the final `Application` class instantiation, where each dependency is properly configured and injected

The separation between the `create_application` factory method and the `Application` class demonstrates Clean Architecture's attention to separation of concerns. The container focuses on component relationships while the factory handles creation details.

Finally, our `main.py` script serves as the tip of our composition root which is the single place where all components are instantiated and wired together at application startup:

```python
def main() -> int:
    """Main entry point for the CLI application."""
    try:
        # Create application with dependencies
        app = create_application(
            notification_service=NotificationRecorder(),
            task_presenter=CliTaskPresenter(),
            project_presenter=CliProjectPresenter(),
        )

        # Create and run CLI implementation
        cli = ClickCli(app)
        return cli.run()

    except KeyboardInterrupt:
        print("\nGoodbye!")
        return 0
    except Exception as e:
        print(f"Error: {str(e)}", file=sys.stderr)
        return 1


if __name__ == "__main__":
    sys.exit(main())
```

This bootstrap process demonstrates how Clean Architecture brings together all the components we've explored throughout this chapter. Notice how the `create_application` call assembles our core components, while `ClickCli(app)` initializes our framework adapter. This separation is significant: we could replace this CLI-specific main with a web application entry point that uses the same `create_application` factory but initializes a different framework adapter like FastAPI or Flask instead of a Click CLI.

The error-handling strategy is also worth noting. The top-level try/except blocks manage both graceful shutdown (KeyboardInterrupt) and unexpected errors at the system boundary, providing a clean exit strategy through the return codes. Throughout this composition, clean architectural boundaries remain intact: the business logic assembled by create_application knows nothing about our CLI implementation, and the ClickCli adapter interacts only with the abstractions provided by our Application container.

The composition patterns we established with repositories extend naturally to all our Frameworks and Drivers layer components, creating a cohesive system that respects clean architectural boundaries while delivering practical functionality.

Let's close the section by acknowledging the end result: a functional CLI that brings together all the components we've explored throughout this chapter.

```
Projects: [type 'np' to create new project]
[1] Project: INBOX
   [a] Buy groceries [TODO] Normal
[2] Project: Chores
   [a] Mow lawn [DONE] Normal
   [b] Clean kitchen [TODO] High

Select a project or task (e.g., '1' or '1.a'):
```

Figure 7.7: The starting CLI for the task management app

As shown in *Figure 7.7*, our Clean Architecture implementation enables users to manage projects and tasks through an intuitive interface, with the inbox project demonstrating how our architectural choices support natural workflow patterns.

The UI's ability to display projects, tasks, their statuses, and priorities while handling user interactions seamlessly demonstrates how Clean Architecture enables us to create practical, user-friendly applications without compromising architectural integrity. Each piece of information displayed, from project names to task priorities, flows through our carefully defined architectural boundaries, proving that Clean Architecture's principles translate into real-world functionality.

Summary

In this chapter, we explored the Frameworks and Drivers layer of Clean Architecture, demonstrating how to integrate external concerns while maintaining clean architectural boundaries. Through our task management system implementation, we saw how to effectively manage frameworks, databases, and external services while keeping our core business logic pristine and protected.

We implemented several key patterns that showcase Clean Architecture's practical benefits:

- Framework adapters that cleanly separate UI concerns from business logic
- Database implementations demonstrating interface flexibility
- External service integration maintaining core independence
- Configuration management that evolves with our system's needs

These implementations demonstrated Clean Architecture's dual strengths: isolating implementation details at the edges while providing clear paths for domain model evolution. We saw this in action twice. First, when implementing external services like SendGrid without touching our core business logic. Second, when evolving our domain model's task–project relationship, which required systematic change across layers. From repositories to framework adapters, careful attention to architectural boundaries helped us create a maintainable system that can adapt to both types of change.

In *Chapter 8* we'll explore how these clean boundaries enable comprehensive testing strategies across all layers of our system.

Further reading

Dependency Injector—Dependency Injection Framework for Python (`https://python-dependency-injector.ets-labs.org/`). For more complex projects, you can consider a dependency injection framework to manage what we've done here with the `Application` class.

Get this book's PDF version and more

Scan the QR code (or go to `packtpub.com/unlock`). Search for this book by name, confirm the edition, and then follow the steps on the page.

Note: Keep your invoice handy. Purchases made directly from Packt don't require an invoice.

8

Implementing Test Patterns with Clean Architecture

In previous chapters, we've built a task management system by carefully implementing each layer of Clean Architecture, from pure domain entities to framework-independent interfaces. For many developers, testing can feel overwhelming, a necessary burden that grows increasingly complex as systems evolve. Clean Architecture offers a different perspective, providing a structured approach that makes testing both manageable and meaningful.

Now that we've worked through all the layers of Clean Architecture, let's step back and examine how this architectural approach transforms our testing practices. By respecting Clean Architecture's boundaries and dependency rules, we create systems that are inherently testable. Each layer's clear responsibilities and explicit interfaces guide us not just in what to test, but how to test effectively.

In this chapter, you'll learn how Clean Architecture's explicit boundaries enable comprehensive test coverage through focused unit and integration tests. Through hands-on examples, you'll discover how Clean Architecture's **separation of concerns** lets us verify system behavior thoroughly while keeping tests maintainable. We'll see how well-defined interfaces and dependency rules lead naturally to test suites that serve as both verification tools and architectural guardrails.

By the end of this chapter, you'll be able to create test suites that are focused, maintainable, and effective at catching issues early. Turning testing from a burden into a powerful tool for maintaining architectural integrity. Along the way we'll be examining the following topics:

- Foundations of testing in Clean Architecture
- Building testable components: a test-driven approach
- Testing across **architectural boundaries**
- Advanced testing patterns for clean systems

Technical requirements

The code examples presented in this chapter and throughout the rest of the book are tested with Python 3.13. For brevity, most code examples in the chapter are only partially implemented. Complete versions of all examples can be found in the book's accompanying GitHub repository at `https://github.com/PacktPublishing/Clean-Architecture-with-Python`.

Foundations of testing in Clean Architecture

The carefully structured layers and explicit dependencies in Clean Architecture don't just make our systems more maintainable, they fundamentally transform how we approach testing. Many teams, faced with complex codebases and unclear boundaries, fall back to end-to-end testing through tools like Selenium or headless browsers. While these tests can provide confidence that critical user workflows function, they're often slow, brittle, and provide poor feedback when failures occur. Moreover, setting up comprehensive unit and integration tests in such systems can feel overwhelming. Where do you even start when everything is tightly coupled?

Clean Architecture offers a different perspective. Instead of relying primarily on end-to-end tests, we can build confidence in our system through focused, maintainable tests that respect architectural boundaries. Rather than fighting complex dependencies and setup, we find that our architectural boundaries provide natural guidance for building effective test suites.

Testing is crucial for maintaining healthy software systems. Through testing, we verify that our code works as intended, catch regressions early, and ensure that our architectural boundaries remain intact. Clean Architecture's explicit boundaries and dependency rules make it easier to write focused, maintainable tests at every level of our system.

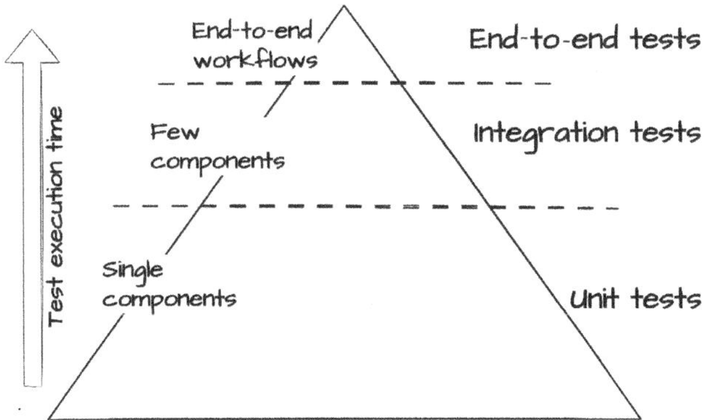

Figure 8.1: Testing pyramid depicting the ideal distribution of test types

The testing pyramid pictured in *Figure 8.1* demonstrates the ideal distribution of test types in a well-designed system. The broad foundation consists of fast **unit tests** that verify individual components in isolation, providing rapid feedback during development. Moving upward, **integration tests** verify interactions between components while remaining reasonably quick to execute. At the top, a small number of end-to-end tests verify critical user workflows, though these tests typically run slower and provide less precise feedback when failures occur.

This architectural approach naturally enables optimal test distribution through its well-defined interfaces and component isolation. Our core business logic, isolated in the Domain and Application layers, is easily verified through focused unit tests without external dependencies. Interface adapters provide clear boundaries for integration tests, letting us verify component interactions without testing entire workflows. This architectural clarity means we can build confidence in our system primarily through fast, focused tests. While end-to-end testing through user interfaces has its place Clean Architecture enables us to build substantial confidence in our system through focused unit and integration tests alone.

Throughout this chapter we'll use `pytest`, Python's standard testing framework, to demonstrate these testing patterns. By leveraging Clean Architecture's boundaries, we'll see how `pytest's` straightforward approach helps us build comprehensive test coverage without complex testing frameworks or browser automation tools. While Clean Architecture's testing benefits apply regardless of tooling choice, using a single, well-established framework lets us focus on architectural principles rather than testing syntax.

Clean Architecture requires more initial setup than simpler approaches, involving additional interfaces and layer separation that might seem unnecessary for small applications. However, this upfront investment transforms testing from a complex technical challenge into straightforward verification. Tightly coupled alternatives might seem faster initially, but soon require coordinating databases and external services just to test basic functionality. The architectural discipline we've established creates systems that are inherently testable, allowing teams to build confidence through focused unit tests rather than slow, brittle end-to-end tests. Teams may adopt these patterns selectively, but understanding the testing benefits helps inform these architectural decisions.

Tests as architectural feedback

Tests are nothing more than clients of our code. If we find that our tests are difficult to write or require complex setup, this often signals that our production code needs improvement. Just as the Dependency Rule guides our production code organization, it similarly informs effective test design. When tests become awkward or brittle, this frequently indicates that we've violated architectural boundaries or mixed concerns that should remain separate.

This architectural feedback loop is one of Clean Architecture's most valuable testing benefits. The explicit boundaries and interfaces align naturally with various testing approaches, including **Test-Driven Development (TDD)**. Whether you write tests first or after implementation, Clean Architecture's layers guide us toward better designs: if writing a test feels awkward, it often reveals a needed architectural boundary. If test setup becomes complex, it suggests we've coupled concerns that should remain separate. These signals serve as early warnings, helping us identify and correct architectural violations before they become deeply embedded in our codebase.

For teams hesitant to adopt comprehensive unit testing due to setup complexity or unclear boundaries, Clean Architecture provides a clear path forward. Each layer defines explicit interfaces and dependencies, providing clear guidance on what should be tested and how to maintain isolation. Throughout the remainder of this chapter, we'll demonstrate these benefits by implementing focused tests for each architectural layer of our task management system, showing how Clean Architecture's boundaries naturally guide us toward maintainable test suites.

From testing complexity to clear boundaries

Many developers struggle with testing codebases that lack clear architectural boundaries. In systems where business logic, persistence, and presentation concerns are tightly coupled, even simple tests become complex technical challenges. Consider a task entity that directly connects to databases and sends notifications on creation. Testing its basic properties requires setting up and managing these external dependencies. This coupling of concerns makes tests slow, brittle, and difficult to maintain. Teams frequently respond by minimizing unit and integration tests in favor of **end-to-end tests**, which while valuable, can't provide the rapid feedback needed during development.

Clean Architecture transforms this landscape by establishing clear boundaries between components. Instead of tests that must coordinate multiple tangled concerns, we can focus on specific responsibilities:

- Domain entities and business rules can be tested in isolation

- Use case orchestration can be verified through explicit interfaces

- Infrastructure concerns remain cleanly separated at system boundaries

The layered structure enhances development workflows in practice. Each architectural boundary provides natural guidance for:

- Isolating bugs to specific components or interactions

- Adding focused tests that capture edge cases

- Building comprehensive coverage incrementally

This clarity dramatically improves development workflows. When bugs are reported, this layered organization guides us directly to the appropriate testing scope. Domain logic issues can be reproduced in unit tests, while integration problems have clear boundaries to examine. This natural organization means our test coverage improves organically as we maintain and debug our system. Each resolved issue leads to focused tests that verify specific behaviors, gradually building a comprehensive test suite that catches edge cases before they reach production.

In the following sections, we'll explore concrete implementations of these testing patterns in our task management system. You'll see how Clean Architecture's boundaries make each type of test more focused and maintainable, starting with unit tests of our Domain layer and progressing through integration tests of our external interfaces.

Testing clean components: unit testing in practice

Let's see how Clean Architecture transforms unit testing from theory into practice. Consider a simple test goal: verifying that new tasks default to medium priority. In a codebase not aligned to a Clean Architecture paradigm, many developers have encountered classes like this, where even simple domain logic becomes tangled with infrastructure:

```python
class Task(Entity):
    """Anti-pattern: Domain entity with
    direct infrastructure dependencies."""
    def __init__(self, title: str, description: str):
        self.title = title
        self.description = description
```

```python
        # Direct database dependency:
        self.db = Database()
        # Direct notification dependency:
        self.notifier = NotificationService()


        self.priority = Priority.MEDIUM
        # Save to database and notify on creation
        self.id = self.db.save_task(self.as_dict())
        self.notifier(f"Task {self.id} created")
```

This tightly coupled code forces us into complex setup to test a simple business rule regarding our Task entity:

```python
def test_new_task_priority_antipattern():
    """An anti-pattern mixing infrastructure concerns
    with simple domain logic."""
    # Complex setup just to test a default value
    db_connection = create_database_connection()
    notification_service = create_notification_service()
    # Just creating a task hits the database and notification service
    task = Task(
        title="Test task",
        description="Test description"
    )
    # Even checking a simple property requires a database query
    saved_task = task.db.get_task(task.id)
    assert saved_task['priority'] == Priority.MEDIUM
```

This test, while functional, exhibits several common problems. It requires complex setup involving databases and services just to verify a simple domain rule. When it fails, the cause could be anything:

- Was there a database connection issue?

- Did the notification service fail to initialize?

- Or was there actually an issue with our priority defaulting logic?

This level of complexity in testing even basic properties highlights why many developers perceive testing as cumbersome and often *not worth the effort*.

Clean Architecture's boundaries eliminate these issues by keeping our domain logic pure and focused. For code following a Clean Architecture approach we can test this same business rule with remarkable clarity:

```python
@dataclass
class Task:
    """Clean Architecture: Pure domain entity."""
    title: str

    description: str
    project_id: UUID
    priority: Priority = Priority.MEDIUM

def test_new_task_priority():
    """Clean test focused purely on domain logic."""
    task = Task(
        title="Test task",
        description="Test description",
        project_id=UUID('12345678-1234-5678-1234-567812345678')
    )
    assert task.priority == Priority.MEDIUM
```

The difference is striking. By keeping our domain entities focused on business rules:

- Our test verifies exactly one thing; new tasks default to medium priority
- Setup requires only the data needed for our test
- If the test fails, there's exactly one possible cause
- The test runs instantly with no external dependencies

This clear separation of concerns demonstrates one of Clean Architecture's key testing benefits: the ability to verify business rules with minimal setup and maximum clarity. Clean Architecture's boundaries create a natural progression for building comprehensive test coverage. Throughout this section, we'll implement focused, maintainable tests that verify behavior while respecting these architectural boundaries. We'll start with the simplest case of testing domain entities and progressively work outward through our architectural layers.

Testing domain entities

Before diving into specific tests, let's establish a pattern that will serve us throughout our testing journey. The **Arrange-Act-Assert (AAA) pattern**, originally proposed by Bill Wake (`https://xp123.com/3a-arrange-act-assert/`), provides a clear structure for organizing tests that aligns naturally with Clean Architecture's boundaries:

- **Arrange**: set up the test conditions and test data
- **Act**: execute the behavior being tested
- **Assert**: verify the expected outcomes

This pattern becomes particularly elegant when testing domain entities because Clean Architecture isolates our core business logic from external concerns. Consider how we test our `Task` entity's completion behavior:

```python
def test_task_completion_captures_completion_time():
    """Test that completing a task records the completion timestamp."""
    # Arrange
    task = Task(
        title="Test task",
        description="Test description",
        project_id=UUID('12345678-1234-5678-1234-567812345678'),
    )

    # Act
    task.complete()

    # Assert
    assert task.completed_at is not None
    assert (datetime.now() - task.completed_at) < timedelta(seconds=1)
```

This test demonstrates the essence of domain entity testing in Clean Architecture. All we need to do is:

1. Set up an initial state (a new task with required attributes)
2. Take an action (complete the task)
3. Verify the final state (completion time was recorded)

The domain test's clarity comes from Clean Architecture's separation of concerns. We don't need to:

- Set up or manage database connections
- Configure notification services
- Handle authentication or authorization
- Manage external system state

We're testing pure business logic: *when a task is completed, it should record when that happened.* This focus makes our tests fast, reliable and readable. If the test fails, there's only one possible cause, our completion logic isn't working correctly.

This focus on pure business rules is one of the key benefits Clean Architecture brings to testing. By isolating our domain logic from infrastructure concerns, we can verify behavior with simple, focused tests that serve as living documentation of our business rules. Next we will see how this clarity of testing continues as we move out from the inner Domain layer.

Test double tools in Python

Before we work with our use case tests, let's understand how Python helps us create **test doubles** which act as dependency replacements for the component under test. When testing code that has dependencies, we often need a way to replace real implementations (like databases or external services) with simulated versions that we can control. Python's `unittest.mock` library, which is seamlessly integrated with `pytest`, provides powerful tools for creating these test doubles:

```python
from unittest.mock import Mock


# Create a mock object that records calls and can return preset values
mock_repo = Mock()
# Configure the response we want
mock_repo.get.return_value = some_task
# Call will return some_task
mock_repo.get(123)
# Verify the call happened exactly once
mock_repo.get.assert_called_once()


# Mocks track all interaction details
# Shows what arguments were passed
print(mock_repo.get.call_args)
# Shows how many times it was called
print(mock_repo.get.call_count)
```

These mocks serve two key purposes in testing:

- They let us control the behavior of dependencies (like ensuring a repository always returns a specific task)

- They let us verify how our code interacts with those dependencies (like ensuring we called save() exactly once)

Testing use case orchestration

As we move outward from the Domain layer, we naturally encounter dependencies on other components of our system. A task completion use case, for instance, needs both a repository to persist changes and a notification service to alert stakeholders. However, Clean Architecture's emphasis on abstraction through interfaces transforms these dependencies from potential testing headaches into straightforward implementation details.

Just as these abstractions let us swap a repository's implementation from file-based storage to SQLite without changing any dependent code, they enable us to replace real implementations with test doubles during testing. Our use cases depend on abstract interfaces like TaskRepository and NotificationPort, not concrete implementations. This means we can provide mock implementations for testing without modifying our use case code at all. The use case neither knows nor cares whether it's working with a real SQLite repository or a test double.

Let's examine how we use mocks to test our use case in isolation:

```python
def test_successful_task_completion():
    """Test task completion using mock dependencies."""
    # Arrange
    task = Task(
        title="Test task",
        description="Test description",
        project_id=UUID('12345678-1234-5678-1234-567812345678'),
    )
    task_repo = Mock()
    task_repo.get.return_value = task
    notification_service = Mock()

    use_case = CompleteTaskUseCase(
        task_repository=task_repo,
        notification_service=notification_service
    )
    request = CompleteTaskRequest(task_id=str(task.id))
```

The Arrange phase demonstrates proper unit test isolation. We mock both the repository and notification service to ensure we're testing the use case's orchestration logic in isolation. This setup guarantees our test won't be affected by database issues, network problems, or other external factors.

The test flow verifies our use case's orchestration responsibilities through distinct mock verifications:

```python
# Act
result = use_case.execute(request)

# Assert
assert result.is_success
task_repo.save.assert_called_once_with(task)
notification_service
  .notify_task_completed
  .assert_called_once_with(task)
```

Notice how the test's assertions focus on orchestration rather than business logic. We verify that our use case coordinates the correct sequence of operations while leaving the implementation details of those operations to our test doubles. This pattern scales naturally as our use cases grow more sophisticated. Whether coordinating multiple repositories, handling notifications, or managing transactions, Clean Architecture's explicit interfaces let us verify complex workflows through focused tests.

In the next section, we'll see how testing interface adapters introduce new patterns for verifying data transformations at our system's boundaries.

Testing interface adapters

As we move to the Interface Adapters layer, our testing focus shifts to verifying proper translation between external formats and our application core. Controllers and presenters serve as these translators, and just as with our unit tests in previous layers, we want to mock anything external to this layer. We don't want database connections, file systems, or even use case implementations to affect our tests of the translation logic. Clean Architecture's explicit interfaces make this straightforward. We can mock our use cases and focus purely on verifying that our adapters properly transform data as it crosses our system's boundaries.

Let's examine how we test a controller's responsibility of converting external string IDs to the UUIDs our domain expects. When web or CLI clients call our system, they typically provide IDs as strings. Our domain, however, works with UUIDs internally. The controller must handle this translation:

```python
def test_controller_converts_string_id_to_uuid():
    """Test that controller properly converts
    string IDs to UUIDs for use cases."""
    # Arrange
    task_id = "123e4567-e89b-12d3-a456-426614174000"
    complete_use_case = Mock()
    complete_use_case.execute.return_value = Result.success(
        TaskResponse.from_entity(
            Task(
                title="Test Task",
                description="Test Description",
                project_id=UUID('12345678-1234-5678-1234-567812345678')
            )
        )
    )
    presenter = Mock(spec=TaskPresenter)

    controller = TaskController(
        complete_use_case=complete_use_case,
        presenter=presenter,
    )
```

The Arrange phase sets up our test scenario. We provide a task ID as a string (like a client would) and create a mock use case that's configured to return a successful result. When creating our presenter mock, we use `spec=TaskPresenter` to create a *strict* mock that knows about our presenter's interface:

```python
# Without spec, any method can be called
loose_mock = Mock()
loose_mock.non_existent_method()  # Works, but could hide bugs
# With spec, mock enforces the interface
strict_mock = Mock(spec=TaskPresenter)
strict_mock.non_existent_method()  # Raises AttributeError
```

This extra **type safety** is particularly valuable in the Interface Adapters layer where maintaining correct interface boundaries is crucial. By using spec, we ensure our tests catch not just behavioral issues but also contract violations.

With our test doubles properly configured to enforce interface boundaries, we can verify our controller's translation logic:

```python
# Act
controller.handle_complete(task_id=task_id)
# Assert
complete_use_case.execute.assert_called_once()
called_request = complete_use_case.execute.call_args[0][0]
assert isinstance(called_request.task_id, UUID)
```

When we call handle_complete, the controller should:

1. Take the string task ID from the client

2. Convert it to a UUID

3. Create a properly formatted request for the use case

4. Pass this request to the use case's execute method

Our assertions verify this flow by:

- Confirming the use case was called exactly once

- Extracting the request that was passed to the use case

- Verifying that the task_id in that request is now a UUID, not a string

This test ensures the controller fulfills its core responsibility: translating external data formats into the types our domain expects. If the controller failed to convert the string identifier to a UUID, the test would fail when checking the type of called_request.task_id.

Similarly, we can test presenters to ensure they format domain data appropriately for external consumption. Let's focus on one specific responsibility: formatting task completion dates into human-readable strings for CLI. This seemingly simple transformation is a perfect example of an interface adapter's role:

```python
def test_presenter_formats_completion_date():
    """Test that presenter formats dates according to
    interface requirements."""
    # Arrange
```

```python
completion_time = datetime(2024, 1, 15, 14, 30, tzinfo=timezone.utc)
task = Task(
    title="Test Task",
    description="Test Description",
    project_id=UUID('12345678-1234-5678-1234-567812345678')
)
task.complete()
# Override completion time for deterministic testing
task.completed_at = completion_time
task_response = TaskResponse.from_entity(task)
presenter = CliTaskPresenter()
```

This test demonstrates how Clean Architecture's layered approach simplifies testing. Because our domain entities have no external dependencies, we can easily create and manipulate them in our tests. We don't need to worry about how the completion time was set in practice. The business rules intrinsic to the Task entity will prevent any illegal states (like setting completion time on an uncompleted task). This isolation makes our presenter tests straightforward and reliable.

```python
# Act
view_model = presenter.present_task(task_response)
# Assert
expected_format = "2024-01-15 14:30"
assert expected_format in view_model.completion_info
```

This test flow demonstrates how Clean Architecture's explicit boundaries make interface adapter testing straightforward. We focus purely on verifying data formatting without entangling persistence, business rules, or other concerns that our unit tests have already verified. Each adapter has a clear, single responsibility that we can test in isolation.

While testing individual formatting concerns is valuable, our presenters often need to handle multiple display aspects simultaneously. Let's see how Clean Architecture's separation of concerns helps us test comprehensive view model creation in a clear methodical manner:

```python
def test_presenter_provides_complete_view_model():
    """Test presenter creates properly formatted view model
    with all display fields."""
    # Arrange
    task = Task(
        title="Important Task",
```

```python
        description="Testing view model creation",
        project_id=UUID('12345678-1234-5678-1234-567812345678'),
        priority=Priority.HIGH
    )
    task.complete()  # Set status to DONE
    task_response = TaskResponse.from_entity(task)
    presenter = CliTaskPresenter()
      # Act
    view_model = presenter.present_task(task_response)

    # Assert
    assert view_model.title == "Important Task"
    assert view_model.status_display == "[DONE]"
    assert view_model.priority_display == "HIGH PRIORITY"
    assert isinstance(view_model.completion_info, str)
```

This test verifies how our presenter transforms multiple aspects of domain state into display-friendly formats. Clean Architecture's separation of concerns means we can verify all our presentation logic (status indicators, priority formatting, and completion information) without entangling business rules or infrastructure concerns.

With these patterns established for testing individual layers, we can now explore how Clean Architecture helps us test interactions across architectural boundaries.

Testing across architectural boundaries

Because our unit tests thoroughly verify business rules and orchestration logic through explicit interfaces, our integration testing can be highly strategic. Where our unit tests used mocks to verify behavior of components in isolation, these integration tests confirm that our concrete implementations work correctly together. Rather than exhaustively testing every combination of components, we focus on key boundary crossings, particularly those involving infrastructure like persistence or external services.

Consider how this changes our testing approach. In our unit tests, we mocked repositories to verify that use cases correctly coordinated task creation and project assignment. Now we'll test that our actual `FileTaskRepository` and `FileProjectRepository` implementations maintain these relationships when persisting to disk.

Let's examine how to test our file system persistence boundary—one of the areas where integration testing provides value beyond our unit test coverage:

```python
@pytest.fixture
def repository(tmp_path): # tmp_path is a pytest builtin for temp dirs
    """Create repository using temporary directory."""
    return FileTaskRepository(data_dir=tmp_path)


def test_repo_handles_project_task_relationships(tmp_path):
    # Arrange
    task_repo = FileTaskRepository(tmp_path)
    project_repo = FileProjectRepository(tmp_path)
    project_repo.set_task_repository(task_repo)

    # Create project and tasks through the repository
    project = Project(name="Test Project",
                      description="Testing relationships")
    project_repo.save(project)

    task = Task(title="Test Task",
                description="Testing relationships",
                project_id=project.id)
    task_repo.save(task)
```

This test setup demonstrates a key integration point where we're creating actual repositories that coordinate through file system storage. Our unit tests already verified the business rules using mocks, so this test focuses purely on verifying that our Infrastructure layer maintains these relationships correctly.

```python
    # Act - Load project with its tasks
    loaded_project = project_repo.get(project.id)

    # Assert
    assert len(loaded_project.tasks) == 1
    assert loaded_project.tasks[0].title == "Test Task"
```

The test verifies behavior we couldn't capture in our unit tests:

- Projects can load their associated tasks from disk
- Task–project relationships survive serialization

This repository coordination becomes particularly important when dealing with **architectural guarantees** that span multiple operations. One such guarantee is our *inbox* project, which is a key infrastructure-level decision made in *Chapter 7* to ensure all tasks have an organizing home.

Another crucial integration point is verifying that our `ProjectRepository` implementations uphold this inbox guarantee. While our unit tests verified the business rules around using the inbox (like preventing its deletion or completion), our integration tests need to verify that the Infrastructure layer properly maintains this special project's existence:

```python
def test_repository_automatically_creates_inbox(tmp_path):
    """Test that project repository maintains inbox project
    across instantiations."""
    # Arrange - Create initial repository and verify Inbox exists
    initial_repo = FileProjectRepository(tmp_path)
    initial_inbox = initial_repo.get_inbox()
    assert initial_inbox.name == "INBOX"
    assert initial_inbox.project_type == ProjectType.INBOX

    # Act - Create new repository instance pointing to same directory
    new_repo = FileProjectRepository(tmp_path)

    # Assert - New instance maintains same Inbox
    persisted_inbox = new_repo.get_inbox()
    assert persisted_inbox.id == initial_inbox.id
    assert persisted_inbox.project_type == ProjectType.INBOX
```

This test verifies behavior that our unit tests couldn't capture because they used mocked repositories. Our concrete repository implementation takes ownership of inbox initialization and persistence. By creating two separate repository instances pointing to the same data directory, we confirm that:

- The repository automatically creates the inbox on first use
- The inbox's special nature (its type and ID) persists correctly
- Subsequent repository instances recognize and maintain this same inbox

This focused integration test verifies a fundamental architectural guarantee that enables our task organization patterns. Rather than testing every possible *Inbox* operation, we verify the core infrastructure behavior that makes these operations possible.

Having verified our repository implementations and infrastructure guarantees, let's examine how Clean Architecture enables focused integration testing at the use case level. Consider our task creation use case. While our unit tests verified its business logic using mocked repositories, we should confirm it works correctly with real persistence. Clean Architecture's explicit boundaries let us do this strategically, testing real persistence while still mocking non-persistence concerns such as notifications:

```python
def test_task_creation_with_persistence(tmp_path):
    """Test task creation use case with real persistence."""
    # Arrange
    task_repo = FileTaskRepository(tmp_path)
    project_repo = FileProjectRepository(tmp_path)
    project_repo.set_task_repository(task_repo)

    use_case = CreateTaskUseCase(
        task_repository=task_repo,
        project_repository=project_repo,
        notification_service=Mock()  # Still mock non-persistence concerns
    )
```

In this test setup we use real repositories to verify persistence behavior while mocking notifications since they're not relevant to this integration test.

```python
    # Act
    result = use_case.execute(CreateTaskRequest(
        title="Test Task",
        description="Integration test"
    ))
    # Assert - Task was persisted
    assert result.is_success
    created_task = task_repo.get(UUID(result.value.id))
    assert created_task.project_id == project_repo.get_inbox().id
```

This test verifies that our use case correctly orchestrates task creation with real persistence:

- The task is properly saved to disk
- The task gets assigned to the Inbox as expected
- We can retrieve the persisted task through the repository

By keeping notifications mocked, we maintain test focus while still verifying critical persistence behavior. This strategic approach to integration testing, which involves testing real implementations of specific boundaries while mocking others, demonstrates how Clean Architecture helps us create comprehensive test coverage without unnecessary complexity.

These integration tests demonstrate how Clean Architecture's explicit boundaries enable focused, effective testing of multi-component concerns. Rather than relying on end-to-end tests that touch every system component, we can strategically test specific boundaries by verifying repository coordination, infrastructure-level guarantees, and use case persistence while ancillary concerns are mocked.

When implementing integration tests in your own Clean Architecture systems:

- Let the architectural boundaries guide what needs integration testing
- Test real implementations only for the boundary being verified
- Trust your unit test coverage of business rules
- Keep each test focused on a specific integration concern

In the next section, we'll explore testing patterns that help maintain test clarity as systems grow more complex.

Tools and patterns for test maintenance

While Clean Architecture's boundaries help us write focused tests, maintaining a comprehensive test suite presents its own challenges. As our task management system grows, so do our tests. New business rules require additional test cases, infrastructure changes need updated verification, and simple modifications can affect multiple test files. Without careful organization, we risk spending more time managing tests than improving our system.

When a test fails, we need to quickly understand what architectural boundary was violated. When business rules change, we should be able to update tests systematically rather than have to hunt through multiple files. When adding new test cases, we want to leverage existing test infrastructure rather than have to duplicate setup code.

Python's testing ecosystem, particularly pytest, provides powerful tools that align naturally with Clean Architecture's goals. We'll explore how to:

- Verify multiple scenarios while keeping test code clean and focused
- Organize test **fixtures** to respect architectural boundaries
- Leverage testing tools that make maintenance easier
- Catch subtle issues that could violate our architectural integrity

Through practical examples, we'll see how these patterns help us maintain comprehensive test coverage without creating a maintenance burden, letting us verify more scenarios with less code while keeping our tests as clean as our architecture.

Structuring test files

Clean Architecture's explicit boundaries provide natural organization for our test files. Whether your team chooses to organize tests by type (unit/integration) or keeps them together, the internal structure should mirror your application's architecture. An example tests directory structure might resemble this:

```
tests/
    domain/
        entities/
            test_task.py
            test_project.py
        value_objects/
            test_deadline.py
    application/
        use_cases/
            test_task_use_cases.py
    # ... Remaining tests by layer
```

This organization reinforces Clean Architecture's dependency rules through file system boundaries. Tests in `tests/domain` shouldn't need to import anything from `application` or `interfaces`, while a test in `tests/interfaces` can work with components from all layers, just as their production counterparts do. This structural alignment also provides early warning of potential architectural violations. If we find ourselves wanting to import a repository into a domain entity test, the awkward import path signals that we're likely violating Clean Architecture's Dependency Rule.

Parameterized testing for comprehensive coverage

When testing across architectural boundaries, we often need to verify similar behavior under different conditions. Consider our task creation use case. We need to test project assignment, priority setting, and deadline validation across multiple input combinations. Writing separate test methods for each scenario leads to duplicated code and harder maintenance. When business rules change, we need to update multiple tests rather than a single source of truth.

The pytest parametrize decorator transforms how we handle these scenarios. Rather than duplicate test code, we can define data variations that exercise our architectural boundaries:

```python
@pytest.mark.parametrize(
    "request_data,expected_behavior",
    [
        # Basic task creation - defaults to INBOX project
        (
            {
                "title": "Test Task",
                "description": "Basic creation"
            },
            {
                "project_type": ProjectType.INBOX,
                "priority": Priority.MEDIUM
            }
        ),
        # Explicit project assignment
        (
            {
                "title": "Project Task",
                "description": "With project",
                "project_id": "project-uuid"
            },
            {
                "project_type": ProjectType.REGULAR,
                "priority": Priority.MEDIUM
            }
        ),
        # High priority task
        # ... data for task
    ],
    ids=["basic-task", "project-task", "priority-task"]
)
```

Then in the test method following the above `parametrize` decorator, the test will run once for each item in the parameters list:

```python
def test_task_creation_scenarios(request_data, expected_behavior):
    """Test task creation use case handles various
    input scenarios correctly."""
    # Arrange
    task_repo = Mock(spec=TaskRepository)
    project_repo = FileProjectRepository(tmp_path)
    # Real project repo for INBOX

    use_case = CreateTaskUseCase(
        task_repository=task_repo,
        project_repository=project_repo
    )

    # Act
    result = use_case.execute(CreateTaskRequest(**request_data))

    # Assert
    assert result.is_success
    created_task = result.value

    if expected_behavior["project_type"] == ProjectType.INBOX:
        assert UUID(created_task.project_id) == (
            project_repo.get_inbox().id
        )
    assert created_task.priority == expected_behavior["priority"]
```

This test demonstrates several key benefits of parameterized testing. The decorator injects each test case's `request_data` and `expected_behavior` into our test method, where `request_data` represents input at our system's edge and `expected_behavior` defines our expected domain rules. This separation lets us define our test scenarios declaratively while keeping the verification logic clean and focused.

The `ids` parameter makes test failures more meaningful: instead of `test_task_creation_scenarios[0]` failing, we see `test_task_creation_scenarios[basic-task]` failed, immediately highlighting which scenario needs attention.

When using parameterized tests, it is best practice to group related scenarios and provide clear scenario identifiers. This approach keeps our test logic focused while our test data varies, helping us maintain comprehensive coverage without sacrificing test clarity.

Having organized our test scenarios, let's explore how `pytest`'s fixture system helps us manage test dependencies across architectural boundaries.

Organizing test fixtures

Throughout our testing examples, we've used `pytest` fixtures to manage test dependencies, from providing clean task entities to configuring mock repositories. While these individual fixtures served our immediate testing needs, as test suites grow, managing test setup across architectural boundaries becomes increasingly complex. Each layer has its own setup needs: domain tests require clean entity instances, use case tests need properly configured repositories and services, and interface tests need formatted request data.

The `pytest` fixture system, particularly paired with its `conftest.py` files, helps us scale this fixture pattern across our test hierarchy while maintaining Clean Architecture's boundaries. By placing fixtures in the appropriate test directory, we ensure each test has access to exactly what it needs without excess dependencies:

```python
# tests/conftest.py - Root fixtures available to all tests
@pytest.fixture
def sample_task_data():
    """Provide basic task attributes for testing."""
    return {
        "title": "Test Task",
        "description": "Sample task for testing",
        "project_id": UUID('12345678-1234-5678-1234-567812345678'),
    }


# tests/domain/conftest.py - Domain layer fixtures
@pytest.fixture
def domain_task(sample_task_data):
    """Provide a clean Task entity for domain tests."""
    return Task(**sample_task_data)


# tests/application/conftest.py - Application layer fixtures
@pytest.fixture
```

```python
def mock_task_repository(domain_task):
    """Provide a pre-configured mock repository."""
    repo = Mock(spec=TaskRepository)
    repo.get.return_value = domain_task
    return repo
```

This organization naturally enforces Clean Architecture's Dependency Rule through our test structure. A test needing both domain entities and repositories must live at the Application layer or higher, as it depends on both layers' fixtures. Similarly, a test using only domain entities can be confident it's not accidentally depending on infrastructure concerns.

The fixtures themselves respect our architectural boundaries:

```python
# tests/interfaces/conftest.py - Interface Layer fixtures
@pytest.fixture
def task_controller(mock_task_repository, mock_notification_port):
    """Provide a properly configured TaskController."""
    return TaskController(
        create_use_case=CreateTaskUseCase(
            task_repository=mock_task_repository,
            project_repository=Mock(spec=ProjectRepository),
            notification_service=mock_notification_port
        ),
        presenter=Mock(spec=TaskPresenter)
    )


@pytest.fixture
def task_request_json():
    """Provide sample request data as it would come from clients."""
    return {
        "title": "Test Task",
        "description": "Testing task creation",
        "priority": "HIGH"
    }
```

When using fixtures across architectural boundaries, structure them to match your production dependency injection. For example, to verify that our controller properly transforms external requests into use case operations:

```python
def test_controller_handles_task_creation(
    task_controller,
    task_request_json,
    mock_task_repository
):
    """Test task creation through controller layer."""
    result = task_controller.handle_create(**task_request_json)

    assert result.is_success
    mock_task_repository.save.assert_called_once()
```

This fixture-based approach pays off in several practical ways:

- Tests stay focused on behavior rather than setup. Our test verifies the controller's responsibility without setup code cluttering the test method.
- Common test configurations are reusable. The same `task_controller` fixture can support multiple controller test scenarios.
- Dependencies are explicit. The test's parameters clearly show what components we're working with.
- Changes to component initialization only need updating in the fixture, not in every test.

Next let's examine how these patterns combine with testing tools to catch subtle architectural violations.

Testing tools and techniques

Even with well-organized tests and fixtures, certain testing scenarios present unique challenges. Some tests can pass in isolation but fail due to hidden temporal or state dependencies, while others may mask architectural violations that only surface under specific conditions. Let's explore some practical tools that help maintain test reliability while respecting our architectural boundaries. From controlling time in our tests to exposing hidden state dependencies to managing test suite execution at scale, these tools help us catch subtle architectural violations before they become deeply embedded in our system.

Managing time in tests

Testing deadline calculations or time-based notifications requires careful handling of time. In our task management system, we have several time-sensitive features. Tasks can become overdue, deadlines trigger notifications when they're approaching, and completed tasks record their completion time. Testing these features without controlling time becomes problematic. Imagine testing that a task becomes overdue after its deadline. We'd either need to wait for actual time to pass (making tests slow and unreliable) or manipulate system time (potentially affecting other tests). Even worse, time-based tests might pass or fail depending on when they're run during the day.

The freezegun library solves these problems by letting us control time in our tests without modifying our domain logic. First, install the library:

```
pip install freezegun
```

The freezegun library provides a context manager that lets us set a specific point in time for code running within its scope. Any code inside the freeze_time(): block will see time as frozen at that moment, while code outside continues with normal time. This lets us create precise test scenarios while our domain entities continue working with real datetime objects:

```python
from freezegun import freeze_time


def test_task_deadline_approaching():
    """Test deadline notifications respect time boundaries."""
    # Arrange
    with freeze_time("2024-01-14 12:00:00"):
        task = Task(
            title="Time-sensitive task",
            description="Testing deadlines",
            project_id=UUID('12345678-1234-5678-1234-567812345678'),
            due_date=Deadline(datetime(
                2024, 1, 15, 12, 0, tzinfo=timezone.utc))
        )

        notification_service = Mock(spec=NotificationPort)
        use_case = CheckDeadlinesUseCase(
            task_repository=Mock(spec=TaskRepository),
```

```
        notification_service=notification_service,
        warning_threshold=timedelta(days=1)
    )
```

In this test arrangement, we freeze time at noon on January 14th to create our task with a due date 24 hours later. This gives us a precise initial state for testing deadline calculations. Our domain entities continue working with standard `datetime` objects, preserving Clean Architecture's separation of concerns. Only the perception of *current time* is affected:

```
# Act
with freeze_time("2024-01-14 13:00:00"):
    result = use_case.execute()
# Assert
assert result.is_success
notification_service.notify_task_deadline_approaching.assert_called_
once()
```

Moving time forward one hour lets us verify that our deadline notification system correctly identifies tasks due within the warning threshold. The test runs instantly while simulating a real-world scenario that would otherwise take hours to validate. Our entities and use cases remain unaware that they're operating in simulated time, maintaining clean architectural boundaries while enabling thorough testing of time-dependent behavior.

This pattern keeps time-dependent logic in our domain while making it testable. Our entities and use cases work with real `datetime` objects, but our tests can verify their behavior at specific points in time.

Exposing state dependencies

Tests that depend on hidden state or execution order can mask architectural violations, particularly around global state. In Clean Architecture, each component should be self-contained, with dependencies explicitly passed through interfaces. However, subtle global state can creep in. Consider our task management system's notification service: it might maintain an internal queue of pending notifications that carries over between tests. A test verifying high-priority task notifications could pass when run alone but fail when run after a test that fills this queue. Or our project repository might cache task counts for performance, leading to tests that pass or fail depending on whether other tests have manipulated this cache.

These hidden state dependencies not only make tests unreliable but often indicate architectural violations where components maintaining state that should be explicit in our interfaces. It is best to expose these issues as soon as possible, so it is highly recommended to adopt the practice of running tests in random order. With `pytest` this can be accomplished by first installing `pytest-random-order`:

```
pip install pytest-random-order
```

Then configure it to run on every test:

```ini
# pytest.ini
[pytest]
addopts = --random-order
```

When tests run in random order, hidden state dependencies surface quickly through test failures. The moment a test relies on global state or execution order; it will fail unpredictably. This is a clear signal that we need to investigate our architectural boundaries. When such a failure occurs, the plugin provides a seed value that lets you reproduce the exact test execution order:

```
pytest --random-order-seed=123456
```

You can then run the tests in the order specified by the seed as many times as needed in order to determine the root cause of the failure.

Accelerating test execution

As your test catalog grows, execution time can become a significant concern. What started as a quick test suite now takes minutes to run. In our task management system, we've built comprehensive coverage across all layers including domain entities, use cases, interface adapters, and infrastructure. Running all these tests sequentially, especially those involving file system operations or time-based behaviors, can create noticeable delays in the development feedback loop.

Fast test execution is crucial for maintaining architectural integrity. Long-running test suites discourage frequent verification during development, increasing the risk that architectural violations might slip through. `pytest-xdist` provides tools to parallelize test execution while maintaining test integrity. First install the plugin with `pip`:

```
pip install pytest-xdist
```

Configure parallel execution in your `pytest.ini`:

```ini
# pytest.ini
[pytest]
addopts = --random-order -n auto  # Combine random order with parallel
execution
```

For any scenarios where tests cannot run in a single parallelized group (for instance, tests sharing known global state or resources), `pytest-xdist` provides several tools:

- Use `@pytest.mark.serial` to mark tests that must run sequentially
- Configure resource scope with `@pytest.mark.resource_group('global-cache')` to ensure tests using the same resources run together

The `-n auto` flag automatically utilizes available CPU cores, though you can specify an exact number like `-n 4` if desired. This approach lets us maintain fast test execution while respecting the constraints of our architectural boundaries. Critical tests that verify our Clean Architecture principles run quickly enough to be part of every development cycle, helping catch architectural violations early.

Summary

In this chapter, we explored how Clean Architecture's principles translate directly into effective testing practices. We learned how architectural boundaries naturally guide our testing strategy, making it clear what to test and how to structure those tests. Through our task management system, we saw how Clean Architecture enables focused testing without heavy reliance on end-to-end tests while keeping our system adaptable and sustainable.

We implemented several key testing patterns that demonstrate Clean Architecture's benefits:

- Unit tests that leverage Clean Architecture's natural boundaries for focused verification
- Integration tests that verify behavior across specific architectural layers
- Tools and patterns for building maintainable test suites at scale

Most importantly, we saw how Clean Architecture's careful attention to dependencies and interfaces makes our tests more focused and maintainable. By organizing our tests to respect architectural boundaries, from file structure to fixtures, we create test suites that grow gracefully with our systems.

In *Chapter 9* we'll explore how to apply Clean Architecture principles to web interface design, showing how our careful attention to architectural boundaries enables us to add a complete Flask-based web interface to our task management system with minimal changes to our core application. This practical demonstration will highlight how Clean Architecture's separation of concerns allows us to maintain our existing CLI while seamlessly introducing new user interfaces.

Further reading

- *Software Testing Guide* (`https://martinfowler.com/testing/`). Collects all the testing articles on Martin Fowler's blog.

- *Just Say No to More End-to-End Tests* (`https://testing.googleblog.com/2015/04/just-say-no-to-more-end-to-end-tests.html`). A blog by Google's testing team, arguing that an over-reliance on end-to-end tests can lead to increased complexity, flakiness, and delayed feedback in software development, advocating instead for a balanced approach that emphasizes unit and integration tests.

- *Python Testing with pytest* (`https://pytest.org/`). The official `pytest` documentation, providing detailed information about the testing tools we've used throughout this chapter.

- *Test-Driven Development* (`https://www.oreilly.com/library/view/test-driven-development/0321146530/`). An essential guide to TDD by Kent Beck, one of its pioneers. This book provides a solid foundation for understanding how TDD can improve your software design and how it naturally aligns with architectural patterns like those found in Clean Architecture.

Get this book's PDF version and more

Scan the QR code (or go to `packtpub.com/unlock`). Search for this book by name, confirm the edition, and then follow the steps on the page.

Note: Keep your invoice handy. Purchases made directly from Packt don't require an invoice.

Part 3

Applying Clean Architecture in Python

The final part demonstrates how to apply Clean Architecture principles in real-world scenarios and diverse contexts. You'll implement a complete web interface, add observability features while maintaining architectural integrity, transform legacy systems through incremental refactoring, and adapt Clean Architecture to different system types and organizational environments. These chapters provide practical guidance for extending Clean Architecture beyond our example application to address complex, real-world challenges.

This part of the book includes the following chapters:

- *Chapter 9, Adding Web UI: Clean Architecture's Interface Flexibility*
- *Chapter 10, Implementing Observability: Monitoring and Verification*
- *Chapter 11, Legacy to Clean: Refactoring Python for Maintainability*
- *Chapter 12, Your Clean Architecture Journey: Next Steps*

Adding Web UI: Clean Architecture's Interface Flexibility

In previous chapters, we established Clean Architecture's foundational patterns through our task management system. We built domain entities, implemented use cases, and created a command line interface (CLI) that demonstrated how Clean Architecture's boundaries enable clear separation between our core business logic and user interfaces. While the CLI provides a functional interface, many applications require web-based access. This presents an excellent opportunity to show how Clean Architecture's principles enable interface evolution without compromising architectural integrity.

Through our task management system, we'll demonstrate one of Clean Architecture's key benefits: the ability to add new interfaces without modifying existing code. Because our domain logic, use cases, and controllers were built with proper architectural boundaries, adding a web interface becomes a purely additive exercise. No refactoring of existing components is required. This same principle that makes adding a web UI straightforward also enables long-term maintenance of multiple interfaces, as each can evolve independently while sharing the same robust core.

By the end of this chapter, you'll understand how to implement additional interfaces while maintaining architectural boundaries. You'll be able to apply these patterns to your own projects, ensuring your applications remain adaptable as interface requirements evolve.

In this chapter, we're going to cover the following main topics:

- Understanding interface flexibility in Clean Architecture
- Web presentation patterns in Clean Architecture
- Integrating Flask with Clean Architecture

Technical requirements

The code examples presented in this chapter and throughout the rest of the book have been tested with Python 3.13. For brevity, most code examples in the chapter are only partially implemented. Complete versions of all examples can be found in the book's accompanying GitHub repository at `https://github.com/PacktPublishing/Clean-Architecture-with-Python`.

Understanding interface flexibility in Clean Architecture

Our task management system's CLI (implemented in *Chapter 7*), demonstrates Clean Architecture's careful separation between core business logic and user interfaces. This separation wasn't just good practice—it was strategic preparation for exactly what we'll accomplish in this chapter: adding a completely new user interface while preserving our existing functionality.

Understanding our web implementation

To implement our web interface, we'll use **Flask**—a lightweight and flexible Python web framework. Flask's explicit request handling and straightforward application structure make it ideal for demonstrating Clean Architecture's boundaries. Its minimal core and extensive ecosystem of optional extensions align well with Clean Architecture's preference for explicit dependencies. While the patterns we'll explore would work equally well with Django, FastAPI, or other web frameworks, Flask's simplicity helps keep our focus on architectural principles rather than framework-specific features.

Through a browser-based interface, users can now manage their projects and tasks with familiar workflows enhanced by web-specific capabilities. When a user visits the application, they're presented with their projects and associated tasks in a clean, hierarchical view:

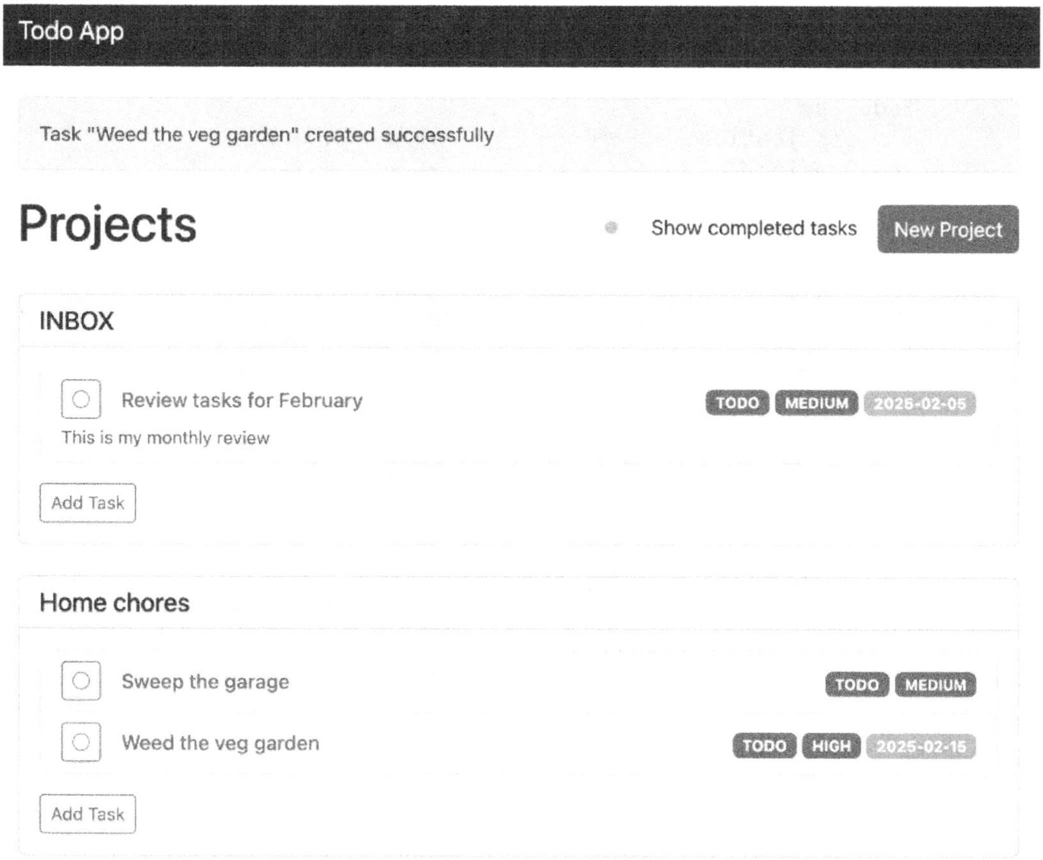

Todo App

Task "Weed the veg garden" created successfully

Projects

Show completed tasks   New Project

INBOX

○ Review tasks for February   TODO MEDIUM 2025-02-05
This is my monthly review

Add Task

Home chores

○ Sweep the garage   TODO MEDIUM

○ Weed the veg garden   TODO HIGH 2025-02-15

Add Task

Figure 9.1: Web UI listing page showing projects and their associated tasks

The web interface enhances our existing task management capabilities through immediate visual feedback and intuitive navigation. Users can create new tasks, update their status, and organize them within projects. The interface adapts our existing business logic to web conventions, using standard patterns such as form submissions for task creation and flash messages for user feedback.

To implement this interface while maintaining our architectural boundaries, our web implementation is organized into distinct components:

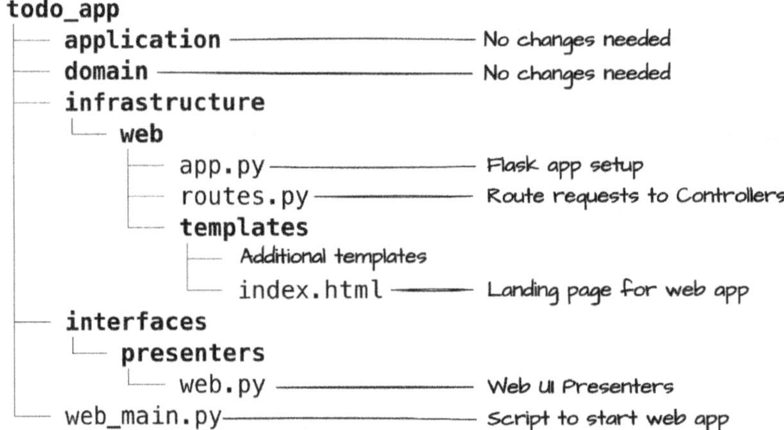

Figure 9.2: Associated files for the Web UI implementation

This structure demonstrates Clean Architecture's separation of concerns in action. In our Adapters and Interfaces (`interfaces`) layer, the web presenters know how to format data for web display by creating HTML-friendly strings and structuring data for templates, but remain completely unaware of Flask or any specific web framework. These presenters could work equally well with Django, FastAPI, or any other web framework.

This separation stands in stark contrast to applications built without clear architectural boundaries. In a less structured application, a request to *add a web interface* often triggers a cascade of changes throughout the codebase. Business logic mixed with presentation concerns requires extensive refactoring. Database queries embedded in display logic need restructuring. Even seemingly simple changes like formatting dates for web display can require modifications across multiple components. In extreme cases, teams find themselves essentially rewriting their application to accommodate the new interface.

Our task management system, by contrast, treats the web interface as a purely additive change. No existing code needs modification: not our business rules, not our use cases, not even our CLI. This ability to add major features without disturbing existing functionality demonstrates Clean Architecture's practical value in evolving systems.

The framework-specific code lives where it belongs—in the `infrastructure/web` directory within our Frameworks and Drivers layer. Here, Flask-specific concerns like route handling, template configuration, and HTTP session management stay isolated at the edges of our system. This separation means we could switch web frameworks without touching our interface adapters or core business logic.

Parallel interface implementations

Before diving into our web implementation details, let's examine how our CLI and web interfaces coexist within our Clean Architecture system. While these interfaces serve users through very different mechanisms (command line versus HTTP), they share the same core components and follow identical architectural patterns.

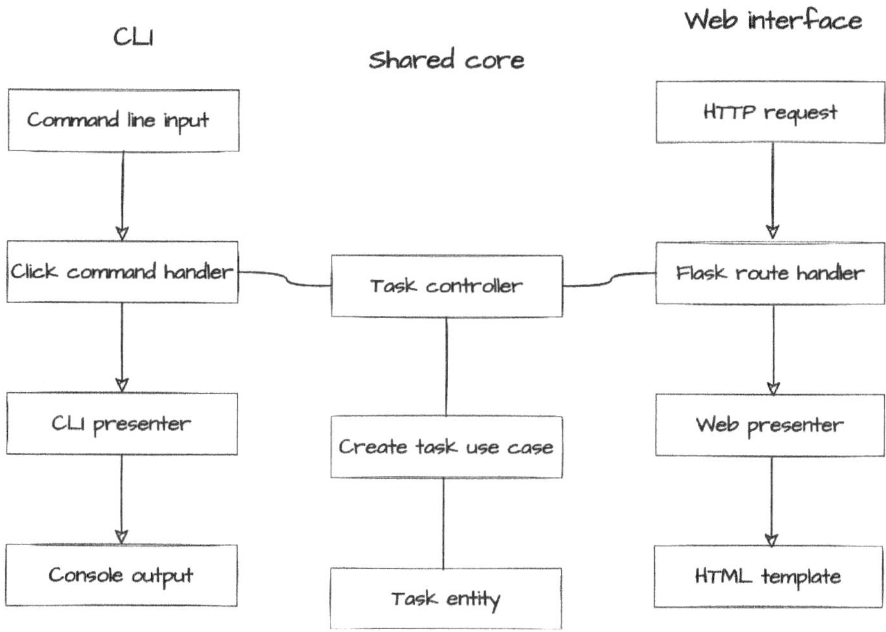

Figure 9.3: Request flow comparison

This diagram illustrates how our architecture maintains clear boundaries while supporting multiple interfaces:

- **CLI** transforms command-line input through Click Command Handler
- **Web interface** processes HTTP requests via Flask Route Handler
- **Shared core** contains our Task Controller, Use Cases, and Entities

Clean Architecture enables this coexistence through strict dependency rules. Both interface handlers connect to the same task controller, but the core components remain completely unaware of how they're being used. This isolation means our core business logic can focus on task creation rules while each interface handles its specific concerns, whether that's parsing command-line arguments or processing form submissions.

To implement this separation, we use a pragmatic dependency injection approach through our Application container:

```python
# todo_app/infrastructure/configuration/container.py
@dataclass
class Application:
    """Container which wires together all components."""
    task_repository: TaskRepository
    project_repository: ProjectRepository
    notification_service: NotificationPort
    task_presenter: TaskPresenter
    project_presenter: ProjectPresenter
```

Note how each component is declared using abstract interfaces (`TaskRepository`, `NotificationPort`, etc.). This enables each interface implementation to provide its own specific dependencies while our application core remains unaware of the concrete implementations it will receive. The application factory demonstrates how this flexibility works in practice.

Our application factory implements Clean Architecture's composition root pattern which serves as the single point where we compose our interface-agnostic core with interface-specific implementations. The factory demonstrates two key architectural principles:

```python
# todo_app/infrastructure/configuration/container.py
def create_application(
    notification_service: NotificationPort,
    task_presenter: TaskPresenter,
    project_presenter: ProjectPresenter,
) -> "Application":
    """Factory function for the Application container."""
    task_repository, project_repository = create_repositories()

    return Application(
        task_repository=task_repository,
```

```
        project_repository=project_repository,
        notification_service=notification_service,
        task_presenter=task_presenter,
        project_presenter=project_presenter,
    )
```

First, the factory demonstrates Clean Architecture's Dependency Inversion Principle in action: interface-specific components (presenters) are passed in as parameters, while core infrastructure (repositories) is constructed internally. This separation means interface implementations can provide their own presenters while the factory ensures everything connects properly to our shared business core.

Second, the factory serves as the composition root that functions as the single point where abstract interfaces meet their concrete implementations.

Our CLI application demonstrates this adaptability to different interfaces. At the application boundary, we wire together our shared core with CLI-specific components:

```python
# cli_main.py
def main() -> int:
    """Main entry point for the CLI application."""
    app = create_application(
        notification_service=NotificationRecorder(),
        task_presenter=CliTaskPresenter(),
        project_presenter=CliProjectPresenter(),
    )
    cli = ClickCli(app)
    return cli.run()
```

Note how `main()` configures a CLI-specific application instance by providing interface-specific implementations (`CliTaskPresenter`, `CliProjectPresenter`) to our generic application container. The `ClickCli` class then wraps this core application, handling the translation between command-line interactions and our application's interface-agnostic operations. This pattern of wrapping interface-specific code around our core application is a fundamental Clean Architecture practice that we'll see mirrored in our web implementation.

By setting up our application this way, we've established a clear pattern for how new interfaces connect to our core application. To add our web interface, we'll need to implement analogous components that fulfill the same roles but for web-specific concerns:

- **Presentation layer**: implementing `WebTaskPresenter` for HTML templates
- **Request handling**: processing form submissions and URL parameters
- **Session state**: managing persistence between requests
- **User feedback**: implementing web-specific error presentation

The key insight is that all interface-specific concerns remain at the edges of our system. Each interface handles its own unique requirements, such as web session management or CLI argument parsing, while our core business logic remains focused and clean.

In the next section, we'll explore specific presentation patterns for web interfaces, seeing how these same principles that kept our CLI implementation clean can guide us in creating maintainable web-specific components.

Common interface boundary violations

Clean Architecture's effectiveness depends on maintaining clear boundaries between layers. A common violation occurs when developers allow interface-specific formatting to creep into controllers, creating problematic dependencies that flow in the wrong direction. Consider this anti-pattern:

```python
# Anti-pattern: Interface-specific logic in controller
def handle_create(self, request_data: dict) -> dict:
    """DON'T: Mixing CLI formatting in controller."""
    try:
        result = self.create_use_case.execute(request_data)
        if result.is_success:
            # Wrong: CLI-specific formatting doesn't belong here
            return {
                "message": click.style(
                    f"Created task: {result.value.title}",
                    fg="green"
                )
            }
```

```python
    except ValueError as e:
        # Wrong: CLI-specific error formatting
        return {"error": click.style(str(e), fg="red")}
```

This implementation violates Clean Architecture's Dependency Rule in a subtle but important way. The controller, which lives in our Interface Adapters layer, directly references Click (a framework that should be constrained to our outermost layer). This creates a problematic coupling, for our controller now depends on both the Application layer (inward) and the Frameworks layer (outward), breaking Clean Architecture's fundamental rule that dependencies should only point inward. Beyond the architectural violation, this coupling has practical consequences: we couldn't reuse this controller for our web interface, and even updating to a newer version of Click would require changes in our Interface Adapters layer.

Instead, our task management system correctly delegates all formatting concerns to interface-specific presenters. Notice how our controller depends only on the abstract Presenter interface. It has no knowledge of whether it's working with CLI, web, or any other concrete presenter implementation:

```python
# Correct: Interface-agnostic controller
def handle_create(self, title: str, description: str) -> OperationResult:
    """DO: Keep controllers interface-agnostic."""
    try:
        request = CreateTaskRequest(title=title, description=description)
        result = self.create_use_case.execute(request)
        if result.is_success:
            view_model = self.presenter.present_task(result.value)
            return OperationResult.succeed(view_model)

        error_vm = self.presenter.present_error(
            result.error.message, str(result.error.code.name)
        )
        return OperationResult.fail(error_vm.message, error_vm.code)
    except ValueError as e:
        error_vm = self.presenter.present_error(
            str(e), "VALIDATION_ERROR")
        return OperationResult.fail(error_vm.message, error_vm.code)
```

This corrected implementation demonstrates several Clean Architecture principles:

- The controller accepts simple types (`str`) rather than framework-specific structures
- Error handling produces framework-agnostic `OperationResult` instances
- All formatting is delegated to the abstract `presenter` interface
- The controller remains focused on coordinating between use cases and presentation

This approach yields significant practical benefits. With our clean implementation, framework changes only affect the outermost layer. We could replace Click with another CLI framework by simply implementing new adapters without touching our controllers, use cases, or domain logic. The same controller handles requests identically regardless of whether they originate from our CLI, web interface, or any future interface we might add.

The Interface Adapters layer acts as a protective boundary, transforming data between our domain core and external interfaces. This architectural boundary enables us to add a web interface without disrupting existing components. Our domain entities focus solely on business rules while interface-specific concerns remain properly isolated at the system edges.

Now that we've established how Clean Architecture's boundaries enable interface flexibility, let's examine the specific presentation patterns needed for web interfaces and how they maintain these same architectural principles.

Web presentation patterns in Clean Architecture

Having established how Clean Architecture enables interface flexibility, we now turn to the specific patterns needed for web presentation. While our CLI directly formatted data for console output, web interfaces must handle more complex presentation requirements: formatting data for HTML templates, managing state across multiple requests, and providing user feedback through form validation and flash messages (temporary notification banners that appear at the top of the page after an action, like the green success message shown in *Figure 9.1*). This section explores these web-specific challenges and shows how Clean Architecture's boundaries guide our implementation choices.

We'll examine how web-specific presenters format domain data for HTML display, ensuring our templates receive properly structured information. We'll see how state management across requests can respect Clean Architecture's boundaries, and how form handling can maintain separation between web concerns and business rules. Through these patterns, we'll demonstrate that web interfaces, despite their complexity, can integrate cleanly with our existing architecture.

Implementing web-specific presenters

To bridge our domain logic and web display requirements, we need presenters that understand web conventions. To understand how our web presenter should work, let's first examine our CLI presenter from *Chapter 7*. Notice how it encapsulates all CLI-specific formatting decisions (bracketed status, colored priorities) while maintaining a clean interface through `TaskViewModel`. This established pattern of transforming domain objects into interface-appropriate view models will guide our web implementation:

```python
# CLI Presenter from Chapter 7
def present_task(self, task_response: TaskResponse) -> TaskViewModel:
    """Format task for CLI display."""
    return TaskViewModel(
        id=task_response.id,
        title=task_response.title,
        # CLI-specific bracketed format:
        status_display=f"[{task_response.status.value}]",
        # CLI-specific coloring.
        priority_display=self._format_priority(task_response.priority)
    )
```

Our web presenter follows the same pattern but adapts the formatting for HTML display:

```python
class WebTaskPresenter(TaskPresenter):

    def present_task(self, task_response: TaskResponse) -> TaskViewModel:
        """Format task for web display."""
        return TaskViewModel(
            id=task_response.id,
            title=task_response.title,
            description=task_response.description,
            status_display=task_response.status.value,
            priority_display=task_response.priority.name,
            due_date_display=self._format_due_date(
                task_response.due_date),
            project_display=task_response.project_id,
            completion_info=self._format_completion_info(
                task_response.completion_date,
```

```
                task_response.completion_notes
        ),
    )
```

Notice how the `WebTaskPresenter` class provides additional fields and formatting specific to web display needs: HTML-friendly status values, date formatting for browser display, and structured completion information for template rendering. This implementation demonstrates how Clean Architecture's presenters serve as a systematic translation layer between domain concepts and presentation needs:

- Translates domain objects into interface-appropriate formats while preserving their business meaning
- Centralizes all presentation decisions in a single, testable component
- Enables each interface to adapt domain data according to its specific needs
- Maintains clear separation between domain logic and display concerns

The presenter doesn't just format data; it serves as the authoritative interpreter of how domain concepts should appear in the interface. Consider our date formatting method:

```python
def _format_due_date(self, due_date: Optional[datetime]) -> str:
    """Format due date for web display."""
    if not due_date:
        return ""


    is_overdue = due_date < datetime.now(timezone.utc)
    date_str = due_date.strftime("%Y-%m-%d")
    return f"Overdue: {date_str}" if is_overdue else date_str
```

The `_format_due_date` method encapsulates all date-related formatting decisions: time zone handling, date format strings, and overdue status checks. By containing these decisions in the presenter, we ensure our domain entities remain focused on business rules (when a task is due) while presentation concerns (how to display that due date) stay in the appropriate architectural layer.

This translation layer allows our templates to remain simple while still delivering rich, contextual information:

```html
<span class="badge
    {% if 'overdue' in task.due_date_display %}bg-danger
    {%else %}bg-info
    {% endif %}">
```

```
    {{ task.due_date_display }}
</span>
```

The template exemplifies Clean Architecture's separation of concerns in action: it focuses purely on HTML structure and styling decisions based on pre-formatted values. All business logic (datetime comparisons) and data formatting remain in the appropriate architectural layers. The template simply adapts the presenter's output for visual display, using simple string checks to apply appropriate CSS classes.

Just as in *Chapter 8*, we can verify this formatting logic through focused unit tests. This test demonstrates a key benefit of Clean Architecture's separation of concerns: we can verify our presentation logic in isolation, without any web framework dependencies. By testing against the presenter directly, we can ensure that our date formatting logic works correctly without setting up a full web environment. The test focuses purely on the transformation from domain data to presentation format:

```python
def test_web_presenter_formats_overdue_date():
    """Test that presenter properly formats overdue dates."""
    # Arrange
    past_date = datetime.now(timezone.utc) - timedelta(days=1)
    task_response = TaskResponse(
        id="123",
        title="Test Task",
        description="Test Description",
        status=TaskStatus.TODO,
        priority=Priority.MEDIUM,
        project_id="456",
        due_date=past_date
    )
    presenter = WebTaskPresenter()

    # Act
    view_model = presenter.present_task(task_response)

    # Assert
    assert "Overdue" in view_model.due_date_display
    assert past_date.strftime("%Y-%m-%d") in view_model.due_date_display
```

This test demonstrates how Clean Architecture's separation enables precise verification of our web formatting logic. We can test complex scenarios, like overdue dates, without any web framework setup. The same pattern applies to future dates:

```python
def test_web_presenter_formats_future_date():
    """Test that presenter properly formats future dates."""
    # Arrange
    future_date = datetime.now(timezone.utc) + timedelta(days=1)
    task_response = TaskResponse(
        id="123",
        title="Test Task",
        description="Test Description",
        status=TaskStatus.TODO,
        priority=Priority.MEDIUM,
        project_id="456",
        due_date=future_date
    )
    presenter = WebTaskPresenter()

    # Act
    view_model = presenter.present_task(task_response)

    # Assert
    assert "Overdue" not in view_model.due_date_display
    assert future_date.strftime("%Y-%m-%d") in view_model.due_date_display
```

This complementary test ensures that our presenter handles future dates appropriately, completing our verification of the date formatting logic. Together with the previous test, we've confirmed both the presence and absence of the 'Overdue' indicator, all without touching any web framework code.

These tests highlight key benefits of Clean Architecture's presenter pattern. Our formatting logic can be verified without complex web setup. No need for Flask test clients, mock databases, or HTML parsing. Changes to date formatting can be tested quickly and precisely, while our templates remain focused purely on display concerns.

This pattern extends across all domain concepts, from task status to priority levels, ensuring consistent translation of business objects into presentation-ready formats. Any template in our system can display task due dates without knowing how those dates are formatted. More importantly, as our formatting logic evolves with additions such as time zone support or new display formats, we only need to update the presenter and its tests. Our templates, controllers, and domain logic remain unchanged.

Presenters versus template-based formatting

Developers familiar with modern web frameworks like React, Vue, or template-oriented patterns in Flask/Django might question our separation of formatting logic into presenters. Many applications embed formatting directly in templates:

```html
<!-- Common pattern in many web frameworks -->
<span class="badge {% if task.due_date < now() %}bg-danger{% else %}bg-info{% endif %}">
    {{ task.due_date.strftime("%Y-%m-%d") }}
    {% if task.due_date < now() %}(Overdue){% endif %}
</span>
```

While this pattern is widespread, it blurs the boundary between presentation decisions and display structure. In Clean Architecture, we recognize formatting as a translation concern that belongs in the Interface Adapters layer, not in the templates themselves.

Even when working with template-oriented frameworks, Clean Architecture principles can still guide implementation decisions by:

- Recognizing where business decisions are leaking into templates
- Extracting formatting logic into dedicated components
- Treating templates purely as display structure

The fundamental architectural principle remains the same: maintain clear boundaries between layers. Whether implemented through our explicit presenter pattern or through template helpers and components, the goal is to ensure that domain concepts are properly translated before they reach the outermost display layer.

Managing web-specific state

Session data and form state present unique challenges for maintaining Clean Architecture's boundaries. Let's examine how our system handles these web-specific concerns while keeping our core domain logic pure. Consider this anti-pattern where a domain entity directly accesses web session data:

```python
# Anti-pattern: Domain entity accessing web state
class Task:
    def complete(self, web_app_contatiner):
        # Wrong: Task shouldn't know about web sessions
        self.completed_by = web_app_contatiner.user.id
        self.completed_at = datetime.now()
```

This demonstrates how mixing web concerns into domain entities creates multiple maintenance challenges:

- Testing requires mocking web session data even for basic domain logic
- Adding new interfaces means updating entity code rather than just adding adapters
- Session handling bugs can ripple through the entire Domain layer
- Entity behavior becomes dependent on web framework implementation details

Our Flask route handlers act as the architectural boundary where web-specific concerns are managed. They translate HTTP concepts into domain-agnostic operations while keeping web state management where it belongs:

```python
# todo_app/infrastructure/web/routes.py
@bp.route("/")
def index():
    """List all projects with their tasks."""
    app = current_app.config["APP_CONTAINER"]
    show_completed = (
        request.args.get("show_completed", "false")
        .lower() == "true"
    )

    result = app.project_controller.handle_list()
    if not result.is_success:
        error = project_presenter.present_error(result.error.message)
```

```python
        flash(error.message, "error")
        return redirect(url_for("todo.index"))

    return render_template(
        "index.html",
        projects=result.success,
        show_completed=show_completed
    )
```

This handler exemplifies Clean Architecture's boundary management in action. At this outer edge of our system, the route captures and processes web-specific state like the show_completed preference, translating HTTP concepts into domain-agnostic operations. Instead of allowing domain entities to access session data directly, the handler extracts only the necessary information before passing it to our core business logic. Web-specific concerns such as user feedback through flash messages and template rendering stay in this outer layer, while our domain logic remains focused purely on its core responsibilities.

Form handling and validation

Form submissions in web applications present an architectural challenge. A common anti-pattern is to spread validation logic across templates, controllers, and domain entities, making it difficult to maintain and evolve validation rules. Let's examine how Clean Architecture guides us to handle forms appropriately using a simple project creation form:

```python
# todo_app/infrastructure/web/routes.py
@bp.route("/projects/new", methods=["GET", "POST"])
def new_project():
    """Create a new project."""
    if request.method == "POST":
        name = request.form["name"]
        app = current_app.config["APP_CONTAINER"]
        result = app.project_controller.handle_create(name)

        if not result.is_success:
            error = project_presenter.present_error(result.error.message)
            flash(error.message, "error")
            return redirect(url_for("todo.index"))
```

```python
        project = result.success
        flash(f'Project "{project.name}" created successfully', "success")
        return redirect(url_for("todo.index"))

    return render_template("project_form.html")
```

The route handler demonstrates Clean Architecture's validation flow:

1. The route extracts web-specific inputs:

    - URL parameters (`project_id`)

    - Form fields (`request.form["title"]`, etc.)

    - Optional fields with defaults (`due_date`)

2. The task controller receives standard Python types:

    - Strings for text fields

    - None for empty optional fields

    - The `project_id` from the URL

3. Domain validation occurs through established layers:

    - Business rules in entities

    - Use case coordination

    - Results returned via our Result type

4. Web-specific responses:

    - Success redirects with flash messages

    - Error handling through flash messages and redirects

Syncing client-side and domain validation

While our domain validation provides the ultimate source of truth, modern web applications often need immediate user feedback. Flask provides mechanisms like WTForms that can mirror domain validation rules in the view layer, enabling responsive UX without duplicating validation logic. The key is to ensure that these view-layer validations remain thin wrappers around our core domain rules rather than introduce parallel validation logic.

This separation ensures that our validation rules stay with our domain logic where they belong, while the web layer focuses on collecting input and presenting feedback.

Integrating Flask with Clean Architecture

Having established our presentation patterns and state management approach, we now turn to the practical integration of Flask into our Clean Architecture system. Building on the application container structure seen earlier in *Understanding interface flexibility in Clean Architecture*, we'll focus on the Flask-specific aspects of our web interface:

- Configuring Flask's application factory pattern
- Managing Flask-specific settings and dependencies
- Connecting Flask routes to our core application logic

Here's how our Flask application factory integrates with our existing architecture:

```python
# todo_app/infrastructure/web/app.py
def create_web_app(app_container: Application) -> Flask:
    """Create and configure Flask application."""
    flask_app = Flask(__name__)
    # Change this in production:
    flask_app.config["SECRET_KEY"] = "dev"
    # Store container in config:
    flask_app.config["APP_CONTAINER"] = app_container

    # Register blueprints
    from . import routes
    flask_app.register_blueprint(routes.bp)

    return flask_app
```

Let's examine the key components of this setup. As shown in *Figure 9.4*, web_main.py acts as our application's entry point, orchestrating the creation and configuration of both our business logic (Application Container) and web interface (Web Container) through Flask. The Application Container holds our core business logic while the Web Container manages Flask-specific concerns like routes and templates.

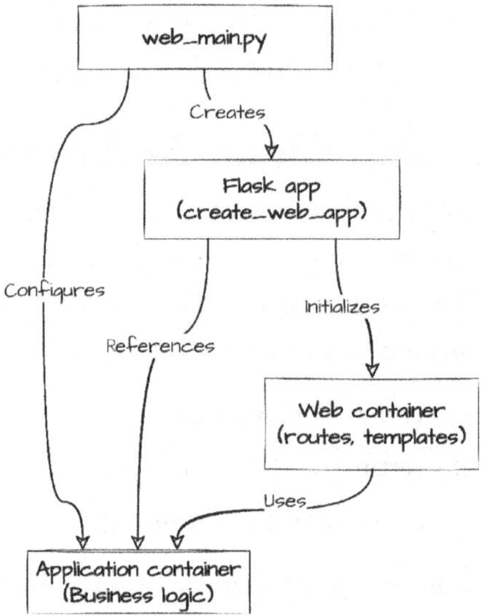

Figure 9.4: Flask application bootstrapping showing container relationships

This structure follows Clean Architecture's principles in several key ways:

- Keeping Flask-specific code isolated in the Web Container

- Maintaining our core Application Container's independence from web concerns

- Enabling clear communication paths between containers through well-defined interfaces

With these containers properly configured and connected, we're ready to implement our routes and templates. These components will build on the presentation patterns we've established, showing how Clean Architecture enables us to create a full-featured web interface while maintaining clear architectural boundaries.

Implementing routes and templates

Earlier in this chapter we examined routes from a data flow perspective: how they represent entry points into our system and translate HTTP requests for our core domain. Now let's look more closely at their implementation to understand how they maintain Clean Architecture's boundaries while delivering web-specific functionality.

Just as our CLI implementation translated command-line arguments into use case inputs, our web routes translate HTTP requests into operations our core application can understand. While the delivery mechanism differs (HTTP requests instead of command-line arguments), the architectural pattern remains the same: external input flows through our interface adapters before reaching our application core.

Consider how our CLI handled task creation:

```python
# todo_app/infrastructure/cli/click_cli_app.py
def _create_task(self):
    """CLI task creation."""
    title = click.prompt("Task title", type=str)
    description = click.prompt("Description", type=str)
    result = self.app.task_controller.handle_create(
        title=title,
        description=description
    )
```

Our web route implements the same architectural pattern as our CLI, though adapted for HTTP's request-response cycle. Just as the CLI handler transformed command-line arguments into domain operations, this route handler serves as a clean boundary between HTTP concepts and our domain logic:

```python
@bp.route("/projects/<project_id>/tasks/new", methods=["GET", "POST"])
def new_task(project_id):
    """Create a new task in a project."""
    if request.method == "POST":
        app = current_app.config["APP_CONTAINER"]
        result = app.task_controller.handle_create(
            project_id=project_id,
            title=request.form["title"],
            description=request.form["description"],
            priority=request.form["priority"],
            due_date=(
                request.form["due_date"]
                if request.form["due_date"] else None
            ),
        )
```

```python
    if not result.is_success:
        error = task_presenter.present_error(result.error.message)
        flash(error.message, "error")
        return redirect(url_for("todo.index"))

    task = result.success
    flash(f'Task "{task.title}" created successfully', "success")
    return redirect(url_for("todo.index"))

return render_template("task_form.html", project_id=project_id)
```

Notice how both implementations:

- Collect input in interface-specific ways (CLI prompts versus form data)

- Transform that input into standard parameters for our controller

- Handle success and error responses appropriately for their interface (CLI output versus HTTP redirects)

This consistent pattern demonstrates how Clean Architecture enables multiple interfaces while keeping our core application focused on business logic.

The route handling goes beyond simple form processing. The `project_id` parameter comes from the URL itself (/projects/<project_id>/tasks/new), while form fields contain task details. Our Clean Architecture layers handle this naturally:

- The route layer manages all web specifics:

    - URL parameter extraction

    - Form data collection

    - Flash messages for user feedback (temporary UI messages shown after redirects)

    - Template selection and rendering

- The controller layer handles:

    - Combining URL and form data into a single operation

    - Coordinating with the appropriate use cases

    - Returning results that our web layer can interpret

The templates represent the outermost layer of our Clean Architecture system, serving as the final transformation point between our domain concepts and user interface. While our presenters handle the logical transformation of domain data into view models, templates focus exclusively on the visual representation of that data:

```
{% extends 'base.html' %}
{% block content %}
    {% for project in projects %}
    <div class="card mb-4">
        <div class="card-header">
            <h2 class="card-title h5 mb-0">{{ project.name }}</h2>
        </div>
        <!-- Template focuses purely on structure and display -->
    </div>
    {% endfor %}
{% endblock %}
```

This template demonstrates our clean separation of concerns in action. It works exclusively with the `ProjectViewModel` provided by our presenters. Notice how it simply references `project.name` without any knowledge of how that data was retrieved or processed. The template has no awareness of repositories, use cases, or even the HTTP layer, but focuses instead solely on rendering the provided view models in a user-friendly format. This mirrors how our CLI presenters formatted data for console output, with each interface handling only its specific display requirements.

This separation means we can completely redesign our templates, whether changing layouts, adding new UI components, or even switching template engines, without touching our core application logic.

Running your Clean Architecture web application

Having implemented our web interface components, let's examine how to bootstrap our Clean Architecture application. The `web_main.py` script serves as our composition root—the single point where abstract interfaces meet their concrete implementations. This entry point orchestrates the creation and connection of our components while maintaining Clean Architecture's dependency rules:

```
def main():
    """Create and run the Flask web application."""
    app_container = create_application(
```

```python
        notification_service=create_notification_service(),
        task_presenter=WebTaskPresenter(),
        project_presenter=WebProjectPresenter(),
    )
    web_app = create_web_app(app_container)
    web_app.run(debug=True)


if __name__ == "__main__":
    main()
```

The Dependency Inversion Principle enables runtime configuration of concrete implementations through environment variables. Just as our CLI application could switch components without code changes, our web interface maintains this flexibility:

```bash
# Repository Configuration
export TODO_REPOSITORY_TYPE="memory"  # or "file"
export TODO_DATA_DIR="repo_data"       # used with file repository


# Optional: Email Notification Configuration
export TODO_SENDGRID_API_KEY="your_api_key"
export TODO_NOTIFICATION_EMAIL="recipient@example.com"
```

This configuration flexibility demonstrates a key benefit of Clean Architecture: the ability to easily switch components. For example, changing `TODO_REPOSITORY_TYPE` from "memory" to "file" switches our entire storage implementation without requiring any code changes. The same pattern that enabled us to add a web interface also enables:

- Adding new storage backends (like PostgreSQL or MongoDB)
- Implementing additional notification services
- Creating new interfaces (such as a desktop or mobile app)
- Supporting alternative authentication methods

Each of these enhancements can be implemented and tested in isolation, then integrated through our clean architectural boundaries. This capability empowers development teams to experiment with new features and technologies while maintaining system stability. Rather than risky 'big bang' code deployments, teams can gradually evolve their applications by adding and testing new components within Clean Architecture's protective boundaries.

To launch the web application, run the main script:

```
> python web_main.py
 * Serving Flask app 'todo_app.infrastructure.web.app'
 * Debug mode: on
 * Running on http://127.0.0.1:5000
Press CTRL+C to quit
 * Restarting with stat
 * Debugger is active!
 * Debugger PIN: 954-447-204
127.0.0.1 - - [05/Feb/2025 13:58:57] "GET / HTTP/1.1" 200 -
```

Visiting `http://127.0.0.1:5000` in your browser presents a web interface that, while radically different in form from our CLI, operates on the exact same core components. Where our CLI interpreted command-line arguments, our web interface now processes form submissions and URL parameters. The same task creation use case that previously responded to CLI commands now handles HTTP POST requests:

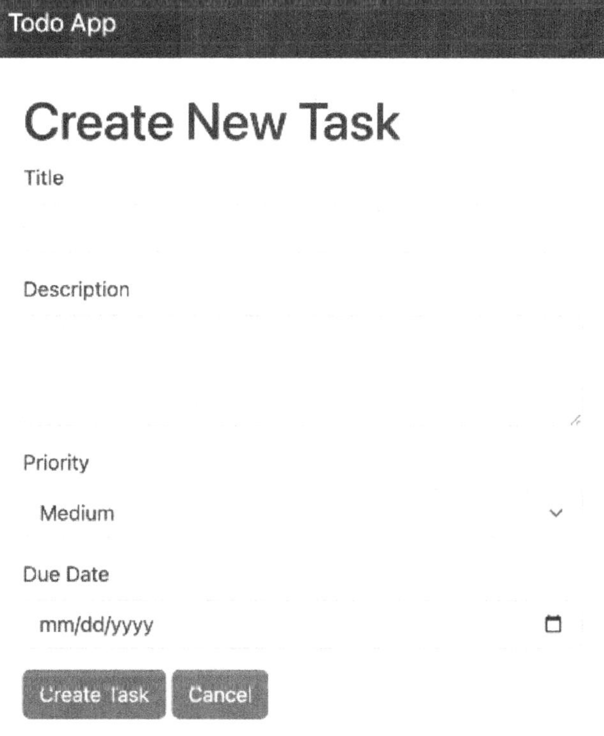

Figure 9.5: Task creation form showing web-specific input handling

This duality showcases Clean Architecture in practice. Our simple command-line application now coexists with a full web interface, complete with forms, dynamic updates, and visual feedback. Both interfaces run independently but share the same core components. The identical task creation use case that previously processed CLI commands now seamlessly handles web form submissions. Our repositories maintain consistent data regardless of which interface creates or updates records. Error handling adapts naturally, with command-line error messages for CLI users, flash messages and form validation for web users.

These aren't just two separate applications that happen to use similar code: they're two interfaces to the exact same application core, each presenting its capabilities in a way that makes sense for its environment. A team member could create a task through the CLI while another updates it through the web interface, with both operations flowing through the same use cases and repositories, demonstrating the practical power of Clean Architecture's boundary rules.

Summary

Our journey from CLI to web interface highlights Clean Architecture's power to enable system evolution without compromising architectural integrity. This capability extends beyond web interfaces to a broader principle: well-designed architectural boundaries create systems that can adapt to changing interface requirements while maintaining a stable core.

The patterns we've explored provide a template for future system evolution. These patterns range from interface-specific presenters to state management at system boundaries. Whether adding mobile interfaces, API endpoints, or entirely new interaction models, these same principles ensure that our core business logic remains focused and protected.

This flexibility doesn't come at the cost of maintainability. By keeping our domain entities focused on business rules and our use cases working with pure domain concepts, we've created a system where each layer can evolve independently. New interface requirements can be met through additional adapters, while our core business logic remains stable and untouched.

In *Chapter 10*, we'll explore how to add logging and monitoring to Clean Architecture systems, ensuring that our applications remain observable and maintainable in production environments.

Further reading

- *Flask Documentation* (`https://flask.palletsprojects.com/en/stable/`). Full documentation for the Flask framework.
- *WTForms* (`https://wtforms.readthedocs.io/en/3.2.x/`). Flexible forms validation and rendering library for Python web development.

10
Implementing Observability: Monitoring and Verification

In previous chapters, we established Clean Architecture's core principles through our task management system. We built domain entities, implemented use cases, and created both CLIs and web interfaces that demonstrate how Clean Architecture's boundaries enable clean separation between our core business logic and external concerns. While these boundaries make our system more maintainable, they serve another crucial purpose. They make our system more observable and its architectural integrity more verifiable.

Through our task management system, we'll demonstrate how Clean Architecture transforms system observability from a cross-cutting concern into a structured capability. Because our system is built with clear architectural layers and explicit interfaces, monitoring becomes a natural extension of our existing structure. This same organization that simplifies monitoring also enables continuous verification, helping ensure our system maintains its architectural integrity as it evolves.

By the end of this chapter, you'll understand how to implement effective observability in Clean Architecture systems and how to verify architectural boundaries remain intact over time. You'll learn practical techniques for detecting and preventing architectural drift, helping ensure your systems maintain their clean structure even as requirements and teams evolve.

In this chapter, we're going to cover the following main topics:

- Understanding observability in Clean Architecture
- Implementing cross-boundary instrumentation
- Maintaining architectural integrity through monitoring

Technical requirements

The code examples presented in this chapter and throughout the rest of the book are tested with Python 3.13. For brevity, most code examples in the chapter are only partially implemented. Complete versions of all examples can be found in the book's accompanying GitHub repository at `https://github.com/PacktPublishing/Clean-Architecture-with-Python`.

Understanding observability boundaries in Clean Architecture

Clean Architecture's explicit layer perimeters provide natural points for system observation which is a significant advantage that many teams overlook. While layered architectures can introduce complexity, these same divisions that help manage dependencies also enable systematic monitoring and observability. Let's first explore how Clean Architecture's fundamental principles create opportunities for better system instrumentation, setting the foundation for the practical implementations we'll explore later. By understanding these concepts, you'll see how Clean Architecture makes systems not only more maintainable but also more observable.

Natural observation points in Clean Architecture

Clean Architecture's layered structure naturally creates strategic points for system observation. Before exploring these observation points, let's understand what we mean by observability in software systems. Modern observability combines logging, metrics, and request tracing to provide a complete picture of system behavior. In traditional systems where these concerns cut across all components, implementing comprehensive monitoring often becomes an exercise in working around tangled dependencies.

Clean Architecture transforms this complexity into clarity by providing consistent observation points at each layer transition. Consider how information flows through our task management system: when a user creates a task through the web interface, we can observe the request as it moves through our architectural layers, from initial HTTP handling, through business operations, to final persistence. Each layer boundary provides specific insight:

- Our web interface tracks incoming requests and their transformations.
- Use cases monitor business operations and their outcomes.
- Domain entities capture state changes and business rule applications.
- Infrastructure components measure resource utilization and external interactions.

This systematic approach ensures we have visibility into every crucial aspect of our system's behavior while maintaining clean separation between technical and business concerns. This transforms not just monitoring but our entire approach to system maintenance. When investigating issues or analyzing performance, we know exactly where to look for relevant information. As we'll see in the following sections, this same structured approach that enables monitoring also provides the foundation for verifying our architectural integrity.

Understanding observability in Clean Architecture

Having seen how Clean Architecture provides natural observation points, let's explore how to effectively leverage these points in practice. While previous chapters focused on establishing core architectural principles, real-world systems require observability from the start. Early instrumentation proves crucial. Without it, debugging becomes more challenging, performance issues go undetected, and understanding system behavior across different environments becomes nearly impossible.

Consider how this plays out in our task management system. *Figure 10.1* shows how a seemingly simple operation like task completion involves multiple architectural transitions, each providing distinct observability needs:

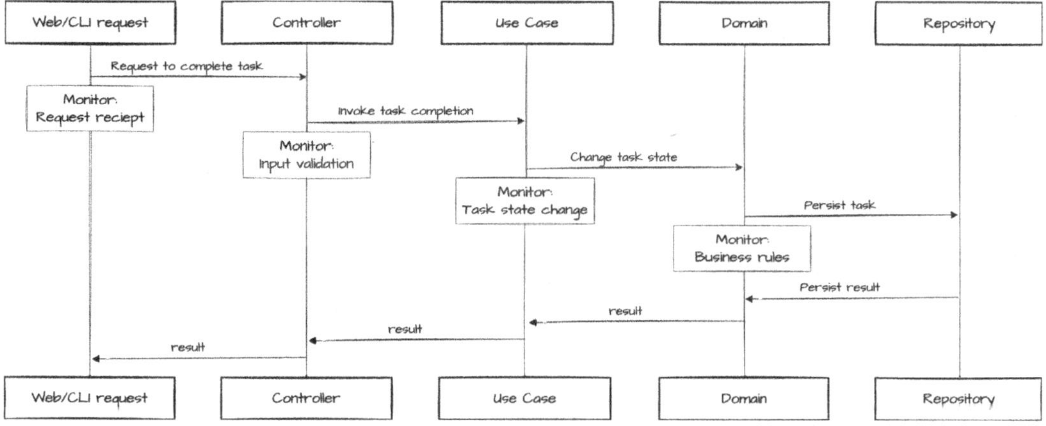

Figure 10.1: Task completion flow with observation points

The figure illustrates how monitoring concerns naturally align with our architectural layers. At each transition, we capture specific aspects of system behavior, from technical metrics at our outer boundaries to business operations in our core layers. This systematic approach ensures we maintain comprehensive visibility while respecting Clean Architecture's separation of concerns.

A layered monitoring approach provides clear benefits. When investigating issues, we can trace operations through our system with precision. If a customer reports intermittent task completion failures, we can follow the operation from web request through business logic to identify exactly where things went wrong. Performance bottlenecks become easier to locate since we know which layer is handling each aspect of the operation.

Each layer contributes what it knows best. Web interfaces track request handling, use cases monitor business operations, and infrastructure captures technical metrics. By respecting these natural divisions, we maintain clean separation between business and technical concerns while ensuring comprehensive visibility into our system's behavior.

These monitoring principles translate directly into implementation patterns. In our task management system, we'll use Python's standard logging framework to implement this layered observability. We'll see how Clean Architecture's boundaries guide us toward simple yet effective monitoring solutions that maintain architectural integrity while providing the insights our system needs.

Implementing cross-boundary instrumentation

Let's translate our understanding of Clean Architecture's observability benefits into practical implementation. Modern web frameworks such as Flask provide their own logging infrastructure, which can tempt developers into tightly coupling business operations with framework-specific logging. We'll see how to work effectively with these framework mechanisms while keeping our core business logic framework-independent. Through a careful implementation of structured logging and request tracing, we'll demonstrate patterns that maintain Clean Architecture's boundaries while delivering comprehensive system observability.

Avoiding framework coupling in logging

As we mentioned, web frameworks often provide their own logging infrastructure. Flask, for instance, encourages direct use of its application logger (`app.logger`):

```python
@app.route('/tasks/new', methods=['POST'])
def create_task():
    task = create_task_from_request(request.form)
    # Framework-specific logging:
    app.logger.info('Created task %s', task.id)
    return redirect(url_for('index'))
```

While convenient, this approach creates problematic coupling between our business operations and framework-specific logging. Using Flask's app.logger would require making the Flask application object accessible throughout our codebase which is a serious violation of Clean Architecture's Dependency Rule. Inner layers would need to reach out to the Framework layer just to perform logging, creating exactly the kind of outward dependency that Clean Architecture aims to prevent.

Instead, Clean Architecture guides us toward framework-independent logging that respects architectural boundaries. Consider how our task creation use case should log operations:

```python
# todo_app/application/use_cases/task_use_cases.py
import logging
logger = logging.getLogger(__name__)


@dataclass
class CreateTaskUseCase:
    task_repository: TaskRepository
    project_repository: ProjectRepository

    def execute(self, request: CreateTaskRequest) -> Result:
        try:
            logger.info(
                "Creating new task",
                extra={"context": {
                    "title": request.title,
                    "project_id": request.project_id
                }},
            )
            # ... implementation continues ...
```

This approach offers several Clean Architecture benefits:

- Use cases remain unaware of logging implementation details
- Logging statements document business operations naturally
- We can change logging infrastructure without modifying business logic
- Framework-specific logging stays at system edges where it belongs

Let's implement this clean logging approach systematically, starting with the proper separation of framework and application logging concerns.

Implementing structured logging patterns

As we've seen, Clean Architecture requires that infrastructure concerns, including logging implementation details, remain isolated in outer layers.

For our implementation, we've chosen structured JSON logging. This is a common practice that enables precise log processing and analysis. Each log entry becomes a JSON object with consistent fields, making it easier to search, filter, and analyze log data programmatically. While we'll demonstrate JSON formatting, the patterns we establish would work equally well with other logging formats: you could adapt the formatter implementation without touching any code in the inner layers.

We organize our logging infrastructure to maintain clean architectural boundaries:

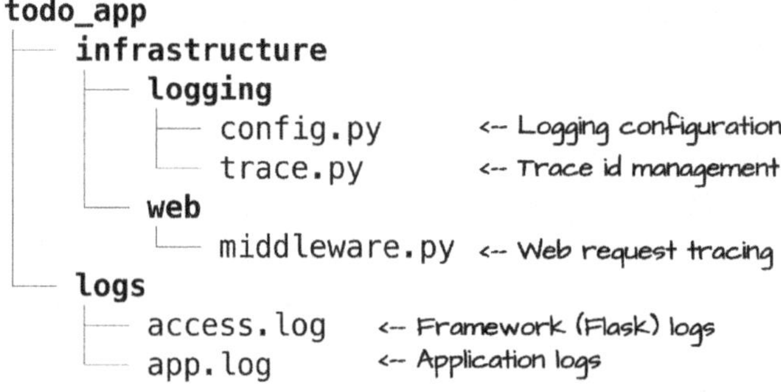

Figure 10.2: Logging files in the Frameworks and Drivers layer

This organization keeps logging configuration where it belongs: in the Frameworks and Drivers layer. The separation between framework logs (`access.log`) and application logs (`app.log`) demonstrates how we maintain clean boundaries even in our log output.

This separation serves two key Clean Architecture objectives:

- **Separation of concerns**: Each layer logs what it knows best. Flask handles HTTP request logging in its standard format, while our application captures business operations in structured JSON. This clean separation means each type of log can evolve independently, using formats and fields appropriate to its purpose.

- **Framework independence**: Our core application logging remains completely unaware of Flask or any other web framework. We could switch to a different framework, or even add new interfaces such as a REST API, while our business operation logging continues unchanged.

We need a way to format our application logs that supports structured data while remaining independent of any framework opinions. Our `JsonFormatter` handles this responsibility:

```python
# todo_app/infrastructure/logging/config.py
class JsonFormatter(logging.Formatter):
    """Formats log records as JSON."""
    def __init__(self, app_context: str):
        super().__init__()
        self.app_context = app_context
        # Custom encoder handles datetime, UUID, sets, and exceptions
        self.encoder = JsonLogEncoder()

    def format(self, record: logging.LogRecord) -> str:
        """Format log record as JSON."""
        log_data = {
            "timestamp": datetime.now(timezone.utc),
            "level": record.levelname,
            "logger": record.name,
            "message": record.getMessage(),
            "app_context": self.app_context,
        }
        # `extra` in the log statement, places `context`
        # on the LogRecord so seek and extract
        context = {}
        for key, value in record.__dict__.items():
            if key == "context":
                context = value
                break
        if context:
            log_data["context"] = context

        return self.encoder.encode(log_data)
```

The formatter encapsulates all JSON formatting logic in a single component, demonstrating the Single Responsibility Principle in action. Each log entry includes essential context like `timestamp` and log level, while remaining completely unaware of web frameworks or other external concerns.

Since Python's logging mechanism directly attaches the extra parameter keys to the `LogRecord` instance, we use a dedicated `context` namespace to prevent collisions with `LogRecord`'s built-in attributes (like `name`, `args`). This simple namespacing strategy lets us safely include structured data with each log message.

With our formatter handling the structure of individual log messages, we now need to configure how these messages flow through our system. This configuration determines which logs go where, maintaining our clean separation between framework and application logging. For clarity, we'll use the Python logger's `dictConfig` to establish these paths, starting with our formatters:

```python
# todo_app/infrastructure/logging/config.py
def configure_logging(app_context: Literal["CLI", "WEB"]) -> None:
    """Configure application logging with sensible defaults."""
    log_dir = Path("logs")
    log_dir.mkdir(exist_ok=True)

    config = {
        "formatters": {
            "json": {"()": JsonFormatter, "app_context": app_context},
            "standard": {"format": "%(message)s"},
        },
        ...
```

Here we define two formatters: our custom JSON formatter for application logs and a simple format for framework logs. This separation lets each type of log maintain its appropriate structure.

Next, we configure handlers that direct logs to their appropriate destinations:

```python
        ...
        },
        "handlers" = {
            "app_file": {
                "class": "logging.FileHandler",
                "filename": log_dir / "app.log",
                "formatter": "json",
            },
            "access_file": {
                "class": "logging.FileHandler",
```

```
                "filename": log_dir / "access.log",
                "formatter": "standard",
            },
        },
        ...
```

Each handler connects a log destination with its appropriate formatter, maintaining our clean separation between framework and application concerns.

Finally, we wire everything together with logger configurations:

```
        ...
        },
        "loggers" = {
            # Application logger
            "todo_app": {
                "handlers": ["app_file"],
                "level": "INFO",
            },
            # Flask's werkzeug logger
            "werkzeug": {
                "handlers": ["access_file"],
                "level": "INFO",
                "propagate": False,
            },
        },
    } // end configure_logging()
```

The todo_app logger captures all application-level operations through our JSON formatter, writing them to app.log. Meanwhile, Flask's built-in Werkzeug logger remains untouched, recording HTTP requests in standard format to access.log. By keeping these logging streams separate, we maintain clean boundaries between framework and business concerns.

This configuration gets activated early in our application startup:

```python
# web_main.py
def main():
    """Configure logging early"""
    configure_logging(app_context="WEB")
    # ...
```

Here we see the main file for the web app; the CLI will be identical except for `app_context="CLI"`.

Most importantly, this configuration means any code in our application can simply use Python's standard logging module without knowing about JSON formatting, file handlers, or any other implementation details. These concerns remain properly contained within our Infrastructure layer.

With our logging infrastructure in place, let's see how Clean Architecture's separation of concerns translates into practical benefit. Our task creation use case demonstrates how business operations can be clearly logged without any awareness of framework specifics:

```python
import logging
logger = logging.getLogger(__name__)
@dataclass
class CreateTaskUseCase:
    task_repository: TaskRepository
    project_repository: ProjectRepository

    def execute(self, request: CreateTaskRequest) -> Result:
        try:
            logger.info(
                "Creating new task",
                extra={"title": request.title,
                       "project_id": request.project_id},
            )
            # ... task creation logic ...
            logger.info(
                "Task created successfully",
                extra={"context":{
                    "task_id": str(task.id),
                    "project_id": str(project_id),
                    "priority": task.priority.name}}
            )
```

When we run our application, we see this in the console:

```
[2025-02-16 14:45:30] INFO werkzeug: 127.0.0.1 - - [16/Feb/2025:14:45:30] "GET /tasks/new HTTP/1.1" 200 -
[2025-02-16 14:45:32] INFO werkzeug: 127.0.0.1 - - [16/Feb/2025:14:45:32] "POST /tasks/new HTTP/1.1" 302 -
{"timestamp": "2025-02-16T14:45:32.123Z", "level": "INFO", "message": "Creating new task...
{"timestamp": "2025-02-16T14:45:32.135Z", "level": "INFO", "message": "Task created successfully",...
```

While we've chosen to display both log streams in the console for development convenience, each type of log is properly separated into its designated file:

```
# logs/access.log
127.0.0.1 - - [16/Feb/2025:14:45:30] "GET /tasks/new HTTP/1.1" 200 -
127.0.0.1 - - [16/Feb/2025:14:45:32] "POST /tasks/new HTTP/1.1" 302 -

# logs/app.log
{"timestamp": "2025-02-16T14:45:32.123Z", "level": "INFO", "message": "Creating...
{"timestamp": "2025-02-16T14:45:32.135Z", "level": "INFO", "logger": "message": "Task created...
```

If we view the formatted *create new task* log statement, we see the injection of the context attribute of the log statement:

```
{
  "timestamp": "2025-02-22T20:10:03.800373+00:00",
  "level": "INFO",
  "logger":
  "todo_app.application.use_cases.task_use_cases",
  "message": "Creating new task",
  "app_context": "WEB",
  "trace_id": "19d386aa-5537-45ac-9da6-3a0ce8717660",
  "context": {
    "title": "New Task",
    "project_id": "e587f1d5-5f6e-4da5-8d6b-155b39bbe8a9"
  }
}
```

Through this implementation, we've seen how Clean Architecture guides us to pragmatic solutions for common infrastructure concerns. By isolating logging configuration in our outermost layer, we enable each part of our system to log appropriately while maintaining proper architectural boundaries. Framework logs and business operations remain cleanly separated, yet both contribute to a comprehensive view of system behavior.

Building cross-boundary observability

Throughout this book, we've seen how Clean Architecture's explicit boundaries provide crucial benefits, from isolating business logic and maintaining testability to enabling interface flexibility and framework independence. However, these same boundaries that keep our system maintainable can make it challenging to trace operations as they flow through our layers.

While structured logging provides insight into individual operations, tracking requests across these architectural boundaries requires additional infrastructure. Let's extend our task management system to implement cross-boundary tracing while maintaining these clean separations.

Consider what happens when a user creates a task through our web interface, an operation that crosses multiple architectural boundaries:

1. A web request arrives at our Flask route handler
2. The request flows through our task controller
3. The controller invokes our use case
4. The use case coordinates with repositories
5. Finally, the result flows back through these layers

Without correlation between these events, debugging and monitoring become challenging. Our solution is straightforward but powerful: we'll generate a unique identifier (trace ID) for each request and include this ID in every log statement related to that request. This allows us to follow a request's journey through all layers of our system, from the initial web request to database operations and back.

To implement this tracing, we'll need to:

1. Create `infrastructure/logging/trace.py` to manage trace ID generation and storage
2. Extend our logging configuration in `infrastructure/logging/config.py` to include trace IDs in log formats
3. Add Flask middleware in `infrastructure/web/middleware.py` to set trace IDs for incoming requests

Because we've built our logging infrastructure following Clean Architecture principles, no changes are needed to application code. Trace IDs will automatically flow through our existing logging calls.

With our approach mapped out, let's start with the foundation: the trace ID management itself. This infrastructure, while living entirely in our outer layer, will enable visibility across all architectural boundaries:

```python
# todo_app/infrastructure/logging/trace.py


# Thread-safe context variable to hold trace ID
trace_id_var: ContextVar[Optional[str]] = ContextVar("trace_id",
                                                      default=None)

def get_trace_id() -> str:
```

```python
    """Get current trace ID or generate new one if not set."""
    current = trace_id_var.get()
    if current is None:
        current = str(uuid4())
        trace_id_var.set(current)
    return current


def set_trace_id(trace_id: Optional[str] = None) -> str:
    """Set trace ID for current context."""
    new_id = trace_id or str(uuid4())
    trace_id_var.set(new_id)
    return new_id
```

The `set_trace_id` function establishes a unique identifier for each request in our system. While it accepts an optional existing ID parameter (primarily used for testing or specialized integrations), in normal operation each request receives a new UUID. This ensures that every operation in our system can be traced independently, regardless of whether it originated from our CLI, web UI, or other entry points.

Why `ContextVar`?

We use Python's `ContextVar` because it provides thread-safe storage that works across async boundaries. While the specific implementation mechanism isn't crucial to Clean Architecture, choosing the right tools helps maintain clean boundaries. For more details on context variables, see Python's documentation: `https://docs.python.org/3/library/contextvars.html`

With trace ID management in place, we next need to ensure our logging configuration includes the trace ID in log formats:

```python
# todo app/infrastructure/logging/config.py
def configure_logging(app_context: Literal["CLI", "WEB"]) -> None:
    config = {
        "formatters": {
            "json": {"()": JsonFormatter, "app_context": app_context},
            "standard": {
                "format": "%(asctime)s [%(trace_id)s] %(message)s",
```

```python
            "datefmt": "%Y-%m-%d %H:%M:%S"
        },
    },
    # ... rest of configuration
}
```

Our logging configuration ensures trace IDs are included with every log message, regardless of the log format. For framework logs, we add trace IDs to the standard format using Python's built-in logging pattern syntax (`%(trace_id)s`). Our JSON formatter automatically includes trace IDs in structured output. This consistency means we can follow operations across all log sources, while each logging stream maintains its appropriate format.

Lastly, our web middleware ensures each request gets a trace ID:

```python
# todo_app/infrastructure/web/middleware.py
def trace_requests(flask_app):
    """Add trace ID to all requests."""
    @flask_app.before_request
    def before_request():
        trace_id = request.headers.get("X-Trace-ID") or None
        # pull trace id from globals
        g.trace_id = set_trace_id(trace_id)


    @flask_app.after_request
    def after_request(response):
        response.headers["X-Trace-ID"] = g.trace_id
        return response
```

This middleware ensures every web request receives a unique trace ID. Though it can accept an existing ID through the `X-Trace-ID` header (useful for testing), it typically generates a new UUID for each request.

To activate this tracing, we integrate the middleware when creating our Flask application:

```python
# todo_app/infrastructure/web/app.py
def create_web_app(app_container: Application) -> Flask:
    """Create and configure Flask application."""
    flask_app = Flask(__name__)
    flask_app.config["SECRET_KEY"] = "dev"
```

```python
    flask_app.config["APP_CONTAINER"] = app_container

    # Add trace ID middleware
    trace_requests(flask_app)
    # ...
```

Recall that web_main.py calls create_web_app, and thus this setup ensures that every request flowing through our system gets traced. This ID is then available throughout request processing and included in response headers for debugging purposes. The trace ID connects all log entries related to processing that specific request, from initial receipt through final response.

```
# logs/access.log
2025-02-16 14:45:32 [abc-123-xyz] 127.0.0.1 - - "POST /tasks/new HTTP/1.1" 302 -

# logs/app.log
{"timestamp": "2025-02-16T14:45:32.123Z", "trace_id": "abc-123-xyz", "level": "INFO", "message": "...
{"timestamp": "2025-02-16T14:45:32.135Z", "trace_id": "abc-123-xyz", "level": "INFO", "message": "...
```

Each request through our system is assigned a unique trace ID, allowing us to follow that specific operation across architectural boundaries. As shown above, the trace ID abc-123-xyz appears in both framework and application logs, connecting all events related to this single task creation request. This tracing enables us to understand exactly what happened during any given request, from initial HTTP handling through business operations to final response.

Our logging and tracing implementation demonstrates how Clean Architecture's boundaries enable comprehensive system observability without compromising architectural principles. Yet implementing these patterns is only half the challenge; we must also ensure these boundaries remain intact as our system evolves. Next, we'll explore how to actively verify our architectural integrity through automated checks and fitness functions.

Verifying architectural integrity through fitness functions

As systems evolve, maintaining architectural integrity becomes increasingly challenging. Even teams committed to Clean Architecture's principles can inadvertently introduce changes that compromise their systems' carefully crafted boundaries. This risk has led architects to develop *fitness functions* which are automated tests that verify that architectural principles are correctly implemented and detect any drift from those principles over time.

The concept of architectural fitness functions, introduced by Neal Ford, Rebecca Parsons, and Patrick Kua in their book *Building Evolutionary Architectures*, provides a systematic approach to maintaining architectural integrity. Just as unit tests verify code behavior, fitness functions verify architectural characteristics. By detecting violations early in the development process (an approach known as *shift left*), these tests help teams maintain Clean Architecture's principles in an automated manner.

While comprehensive architectural validation frameworks exist, Python enables us to implement effective verification in a simpler, more pragmatic way using the language's built-in capabilities. Through our architectural verification approach, we'll focus on two key aspects: ensuring our source structure maintains Clean Architecture's layered organization, and detecting any violations of the fundamental Dependency Rule that requires dependencies to only flow inward. These complementary checks help teams maintain architectural integrity as systems evolve.

Verifying layer structure

Let's start by defining our expected architectural structure. While every team's specific implementation of Clean Architecture may vary slightly, the core principle of explicit layer organization remains constant. We can capture our particular interpretation in a simple configuration:

```python
class ArchitectureConfig:
    """Defines Clean Architecture structure and rules."""

    # Ordered from innermost to outermost layer
    LAYER_HIERARCHY = [
        "domain",
        "application",
        "interfaces",
        "infrastructure"
    ]
```

This configuration serves as our architectural contract, by defining how we expect our codebase directories to be organized. Your team might choose different layer names or add additional organizational rules, but the principle remains the same: Clean Architecture requires explicit, well-defined layers with clear responsibilities.

With our structure defined, we can implement verification tests that ensure our codebase maintains this organization:

```python
def test_source_folders(self):
    """Verify todo_app contains only Clean Architecture layer folders."""
    src_path = Path("todo_app")
    folders = {f.name for f in src_path.iterdir() if f.is_dir()}

    # All layer folders must exist
    for layer in ArchitectureConfig.LAYER_HIERARCHY:
        self.assertIn(
            layer,
            folders,
            f"Missing {layer} layer folder"
        )

    # No unexpected folders
    unexpected = folders - set(ArchitectureConfig.LAYER_HIERARCHY)
    self.assertEqual(
        unexpected,
        set(),
        f"Source should only contain Clean Architecture layers.\n"
        f"Unexpected folders found: {unexpected}"
    )
```

This simple check enforces a fundamental Clean Architecture principle: our source code must be explicitly organized into well-defined layers. The `ArchitectureConfig` class allows us to customize these tests to your particular preferences. We're specifically examining the top-level folders within `todo_app`, ensuring they match our expected architectural structure. This isn't about the contents of these folders (we'll get to that with dependency checking), but rather verifying the basic organizational foundation of our Clean Architecture implementation.

Consider a common scenario: a team is adding email notification capabilities to the task management system. A new developer, not yet familiar with Clean Architecture, creates a new notifications folder at the root level:

```
todo_app
├── application
├── domain
├── infrastructure
├── interfaces
└── notifications        <-- Violation: new top level folder
    ├── email.py
    └── templates
```

This seemingly innocent organization choice represents the start of architectural drift. The notifications code should live in the Infrastructure layer since it's an external concern. By creating a new top-level folder, we've:

- Created confusion about where notification-related code belongs

- Started bypassing Clean Architecture's explicit layering

- Set a precedent for creating new top-level folders when developers are unsure about proper placement

Our simple structural check catches this early (literally within seconds if tests are run on the developer's machine):

```
> pytest tests/architecture
========== test session starts ===================
tests/architecture/test_source_structure.py F
E    AssertionError: Items in the first set but not the second:
E    'notifications' : Source should only contain Clean Architecture
layers.
E    Unexpected folders found: {'notifications'}
```

This warning prompts the new developer to properly integrate the notification code into the Infrastructure layer:

```
todo_app
├── application
├── domain
├── infrastructure
│   └── notifications      <-- correct: part of
│       ├── email.py           Frameworks and
│       └── templates          Drivers layer
└── interfaces
```

These simple structural checks catch architectural drift before it can compromise system maintainability. However, proper structure is only part of Clean Architecture's requirements. We must also ensure that dependencies between these layers flow in the right direction. Let's examine how to verify Clean Architecture's fundamental Dependency Rule.

Enforcing dependency rules

With our layer structure verified, we must ensure that these layers interact correctly according to Clean Architecture's principles. The most fundamental of these is the Dependency Rule, which states that dependencies must only point inward toward more central layers. Even a small violation of this rule can compromise the architectural integrity we've carefully built.

Building on our structural verification, let's examine how to detect violations of the Dependency Rule. This rule is crucial for maintaining a clean separation of concerns, yet it can be subtly violated during development.

Our Dependency Rule verification takes a direct approach, examining Python import statements to ensure they only flow inward through our architectural layers. While more sophisticated static analysis tools exist (see *Further reading*), this straightforward implementation catches the most common violations:

```python
def test_domain_layer_dependencies(self):
    """Verify domain layer has no outward dependencies."""
    domain_path = Path("todo_app/domain")
    violations = []

    for py_file in domain_path.rglob("*.py"):
        with open(py_file) as f:
            tree = ast.parse(f.read())

        for node in ast.walk(tree):
            if isinstance(node, ast.Import) or isinstance(
                node, ast.ImportFrom
            ):
                module = node.names[0].name
                if module.startswith("todo_app."):
                    layer = module.split(".")[1]
                    if layer in [
                        "infrastructure",
                        "interfaces",
                        "application"
                    ]:
                        violations.append(
                            f"{py_file.relative_to(domain_path)}: "
```

```
                        f"Domain layer cannot import from "
                        f"{layer} layer"
                )
        self.assertEqual(
            violations,
            [],
            "\nDependency Rule Violations:\n" + "\n".join(violations)
        )
```

This test implementation leverages Python's built-in ast module to analyze import statements in our Domain layer code. It works by:

1. Recursively finding all Python files in the Domain layer

2. Parsing each file into an Abstract Syntax Tree (AST)

3. Walking the AST to find Import and ImportFrom nodes

4. Checking each import to ensure it doesn't reference outer layers

While more complex static analysis is possible, this focused check effectively catches the most critical dependency violations, which are those that would compromise our core Domain layer's independence.

Consider a real-world scenario: a developer is implementing task completion notifications. They notice that the NotificationService in the Infrastructure layer already has the logic they need. Instead of following Clean Architecture's patterns, they take a shortcut that violates our fundamental Dependency Rule:

```
# todo_app/domain/entities/task.py
# Dependency Rule Violation!
from todo_app.infrastructure.notifications.recorder import
NotificationRecorder


class Task:
    def complete(self):
        self.status = TaskStatus.DONE
        self.completed_at = datetime.now()


        # Direct dependency on infrastructure -
        # violates Clean Architecture
        notification = NotificationRecorder()
        notification.notify_task_completed(self)
```

This change might seem innocent because it gets the job done. However, it creates exactly the kind of outward dependency that Clean Architecture prohibits. Our domain entity now depends directly on an infrastructure component, meaning:

- The Task entity can no longer be tested without `NotificationService`
- We can't change notification implementations without modifying domain code
- We've created a precedent for mixing infrastructure concerns with domain logic

Our dependency check catches this violation immediately during testing:

```
> pytest tests/architecture
======================== test session starts ==========
...
E    'entities/task.py: Domain layer cannot import from infrastructure
layer'
E     Dependency Rule Violations:
E      entities/task.py: Domain layer cannot import from infrastructure
layer

======================== 2 passed in 0.01s =============
```

The error message clearly identifies:

- The file containing the violation
- Which architectural rule was broken
- How to fix it (Domain layer can't import from infrastructure)

These simple but powerful verifications help teams maintain alignment with Clean Architecture's principles as systems evolve. While we've focused on two fundamental checks (structural organization and dependency rules), teams can expand this approach to verify other architectural characteristics:

- **Interface conformance**: Verify that interface adapters properly implement their declared contracts
- **Repository implementations**: Confirm that repository implementations properly extend their abstract bases
- **Layer-specific rules**: Add custom rules for how each layer should structure and expose its components

The key is starting with focused, high-impact checks that verify your most crucial architectural boundaries. You can then evolve these fitness functions alongside your architecture, adding verification for new patterns and constraints as your system grows.

By catching structural and dependency violations early, we prevent the gradual erosion of architectural boundaries that can occur during rapid development. While these checks can't replace architectural understanding, they provide immediate, actionable feedback when architectural rules are violated, thereby helping teams build and preserve clean, maintainable systems.

Summary

In this chapter, we've explored how Clean Architecture's explicit boundaries enable systematic monitoring and verification of our systems. Through our task management system, we've demonstrated how to implement effective observability while maintaining architectural integrity. We've seen how Clean Architecture transforms monitoring from a cross-cutting concern into a natural part of our system's structure.

We implemented several key observability patterns that demonstrate Clean Architecture's benefits:

- Framework-independent logging that respects architectural boundaries while enabling comprehensive system visibility
- Cross-boundary request tracing that maintains clean separation between technical and business concerns
- Automated architectural verification that helps teams maintain Clean Architecture's principles as systems evolve

Most importantly, we've seen how Clean Architecture's careful attention to boundaries makes our systems not just maintainable but also observable and verifiable. By organizing our logging and monitoring infrastructure according to Clean Architecture principles, we create systems that are easier to understand, debug, and maintain over time.

In *Chapter 11*, we'll explore how to apply Clean Architecture principles to existing systems, showing how these same boundaries and patterns can guide the transformation of legacy codebases into clean, maintainable architectures.

Further reading

- *Python Logging Cookbook* (`https://docs.python.org/3/howto/logging-cookbook.html`). A collection of logging related code recipes.

- *Building Evolutionary Architectures* (`https://www.oreilly.com/library/view/building-evolutionary-architectures/9781491986356/`). Excellent software architecture book where the term *Fitness Function* was first coined.

- *PyTestArch* (`https://github.com/zyskarch/pytestarch`). Open-source framework enabling you to define architectural rules in code and run as tests.

Get this book's PDF version and more

Scan the QR code (or go to `packtpub.com/unlock`). Search for this book by name, confirm the edition, and then follow the steps on the page.

Note: Keep your invoice handy. Purchases made directly from Packt don't require an invoice.

11

Legacy to Clean: Refactoring Python for Maintainability

While previous chapters demonstrated Clean Architecture principles through greenfield development, real-world systems often present a different challenge. Existing applications, built under time pressure or before architectural best practices were established, frequently violate Clean Architecture's fundamental principles. Their domain logic becomes tangled with frameworks, business rules mix with infrastructure concerns, and dependencies flow in all directions. Yet these systems often serve critical business needs and cannot simply be replaced.

Through our exploration of Clean Architecture transformation, we'll discover how to systematically evolve legacy systems while maintaining their business value. We'll see how Clean Architecture's explicit boundaries and dependency rules provide clear guidance for improving existing systems, even under real-world constraints. You'll learn how to identify architectural violations, establish clean boundaries incrementally, and maintain system stability during transformation.

By the end of this chapter, you'll understand how to apply Clean Architecture principles to legacy systems through staged implementation. You'll be able to evaluate existing systems through Clean Architecture's lens and implement bounded transformations that respect business constraints while maintaining system stability.

In this chapter, we're going to cover the following main topics:

- Evaluating and planning architectural transformation
- Progressive Clean Architecture implementation

Technical requirements

The code examples presented in this chapter and throughout the rest of the book are tested with Python 3.13. For brevity, most code examples in the chapter are only partially implemented. Complete versions of all examples can be found in the book's accompanying GitHub repository at `https://github.com/PacktPublishing/Clean-Architecture-with-Python`.

Evaluating and planning architectural transformation

Improving maintainability and reducing risk in complex applications requires a systematic approach to architectural evolution. Applications with tangled dependencies and blurred responsibilities consume disproportionate maintenance effort. Feature additions that should take days stretch into weeks; bug fixes trigger unexpected, persistent failures; and developer onboarding becomes painfully slow. These symptoms don't just reflect technical issues; they also have direct business impacts that need addressing.

Throughout previous chapters, we've seen how Clean Architecture naturally minimizes maintenance burdens through clear boundaries and explicit dependencies. Now, we can apply this same architectural lens to evaluate existing systems, identifying where violations occur and how to address them systematically. This doesn't mean forcing an ideal Clean Architecture onto legacy systems all at once but, rather, taking a balanced, incremental approach that respects business constraints while progressively improving the system.

By analyzing legacy code through Clean Architecture principles, we can uncover natural system boundaries waiting to be established, domain concepts ready to be isolated, and interfaces eager to emerge. This evaluation forms the foundation for our transformation strategy, guiding decisions about what to change, when to change it, and how to minimize risk throughout the process. With each incremental improvement, we reduce both the maintenance burden and the instability associated with future changes, creating measurable business value beyond the technical improvements.

Evaluating through a Clean Architecture lens

Transforming an existing system begins with evaluating its current state with respect to Clean Architecture principles. This evaluation isn't about documenting every detail, but rather aims at identifying key architectural violations and gauging their business impact. Since wholesale transformation introduces unacceptable risk, we need a balanced approach that provides enough understanding to inform stakeholder discussions while enabling meaningful progress. This measured assessment creates the foundation for deeper collaborative analysis once initial stakeholder support is secured.

Conducting preliminary architectural analysis

Before engaging stakeholders, we need to conduct a targeted preliminary architectural analysis focused on identifying key technical issues that can be effectively communicated to non-technical audiences. This initial assessment isn't exhaustive but provides enough insight to illustrate architectural problems in business-relevant terms.

A focused preliminary analysis might include:

- **Architectural inventory**: Identify major components and their interactions, creating a baseline understanding without documenting every detail.

- **Dependency mapping**: Sketch high-level dependency flows that reveal the most problematic circular dependencies and framework coupling that violates Clean Architecture's principles.

- **Framework penetration assessment**: Spotlight examples where framework code has significantly permeated business logic, focusing on areas with visible impact on maintenance or flexibility.

- **Domain logic dispersion**: Identify a few clear examples where business rules are fragmented across the codebase, particularly those affecting functionality that changes frequently.

For example, in analyzing a Python e-commerce system, we might discover that Django models contain critical business rules, validation logic is duplicated across multiple views, and payment processing code directly references native database queries. This preliminary analysis provides concrete examples that non-technical stakeholders can understand: *When we need to change how pricing works, we currently have to modify code in seven different places across three different modules.*

This analysis serves as a communication tool, translated into business impact terms like increased time-to-market, elevated bug rates, and diminished ability to respond to changing requirements. By framing architectural issues in business terms before beginning the transformation, we create the foundation for stakeholder support and appropriate resource allocation.

This preliminary architectural assessment serves as an entry point for transformation, not an exhaustive blueprint. Focus on identifying just enough specific violations to engage stakeholders with credible examples that illustrate business impact. Resist the temptation to diagram every relationship at this stage. Your understanding will deepen substantially during the collaborative domain analysis that follows. The goal is to gather sufficient evidence to make the case for transformation while setting the stage for deeper exploration with stakeholders.

Building stakeholder alignment

With the preliminary architectural analysis complete and key issues identified, the next step is communicating these findings to stakeholders and securing initial buy-in for transformation. This initial engagement isn't about getting final approval for specific changes, but rather aims to build shared awareness of architectural issues and establish support for a more collaborative discovery process. The insights gained from our analysis must now be translated into business-impact terms that resonate with different stakeholder groups, creating the foundation for the deeper collaborative analysis that will follow.

The first step is involving the right stakeholders:

- **Engineering teams** who understand the technical details and implementation constraints
- **Product owners** who can articulate business priorities and validate the value of architectural changes
- **Operations personnel** who manage system deployment and reliability concerns
- **End users** who can share pain points related to system stability and feature delivery

The scope of stakeholder involvement should correspond directly to the scale of transformation planned. Smaller refactorings might only require coordination with your immediate team, while system-wide architectural overhauls may need engagement all the way up to the CTO or VP of Engineering.

Once you have stakeholders aligned around a shared transformation vision, the next critical step is establishing baseline measurements that will track progress and demonstrate value. These metrics create accountability and provide clear evidence of improvement throughout the transformation journey:

- **Maintenance metrics**: time spent on bug fixes, feature delivery lead time
- **Quality indicators**: defect rates, test coverage, static analysis scores
- **Team effectiveness**: developer onboarding time, deployment frequency
- **Business outcomes**: customer satisfaction, feature adoption rates

These metrics serve multiple purposes throughout the transformation. Initially, they justify the effort and help secure leadership support. As work progresses, they validate effectiveness and highlight areas needing adjustment. They also help define what *done* means for the transformation, recognizing that the goal is sustainable improvement rather than architectural perfection. Most importantly, metrics translate technical improvements into business value language, creating a feedback loop that keeps the transformation aligned with both technical goals and business priorities.

Deeper domain analysis

Business domains naturally evolve over time, making architectural transformation an ideal opportunity to realign systems with current business needs. After securing initial stakeholder support, the next step is deepening our understanding through collaborative domain discovery techniques. This phase connects our technical insights with business domain knowledge, identifying meaningful boundaries while solidifying stakeholder buy-in through active involvement. Where our preliminary analysis focused on technical issues, collaborative discovery bridges these findings with evolving business requirements, ensuring the transformed system not only has better architecture but also better serves current needs.

Several collaborative approaches can help bridge technical understanding with domain expertise:

- **Event storming workshops** to map business processes and domain events (`https://www.eventstorming.com/`)

- **Domain storytelling sessions** where stakeholders narrate key workflows (`https://domainstorytelling.org/`)

- **Context mapping exercises** to identify system boundaries and integration points (`https://contextmapper.org/`)

Among these approaches, **event storming** stands out as particularly valuable for Clean Architecture transformations. It brings together stakeholders in facilitated workshops to validate domain understanding and identify architectural boundaries. Participants use color-coded sticky notes on a shared modeling space, creating a visual timeline of business processes. The color coding intentionally maps to Clean Architecture layers: orange domain events represent core entities at the center of the architecture, blue commands align with use cases in the Application layer, and purple business rules reflect domain rules that remain independent of external concerns. Typical domain events include *Order Placed*, while commands might include actions like *Process Payments*. This visual approach makes architectural boundaries tangible to all stakeholders, helping identify natural separation points when transforming legacy systems. While specific color schemes may vary between teams, maintaining a consistent visual language is what matters most.

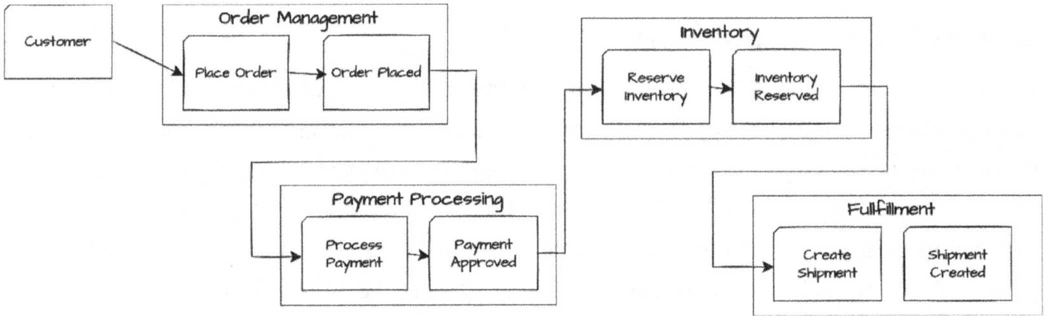

Figure 11.1: Event storming visualization for an e-commerce system, showing domain events, commands, actors, and potential bounded contexts

This collaborative approach builds directly on the domain modeling principles from *Chapter 4*, applying them to discover boundaries in existing systems. The same concepts of Entities, Value Objects, and Aggregates now help identify what the legacy system *should* have separated but didn't. For example, an event storming session might reveal that the *Order Processing* domain contains distinct events like *Order Placed, Payment Approved, Inventory Reserved,* and *Shipment Created.* Be sure to separate business concerns that could be cleanly divided into discrete use cases rather than handled by a monolithic Order Controller.

The resulting visual artifacts serve as powerful communication tools, helping stakeholders see how architectural boundaries translate to business benefits like faster delivery or reduced errors. This shared language often reveals insights that technical analysis alone would miss, such as Order and Payment processing having different change patterns that indicate natural separation points. With these boundaries identified through stakeholder collaboration, we can move from discovery to action, translating insights into a prioritized roadmap for architectural improvement.

Creating a staged implementation roadmap

With architectural boundaries identified and prioritized based on business value, the focus now shifts to tactical execution planning. Transforming legacy systems isn't just about knowing what to change, it's about organizing the work into manageable, low-risk increments that maintain system stability while progressively improving architecture.

Effective transformation planning requires breaking down the work into distinct stages with clear deliverables. Rather than overwhelming teams with a massive refactoring effort, a staged implementation creates natural checkpoints to validate progress, gather feedback, and adjust course as needed.

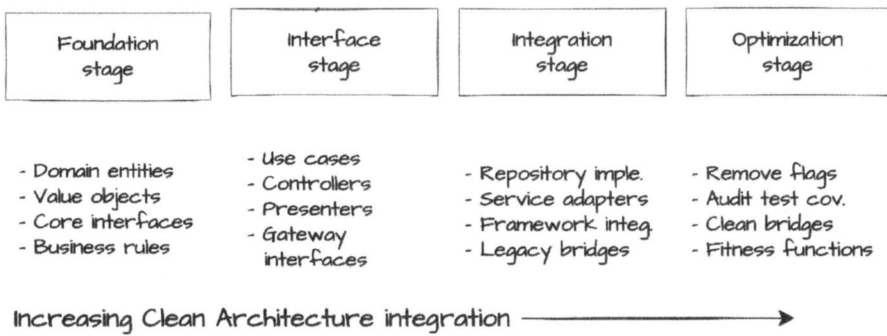

Figure 11.2: Clean Architecture transformation stages showing progression from foundation to optimization

The **foundation stage** establishes core domain concepts and abstractions that serve as building blocks for later work. This often begins with creating clean entity models alongside existing implementations and defining interfaces for repositories and services. By starting with these core elements, teams establish a clear target architecture while minimizing initial changes to the running system.

As the foundation takes shape, the **interface stage** focuses on implementing adapters that bridge the clean core and external concerns. This includes building repository implementations that work with existing databases, creating service adapters for third-party integrations, and developing controllers that translate between frameworks and the domain. These adapters create a protective layer around the emerging Clean Architecture.

The **integration stage** gradually migrates existing functionality to the new architecture. Teams replace direct database access with repository implementations, substitute hard-coded business rules with domain services, and integrate new components with legacy systems through appropriate adapters. This stage often progresses feature by feature or domain by domain, allowing for controlled, incremental changes.

Finally, the **optimization stage** refines and enhances the architecture based on real-world experience. Teams address performance considerations in repository implementations, expand test coverage, and improve error handling and resilience patterns. This stage acknowledges that the target architecture isn't achieved in one pass, but rather through continuous refinement.

Throughout this staged approach, the baseline metrics established earlier serve a crucial role in validating progress and communicating the transformation's impact. By tracking metrics such as maintenance time, defect rates, and feature delivery speed before, during, and after each transformation stage, teams can demonstrate tangible improvements and adjust their approach based on actual results rather than assumptions. These metrics also help teams identify when they've reached acceptable levels of architectural improvement, allowing organizations to balance architectural refinement with ongoing business needs.

Approaches for doing the transformation work

The execution complexity of architectural transformation requires careful logistics planning beyond the technical aspects. Teams must decide how to organize the work alongside ongoing feature development and maintenance. Several approaches are worth considering:

- **Dedicated transformation iterations** allocate specific sprint cycles exclusively to architectural work. This approach provides focused time for complex refactoring but may delay feature delivery. It works well for components that need significant changes but which can be completed within one or two iterations.

- **Parallel transformation tracks** create dedicated teams focused on architectural improvements while other teams continue feature development. This approach maintains delivery velocity but requires careful coordination to prevent conflicts. It's particularly effective for larger systems where transformation will span multiple quarters.

- **Opportunity-based transformation** integrates architectural improvements with feature work in related areas. As new features touch a component, teams refactor it toward Clean Architecture. This approach minimizes isolated refactoring risk but makes progress dependent on feature priorities and may result in uneven transformation.

Most successful transformations combine these approaches based on business priorities and team structure. Critical components might warrant dedicated efforts, while less frequently changed areas can evolve through opportunity-based transformation. The key is to explicitly plan how each component will be transformed rather than assume a one-size-fits-all approach.

Navigating the in-flight transformation

During transformation, the system will temporarily contain a mixture of old and new architectural approaches. Careful planning of these transitional states is crucial to maintain system stability. For each component being transformed, the plan should address:

- **Parallel operation strategy**: How old and new implementations will coexist
- **Verification approach**: Methods to confirm functional equivalence
- **Cutover criteria**: Clear conditions for switching to the new implementation
- **Rollback procedures**: Safety mechanisms if issues emerge

Comprehensive testing strategies are essential during these transitions. Regression test suites validate that new implementations maintain existing functionality, while interface compatibility tests ensure that transformed components correctly integrate with the broader system. **Feature flags** provide an effective cutover mechanism, allowing teams to selectively enable new implementations for specific users or scenarios while maintaining the ability to instantly revert if issues arise.

It's important to recognize that while this section outlines a general approach to transformation planning, every legacy system presents unique challenges based on its size, complexity, technology stack, and business constraints. The scale of work will differ dramatically between systems, and teams should adapt these guidelines to their specific circumstances. Additional research into techniques specific to your technology stack or domain will help you tailor this approach to your needs. The key is to maintain a pragmatic mindset, taking Clean Architecture principles as a guide rather than a rigid prescription.

With a comprehensive transformation plan that addresses both the technical changes and their implementation logistics, teams are well-positioned to begin the actual transformation work. The subsequent sections will explore concrete techniques for implementing these plans, starting with establishing core domain boundaries and progressively refactoring toward a Clean Architecture.

Progressive Clean Architecture implementation

With our evaluation complete and transformation strategy established, we now turn to practical implementation. This section demonstrates how to progressively transform a legacy system through carefully staged improvements that deliver the greatest architectural value. Rather than attempting to cover the transformation process exhaustively, which would require a book of its own, we'll highlight strategic refactoring patterns that establish Clean Architecture boundaries incrementally while maintaining system stability.

The following examples, drawn from an order processing system rather than our previous task management application, illustrate how to apply Clean Architecture principles to legacy code in a practical manner. Each implementation stage builds on the previous one, gradually moving from tangled dependencies toward clean separation of concerns, from establishing domain boundaries to creating interfaces that bridge old and new architectures.

Initial system analysis

In this hypothetical scenario, you find yourself responsible for an order processing subsystem that has evolved over several years. What started as a simple Flask application for managing customer orders has grown to include payment processing and basic order fulfillment. While functionally complete, the codebase exhibits significant technical debt, with tangled dependencies, blurred responsibilities, and architectural inconsistencies that make even simple changes risky and time-consuming.

The team faces recurring issues that highlight the architectural problems: a simple change to the order calculation logic requires modifications in three different files; adding a new payment method takes three weeks instead of three days; and every deployment comes with the fear of unexpected side effects. Most telling, new developers need months to become productive, frequently breaking functionality in seemingly unrelated areas when making changes.

Building on the preliminary architectural analysis and domain discovery phases described in the first section of this chapter, we've identified key architectural issues to address in our transformation. Let's begin by examining the current state of the system through the lens of Clean Architecture, identifying specific violations and architectural boundaries that need reinforcement.

Let's examine one such file that handles order creation—a central piece of the system's functionality and a prime candidate for our transformation efforts:

```python
# order_system/app.py
from flask import Flask, request, jsonify
import sqlite3
import requests

app = Flask(__name__)

def get_db_connection():
    conn = sqlite3.connect('orders.db')
    conn.row_factory = sqlite3.Row
    return conn

@app.route('/orders', methods=['POST'])
def create_order():
    data = request.get_json()
```

```python
    # Input validation mixed with business logic
    if not data or not 'customer_id' in data or not 'items' in data:
        return jsonify({'error': 'Missing required fields'}), 400


    # Direct database access in route handler
    conn = get_db_connection()
```

The beginning of this file already reveals several architectural issues. The route handler imports SQLite and requests directly, establishing hard dependencies on these specific implementations. The get_db_connection function creates a direct connection to a specific database, with no abstraction layer. These structural choices violate Clean Architecture's Dependency Rule by allowing outer-layer concerns (web framework, database) to penetrate into business logic.

Continuing down the create_order function, let's examine how the route handler processes orders:

```python
  # def create_order(): <continued>
    # Business logic mixed with data access
    total_price = 0
    for item in data['items']:
        # Inventory check via direct database query
        product = conn.execute('SELECT * FROM products WHERE id = ?',
                               (item['product_id'],)).fetchone()
        if not product or product['stock'] < item['quantity']:
            conn.close()
            return jsonify({
                'error': f'Product {item["product_id"]} out of stock'
            }), 400


        # Price calculation mixed with HTTP response preparation
        price = product['price'] * item['quantity']
        total_price += price


    # External payment service call directly in route handler
    payment_result = requests.post(
        'https://payment-gateway.example.com/process',
        json={
            'customer_id': data['customer_id'],
            'amount': total_price,
```

```python
        'currency': 'USD'
    }
)
```

This middle section demonstrates several Clean Architecture violations. Core business logic like inventory checking and price calculation is mixed directly with database access. The payment processing logic makes direct HTTP calls to an external service, creating a hard dependency that would be difficult to test or change. These implementation details should be hidden behind interfaces, in accordance with Clean Architecture principles, not exposed directly in business logic.

Finally, closing out the `create_order` function, we complete the order processing:

```python
# def create_order(): <continued>
    if payment_result.status_code != 200:
        conn.close()
        return jsonify({'error': 'Payment failed'}), 400

    # Order creation directly in route handler
    order_id = conn.execute(
        'INSERT INTO orders (customer_id, total_price, status) '
        'VALUES (?, ?, ?)',
        (
            data['customer_id'],
            total_price, 'PAID'
        )
    ).lastrowid

    # Order items creation and inventory update
    for item in data['items']:
        conn.execute(
            'INSERT INTO order_items (order_id, product_id, '
            'quantity, price) VALUES (?, ?, ?, ?)',
            (order_id, item['product_id'], item['quantity'], price)
        )
        conn.execute( # Update inventory
            'UPDATE products SET stock = stock - ? WHERE id = ?',
            (item['quantity'], item['product_id'])
        )
```

```
    conn.commit()
    conn.close()
    return jsonify({'order_id': order_id, 'status': 'success'}), 201
```

The code analysis reveals fundamental architectural problems throughout this handler. Direct SQL statements are intertwined with business logic, HTTP responses, and external service calls, which are all crammed into a single function with no separation of concerns. This structure violates the Single Responsibility Principle we discussed in *Chapter 2* and makes changes extremely risky, as modifications in one area frequently affect seemingly unrelated functionality.

The system lacks the rich domain model we established in *Chapter 4* as orders and products exist only as database records and dictionaries rather than as proper entities with encapsulated behavior and business rules.

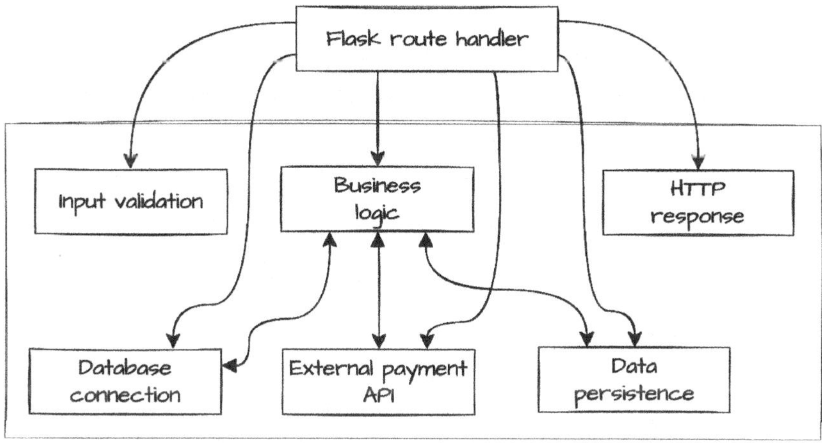

Figure 11.3: Entangled responsibilities in the current order processing handler

Figure 11.3 illustrates how a single Flask route handler encompasses multiple responsibilities that should be separated according to Clean Architecture principles. The business logic is directly connected to infrastructure concerns such as database connections and external APIs, violating the Dependency Rule we explored in *Chapter 1*.

Based on our analysis, we've identified key architectural issues to address in our transformation:

- **Boundary violations**: The route handler crosses multiple architectural boundaries, mixing web, business logic, and infrastructure concerns

- **Missing domain model**: We need to establish proper domain entities like Order and Product as the core of our system

- **Dependency inversion needed**: Direct infrastructure dependencies should be replaced with abstractions following the principles from *Chapter 2*
- **Interface separation required**: Clear interfaces between architectural layers will help maintain proper boundaries

There are key architectural issues in our order creation process; we can see a system that evolved without architectural guidance. Business logic, data access, and external services are tightly coupled, with no clear boundaries between concerns. The system works, but its structure makes it increasingly difficult to maintain, extend, or test.

With this understanding of the current system, we're now ready to begin our transformation journey. We'll start by establishing a clean domain model in the next section, creating proper boundaries between layers as we progressively refactor toward a Clean Architecture.

Stage 1: establishing domain boundaries

Having analyzed our legacy system, we begin our transformation by establishing a clean domain model that will serve as our architectural foundation. Starting with the Domain layer provides a stable core around which we can progressively rebuild the outer layers of our system.

In our order processing system, we need to extract the implicit domain concepts buried in our database queries and controller logic. The most critical entities in our system appear to be:

- **Order**: The central business entity
- **Customer**: The buyer placing the order
- **Product**: Items being purchased
- **OrderItem**: The association between orders and products

Let's begin by implementing the Order entity and its related value objects:

```python
# order_system/domain/entities/order.py


class OrderStatus(Enum):
    CREATED = "CREATED"
    PAID = "PAID"
    FULFILLING = "FULFILLING"
    SHIPPED = "SHIPPED"
    DELIVERED = "DELIVERED"
    CANCELED = "CANCELED"
```

```python
@dataclass
class OrderItem:
    product_id: UUID
    quantity: int
    price: float

    @property
    def total_price(self) -> float:
        return self.price * self.quantity
```

Here we've defined an `OrderStatus` enum to replace the string constants previously used throughout the code. We've also created an `OrderItem` value object to represent the relationship between orders and products. This approach aligns with the value object pattern we explored in *Chapter 4*, creating immutable objects that represent important domain concepts.

Now let's implement the `Order` entity itself:

```python
@dataclass
class Order:
    customer_id: UUID
    items: List[OrderItem] = field(default_factory=list)
    id: UUID = field(default_factory=uuid4)
    status: OrderStatus = OrderStatus.CREATED
    created_at: datetime = field(default_factory=lambda: datetime.now())
    updated_at: Optional[datetime] = None

    @property
    def total_price(self) -> float:
        return sum(item.total_price for item in self.items)

    def add_item(self, item: OrderItem) -> None:
        self.items.append(item)
        self.updated_at = datetime.now()

    def mark_as_paid(self) -> None:
        if self.status != OrderStatus.CREATED:
            raise ValueError(
                f"Cannot mark as paid: order is {self.status.value}"
            )
```

```python
        self.status = OrderStatus.PAID
        self.updated_at = datetime.now()
```

Our `Order` entity now properly encapsulates core business concepts that were previously scattered throughout the codebase. We've implemented methods that enforce business rules, such as validating state transitions when marking an order as paid. These validations were previously buried in controller logic but now reside in their proper home within the entity itself.

We need to create the remaining domain entities to complete our core model:

```python
# order_system/domain/entities/product.py


@dataclass
class Product:
    name: str
    price: float
    stock: int
    id: UUID = field(default_factory=uuid4)


    def decrease_stock(self, quantity: int) -> None:
        if quantity <= 0:
            raise ValueError("Quantity must be positive")
        if quantity > self.stock:
            raise ValueError(
                f"Insufficient stock: requested {quantity}, "
                f"available {self.stock}")
        self.stock -= quantity
```

The `Product` entity now encapsulates inventory management logic that was previously spread across controller methods. It enforces business rules such as preventing negative stock or excessive withdrawals. This is an example of the *tell, don't ask* principle that helps maintain domain integrity.

With our core domain entities defined, we need to create abstractions for the supporting services and repositories. Following the Dependency Inversion Principle we'll define interfaces that the domain needs without coupling to specific implementations:

```python
# order_system/domain/repositories/order_repository.py
from order_system.domain.entities.order import Order


class OrderRepository(ABC):
```

```python
    @abstractmethod
    def save(self, order: Order) -> None:
        """Save an order to the repository"""
        pass

    @abstractmethod
    def get_by_id(self, order_id: UUID) -> Optional[Order]:
        """Retrieve an order by its ID"""
        pass

    @abstractmethod
    def get_by_customer(self, customer_id: UUID) -> List[Order]:
        """Retrieve all orders for a customer"""
        pass
```

This abstract `OrderRepository` defines the operations our Domain layer needs without specifying how they're implemented. We'll create similar interfaces for `ProductRepository` and other necessary repositories. These abstractions are a crucial element of Clean Architecture, as they allow our Domain layer to remain independent of specific persistence mechanisms.

If you recall the task management system from previous chapters, we established similar repository interfaces such as `TaskRepository` in *Chapter 5*. Both follow the same pattern: defining abstract methods that domain components require without specifying implementation details. This consistency demonstrates how Clean Architecture's principles apply across different domains and applications, creating a reliable pattern for maintaining proper boundaries.

Next, let's define service interfaces for external operations like payments and notifications:

```python
# order_system/domain/services/payment_service.py
from order_system.domain.entities.order import Order

@dataclass
class PaymentResult:
    success: bool
    error_message: Optional[str] = None

class PaymentService(ABC):
    @abstractmethod
```

```python
def process_payment(self, order: Order) -> PaymentResult:
    """Process payment for an order"""
    pass
```

With these core domain components defined, we've created a clean foundation for our system. The business rules and concepts that were previously scattered across controllers and utility functions now have a proper home in a well-structured domain model. This transformation provides several immediate benefits:

- **Business rules centralization**: Rules like *cannot mark a non-CREATED order as PAID* are now explicitly defined in the domain model

- **Improved testability**: Domain entities and services can be tested in isolation without requiring database connections or web frameworks

- **Clearer boundaries**: The separation between core business concepts and infrastructure concerns is now explicit

- **Richer domain model**: We've moved from anemic database records to a rich domain model with behavior

Let's take a moment to review this new Domain layer:

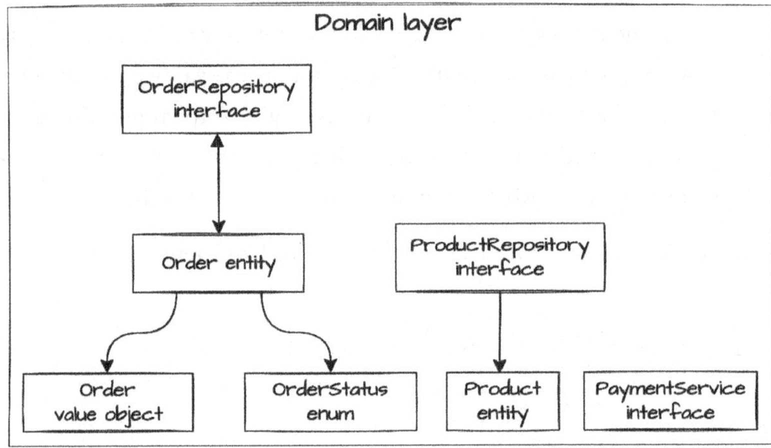

Figure 11.4: The newly established domain model with clean boundaries

This diagram illustrates our first major transformation step: establishing a proper Domain layer with clean boundaries. We've created entities, value objects, and service interfaces that encapsulate our core business concepts and rules. Comparing this with *Figure 11.2*, we can see significant progress toward untangling the responsibilities that were previously mixed in our legacy controller implementation.

Incremental integration strategies

In real-world transformations, a common pitfall is attempting to implement the entire Clean Architecture in isolation before integration. This *big bang release* approach introduces significant risk since by the time integration occurs, the production system may have evolved substantially, creating complex merge conflicts and unexpected behavior changes.

To mitigate this risk, several incremental integration strategies can be employed:

- **Adapter pattern**: Create adapters that bridge legacy components and new domain entities, allowing them to coexist within the running system. This enables gradual adoption without disrupting existing functionality.

- **Parallel implementation**: Implement new functionality using Clean Architecture alongside legacy code, with feature flags controlling which implementation handles requests. This provides an easy rollback mechanism if issues arise.

- **Strangler Fig pattern**: Incrementally replace pieces of the legacy application while maintaining the same external interfaces, gradually supplanting the old implementation until it can be safely removed (`https://martinfowler.com/bliki/StranglerFigApplication.html`).

- **Shadow mode**: Run new implementations alongside the production code by use of a proxy that duplicates all requests. This gives the new implementation the opportunity to process its copy of the request and we compare the outputs with the legacy system. This validates behavior without affecting users.

Throughout this incremental transformation, comprehensive **regression testing** is absolutely essential. Before making any architectural changes, establish a thorough test suite that captures existing system behavior. These tests serve multiple purposes:

- They verify that refactoring hasn't broken existing functionality

- They document current system behavior for reference

- They provide confidence to stakeholders that the transformation is proceeding safely

As we discussed in *Chapter 8*, testing provides crucial safety nets during architectural transformation. For our order processing system, we would establish **end-to-end tests** that verify complete order flows before beginning our transformation, then supplement these with more granular tests as we establish clean architectural boundaries.

By adopting these incremental strategies and prioritizing regression testing, we can transform our system while maintaining stability and continuing to deliver business value. In the next section, we'll begin implementing the production integration approach described above, building on our domain model by implementing the Interface Adapters layer.

Stage 2: Interface layer implementation

With our domain entities and interfaces established, we now face a critical transition challenge: integrating this clean foundation with our existing codebase. Unlike greenfield development, transformation requires us to evolve our system incrementally while maintaining continuous operation. The **Interface layer** provides our first opportunity to bridge old and new architectures.

Identifying transformation boundaries

The first step in our transformation is identifying viable seams where we can introduce clean interfaces without overly disrupting the existing system. Looking back at our legacy controller, the order creation process stands out as a natural boundary:

```python
# order_system/app.py
@app.route('/orders', methods=['POST'])
def create_order():
    data = request.get_json()

    # Input validation mixed with business logic
    if not data or not 'customer_id' in data or not 'items' in data:
        return jsonify({'error': 'Missing required fields'}), 400

    # Direct database access in route handler
    conn = get_db_connection()

    # Business logic implementation
    # ... existing implementation ...

    return jsonify({'order_id': order_id, 'status': 'success'}), 201
```

This controller method represents a self-contained workflow with clear inputs and outputs, making it an ideal candidate for our initial transformation. Before modifying this code, we need to establish comprehensive test coverage that captures its current behavior. These tests will serve as our safety net during refactoring, ensuring we maintain functionality while improving architecture:

```python
# test_order_creation.py
def test_create_order_success():
    # Setup test data and expected results
    response = client.post('/orders', json={
        'customer_id': '12345',
        'items': [{'product_id': '789', 'quantity': 2}]
    })

    # Verify status code and response structure
    assert response.status_code == 201
    assert 'order_id' in response.json

    # Verify database state - order was created with correct values
    conn = get_db_connection()
    order = conn.execute('SELECT * FROM orders WHERE id = ?',
                         (response.json['order_id'],)).fetchone()
    assert order['status'] == 'PAID'

# Additional order creation test scenarios ...
```

With tests in place, we can begin implementing the Interface layer components that will bridge our clean domain model and the existing infrastructure.

Implementing repository adapters

Our first step is creating **repository adapters** that satisfy our clean domain interfaces while interacting with the existing database schema. This crucial component bridges our domain entities and legacy infrastructure.

```python
# order_system/infrastructure/repositories/sqlite_order_repository.py
class SQLiteOrderRepository(OrderRepository):

    # ... truncated implementation
```

```python
    def save(self, order: Order) -> None:
        conn = sqlite3.connect(self.db_path)

        try:
            cursor = conn.cursor()
            # Check if order exists and perform insert or update
            if self._order_exists(conn, order.id):
                # ... SQL update operation ...
            else:
                # ... SQL insert operation ...


                # ... SQL operations for order items ...
            conn.commit()
        except Exception as e:
            conn.rollback()
            raise RepositoryError(f"Failed to save order: {str(e)}")
        finally:
            conn.close()
```

This repository adapter plays a vital role in our transformation strategy. You may recall from *Chapter 6* that we introduced similar repository implementations for our task management system. Like those examples, this adapter implements our clean `OrderRepository` interface (from *Stage 1*) while handling the details of our existing database schema. The adapter translates between domain entities and database records, managing the impedance mismatch between our rich domain model and the flat relational structure.

We would also implement a similar `SQLiteProductRepository` that follows the same pattern, implementing a clean domain interface while interacting with the existing database schema. These repository implementations handle all database access details, connection management, and error handling, providing a clean interface to the rest of our architecture.

Additionally, we would implement adapters for external services like payment processing. These service adapters would follow the same pattern, implementing our clean domain interfaces while encapsulating the details of external service interactions. For brevity, we won't show these implementations here, but the complete code is available in the book's GitHub repository.

With these infrastructure adapters in place, we now have a bridge between our clean domain model and the legacy infrastructure. This enables us to implement use cases that work with proper domain entities while seamlessly interacting with the existing database and external services via interfaces versus interacting directly with concrete implementations.

Building clean use cases

Now that we have repository and service adapters that connect to our existing infrastructure, we can implement the use cases that orchestrate our business logic. In *Chapter 5*, we established that use cases serve as application-specific business rules that coordinate domain entities to fulfill specific user requirements. Following this pattern, let's look at the order creation use case that will replace our tangled legacy implementation:

```python
# order_system/application/use_cases/create_order.py
@dataclass
class CreateOrderRequest:
    customer_id: UUID
    items: List[Dict[str, Any]]


@dataclass
class CreateOrderUseCase:
    order_repository: OrderRepository
    product_repository: ProductRepository
    payment_service: PaymentService

    def execute(self, request: CreateOrderRequest) -> Order:
        # Create order entity with basic information
        order = Order(customer_id=request.customer_id)

        # Add items to order, checking inventory
        for item_data in request.items:
            product_id = UUID(item_data['product_id'])
            quantity = item_data['quantity']

            # ... inventory validation logic ...

            # Update inventory
            product.decrease_stock(quantity)
            self.product_repository.update(product)
```

The execute method of our use case begins by creating an `Order` entity and adds items to it, checking inventory availability in the process. Note how it works with proper domain entities rather than raw database records.

Let's now examine the remainder of the execute method:

```python
# order_system/application/use_cases/create_order.py
    # def execute <continued>


        # Process payment
        payment_result = self.payment_service.process_payment(order)
        if not payment_result.success:
            raise ValueError(
                f"Payment failed: {payment_result.error_message}"
            )


        # Mark order as paid and save
        order.mark_as_paid()
        self.order_repository.save(order)


        return order
```

The second half of our execute method continues the order creation process by handling payment processing, updating the order status, and saving the completed order.

This use case demonstrates Clean Architecture's separation of concerns in action. It orchestrates the order creation process by:

1. Creating an `Order` entity with basic information
2. Adding items to the order, checking inventory
3. Processing payment
4. Updating the order status and saving it

Each step interacts with the domain model through well-defined interfaces, without knowledge of the underlying infrastructure. The use case depends on abstract `OrderRepository`, `ProductRepository`, and `PaymentService` interfaces, not on concrete implementations.

Notice how the business rules are now explicit and centralized in this use case. Inventory checking, payment processing, and order status management all flow through a clean, organized process rather than being scattered across controller methods and utility functions. This clarity makes the code more maintainable and adaptable to changing requirements.

Implementing clean controllers

With our repositories and use cases in place, we now implement **controllers** that bridge our web framework and application core. As we established in *Chapter 6*, controllers serve as translation layers at the boundary of our architecture, converting external request formats into inputs our use cases can process. These controllers maintain the separation between our application core and delivery mechanisms, ensuring that web-specific concerns don't penetrate our Clean Architecture:

```python
# order_system/interfaces/controllers/order_controller.py
@dataclass
class OrderController:
    create_use_case: CreateOrderUseCase

    def handle_create_order(
        self, request_data: Dict[str, Any]
    ) -> Dict[str, Any]:
        try:
            # Transform web request to domain request format
            customer_id = UUID(request_data['customer_id'])
            items = request_data['items']

            request = CreateOrderRequest(
                customer_id=customer_id,
                items=items
            )

            # Execute use case
            order = self.create_use_case.execute(request)

            # Transform domain response to web response format
            return {
```

```python
            'order_id': str(order.id),
            'status': order.status.value
        }
    except ValueError as e:
        # ... exception logic
```

This controller shows Clean Architecture boundaries at work, functioning as a translation layer between external requests and our domain operations. The heart of this controller is the single line order = `self.create_use_case.execute(request)`, which represents the critical boundary between our Interface layer and application core. Notice how the controller doesn't reference Flask, HTTP status codes, or JSON formatting. These web-specific concerns are handled at the framework boundary, maintaining a clean separation between our application logic and delivery mechanism. This framework independence allows our controller to remain focused on its core responsibility, transforming external requests into domain operations and translating results back to a format suitable for the caller.

Stage 3: integration strategy: bridging legacy and clean implementations

Now comes the crucial step: integrating our clean implementation with the existing system. Rather than immediately replacing the entire legacy route handler, we'll modify it to delegate to our clean controller using the adapter pattern:

```python
# Modified route in order_system/app.py
@app.route('/orders', methods=['POST'])
def create_order():
    data = request.get_json()

    # Basic input validation remains in the route handler
    if not data or not 'customer_id' in data or not 'items' in data:
        return jsonify({'error': 'Missing required fields'}), 400

    try:
        # Feature flag to control which implementation handles the request
        if app.config.get('USE_CLEAN_ARCHITECTURE', False):
            # Use the clean implementation
            result = order_controller.handle_create_order(data)
            return jsonify(result), 201
```

```python
    else:
        # ... original implementation remains here ...
except ValidationError as e:
    return jsonify({'error': str(e)}), 400
except SystemError:
    return jsonify({'error': 'Internal server error'}), 500
```

The key portion of this modification is the feature flag conditional. When `USE_CLEAN_ARCHITECTURE` is enabled, we delegate order processing to our new controller, which then invokes the clean use case. This creates a controlled pathway into our Clean Architecture implementation without disturbing the existing code path. The feature flag gives us a simple mechanism to toggle between implementations, either globally or for specific requests.

This modified route handler demonstrates several key transformation patterns:

- **Feature flag control**: We use a configuration setting to determine which implementation processes the request, allowing us to gradually transition traffic.

- **Consistent interfaces**: Both implementations produce identical response formats, ensuring a seamless transition from the user's perspective.

- **Incremental migration**: The legacy code remains fully functional, serving as a fallback if issues arise with the clean implementation.

- **Exception translation**: We map domain-specific exceptions to appropriate HTTP responses at the framework boundary.

When integrating with specific frameworks like Flask, we must attend to framework-specific details at the system boundaries. In the case of Flask, we need to configure our dependency injection container, register our Clean Architecture components, and establish the feature flagging mechanism. We create a central configuration point that instantiates all necessary components (repositories, services, use cases, and controllers) and wires them together according to Clean Architecture's dependency rules. This configuration happens at application startup, keeping all framework-specific initialization code at the system's edge where it belongs. We saw this in action in our task management application in *Chapter 7*.

Incremental transformation approach

During this transformation process, comprehensive testing is absolutely essential. We leverage our regression test suite to ensure that refactoring hasn't broken existing functionality. These tests verify both the legacy implementation and our new Clean Architecture components, providing confidence that the transformation maintains functional parity.

Each step of our transformation is carefully validated before proceeding to the next. We don't move forward until we've verified that our changes maintain system behavior and stability. This incremental approach minimizes risk and allows us to deliver value continuously throughout the transformation process.

At a high level, our approach aligns with the Strangler Fig pattern (`https://martinfowler.com/bliki/StranglerFigApplication.html`), where we gradually replace pieces of the legacy application while maintaining the same external interfaces. This approach minimizes risk by allowing incremental validation and rollback if needed.

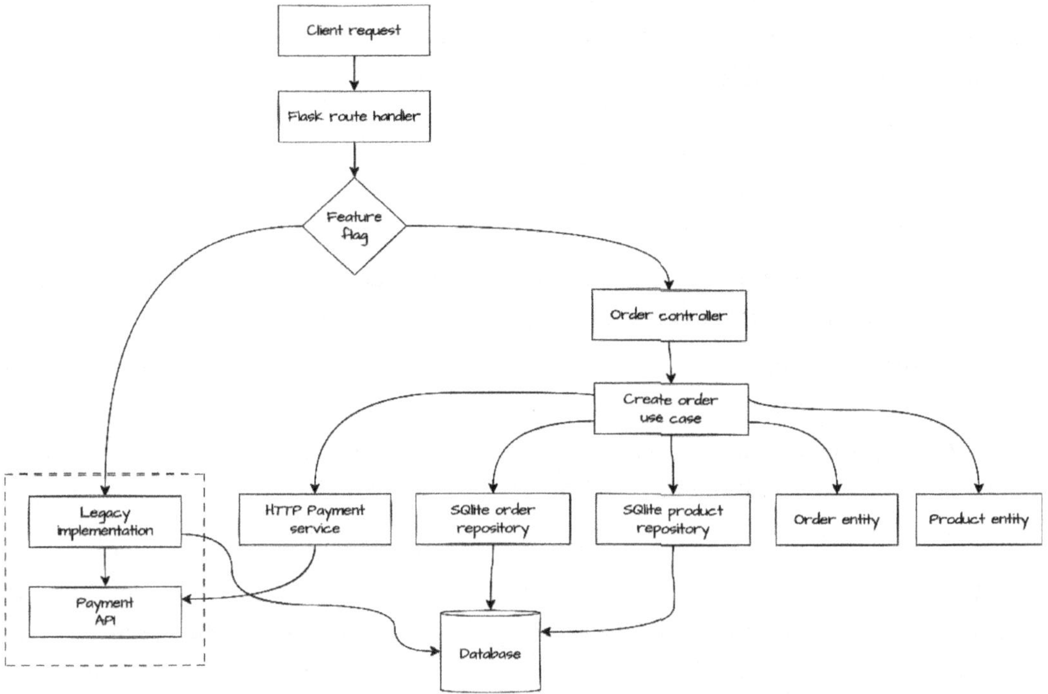

Figure 11.5: Current system architecture showing parallel implementations

Figure 11.5 illustrates our current architectural state, with both legacy and clean implementations coexisting in the system. The legacy components represent the tangled, unstructured code that directly mixes business logic with infrastructure concerns. In contrast, the Clean Architecture implementation shows proper separation of concerns with distinct layers and well-defined interfaces.

Through this incremental implementation approach, we've made significant progress in our transformation journey:

1. We've established a clean domain model with proper entities and value objects
2. We've implemented repository adapters that bridge our domain model and the existing database
3. We've created use cases that orchestrate the business logic using our domain model
4. We've built controllers that translate between web requests and our domain language
5. We've integrated our clean implementation alongside the legacy code using the adapter pattern

Through this incremental implementation approach, we've demonstrated how to transform a legacy system using Clean Architecture principles while maintaining system stability and functionality throughout the process.

Stage 4: optimization stage

While our example has focused primarily on the foundation, interface, and integration stages, a complete transformation would eventually include an optimization stage. This final phase typically involves performance tuning, expanded test coverage, and improved error-handling patterns based on real-world usage.

Rather than providing detailed examples of this stage, we'll note that optimization should be approached with the same incremental mindset. Teams should prioritize optimizations that deliver the greatest business value, gradually removing feature flags as clean implementations prove stable, and ultimately decommissioning legacy code paths entirely.

The optimization stage acknowledges that architectural transformation is not a one-time effort but rather a continuous refinement process that balances technical excellence with business priorities. Teams should define clear metrics for when *good enough* has been achieved, avoiding the trap of endless perfectionism.

Summary

In this chapter, we've explored how to apply Clean Architecture principles to legacy systems through systematic transformation. We began by examining how to evaluate existing systems through Clean Architecture's lens, identifying architectural violations, and creating a staged approach to transformation.

We established a framework for building stakeholder alignment by translating technical debt into business impact terms and gathering deeper domain understanding through collaborative techniques like event storming. This collaborative approach directly informed our staged implementation plan, grounding our architectural decisions in business priorities.

Through our order processing example, we demonstrated a progressive implementation approach that maintains system stability while establishing clean architectural boundaries. We started with the Domain layer, creating proper entities and value objects that encapsulate business rules previously scattered throughout the codebase. We then implemented repository interfaces that protect our domain from infrastructure details, followed by use cases that orchestrate business operations.

The Interface Adapters layer provided a bridge between our clean implementation and legacy code, enabling incremental adoption through feature flags and adapter patterns. This staged approach allowed us to validate our transformation while minimizing risk, demonstrating how Clean Architecture can be applied pragmatically to real-world systems.

By following these transformation patterns, you can systematically improve architectural quality in existing systems, reducing maintenance costs and increasing adaptability while continuing to deliver business value. This approach embodies Clean Architecture's core principles while recognizing the practical constraints of evolving production systems.

Further reading

- *Working Effectively with Legacy Code* (`https://www.oreilly.com/library/view/working-effectively-with/0131177052/`) by Michael Feathers. Provides techniques for working with existing codebases, including strategies for safely introducing tests and making incremental improvements.
- *Event Storming* (`https://www.eventstorming.com`). A great resource for learning more about and planning event storming sessions.

12

Your Clean Architecture Journey: Next Steps

As we reach the conclusion of our exploration, it's time to look beyond our task management implementation to the broader application of Clean Architecture principles. Throughout this journey, we've seen how Clean Architecture creates systems that are adaptable, maintainable, and resilient to change. Now we'll examine how these same principles can be applied across different architectural contexts and how you can lead this application in your own teams and organizations.

Clean Architecture isn't a rigid formula but a flexible set of principles that can be adapted to various system types and organizational contexts. The true power of these principles emerges not when followed dogmatically, but when applied thoughtfully to address the specific challenges your systems face.

In this final chapter, we'll examine Clean Architecture from three perspectives: as a cohesive whole transcending our specific implementation, as an adaptable approach for different architectural styles, and as a foundation for technical leadership. These perspectives will help you apply Clean Architecture principles effectively in your unique context.

In this chapter, we're going to cover the following main topics:

- Clean Architecture in retrospect: a holistic view
- Adapting Clean Architecture across system types
- Architectural leadership and community engagement

Clean Architecture in retrospect: a holistic view

Throughout our journey with the task management system, we've constructed a comprehensive implementation of Clean Architecture piece by piece. Each chapter has built upon the previous ones, adding new layers and capabilities while maintaining the core architectural principles. As we review Clean Architecture from a high-level, holistic perspective, let's review what makes this architectural approach so powerful and adaptable.

The journey through architectural layers

Our journey began with SOLID principles and type-enhanced Python, establishing a foundation for maintainable, adaptable code. We then moved inward to outward through the architectural layers: from domain entities encapsulating core business concepts, to use cases orchestrating business operations, to interface adapters translating between our core and external concerns, and finally to frameworks that connect our system to the outside world.

What makes this layered approach powerful isn't just the separation of concerns it provides, but how it enables controlled communication between layers through well-defined interfaces. Throughout our implementation, we've seen how these architectural boundaries create a system that's both flexible and resilient to change. When we added a web interface in *Chapter 9*, our core business logic remained untouched. When we implemented observability in *Chapter 10*, our monitoring capabilities integrated cleanly with existing components without disrupting their responsibilities.

This architectural resilience stems from our consistent application of the Dependency Rule. This ensures that dependencies always point inward toward more stable abstractions. By inverting traditional dependencies through interfaces and dependency injection, we've created a system where external changes don't ripple through our core business logic. While we'll explore some pragmatic situations later in this chapter where selectively bending this rule might be warranted, the fundamental principle has served us well. This protection isn't just theoretical; we've demonstrated it through practical implementations across multiple interfaces and storage mechanisms.

Python's natural fit with Clean Architecture

Python has proven to be an ideal language for implementing Clean Architecture. Its dynamic nature combined with type hinting gives us the perfect balance of flexibility and structure. Throughout our implementation, we've leveraged Python-specific features that align naturally with Clean Architecture principles:

- **Duck typing** allows us to create flexible interfaces that focus on behavior rather than rigid inheritance hierarchies
- **Type hinting** provides clarity at architectural boundaries without sacrificing Python's dynamic nature
- **Abstract base classes** and **Protocols** establish clear contracts between layers
- **Dataclasses** simplify entity implementation while maintaining proper encapsulation

This synergy between Python's philosophy of simplicity and Clean Architecture's emphasis on clarity creates systems that are both maintainable and expressive. Python's readability naturally aligns with Clean Architecture's goal of making system intent clear, while its flexibility enables implementing architectural patterns without excessive boilerplate.

Perhaps the most valuable insight from our journey is that Clean Architecture isn't about rigid structural rules but about creating systems where components can evolve independently yet work together cohesively. The boundaries we've established don't just separate concerns, they actively manage translation between different contextual needs, ensuring that each layer can focus on its specific responsibilities.

As we explore broader applications of Clean Architecture beyond our task management example, remember that the patterns and principles we've implemented are tools in your architectural toolkit. While specific structures may vary based on context, core principles of separation of concerns, dependency inversion, and clear boundaries remain valuable across diverse system types. Throughout this book, we've demonstrated a comprehensive implementation to showcase the full potential of these principles, but teams should select the boundaries and abstractions that provide the most value for their specific context and constraints.

Adapting Clean Architecture across system types

Clean Architecture has proven its value through our task management system implementation. Now let's explore how these same principles adapt to different architectural contexts. Rather than rigid application of patterns, we'll focus on how Clean Architecture's core tenets—the Dependency Rule, clear boundaries, and separation of concerns—can be tailored to these specialized domains while maintaining architectural integrity.

Clean Architecture in API systems

Pure API systems present a fundamental architectural shift compared to our task management application. In our previous implementation of the task application, we created an *internal API* through our controllers and request/response models, but these were only consumed by presentation layers we controlled completely (CLI and web UI). This gave us significant freedom to modify these interfaces, since we could simultaneously update both sides of the interaction.

API-first systems remove this safety net by exposing these interfaces directly to external clients we don't necessarily control. It's as if we're taking the controllers and request/response models from our task management system and making them public, allowing other developers to build applications that depend directly on their structure and behavior.

This shift fundamentally changes how we must approach our architectural boundaries. Consider the following example from our task management system:

```python
# Task management Request model - internal only
class CreateTaskRequest:
    """Data structure for task creation requests."""
    title: str
    description: str
    project_id: Optional[str] = None

    def to_execution_params(self) -> dict:
        """Convert validated request data to use case parameters."""
        return {
            'title': self.title.strip(),
            'project_id': UUID(self.project_id)
            if self.project_id else None,
            'description': self.description.strip()
        }
```

In our task management system, this model was safely hidden behind our presentation layer. When we needed to change it to better align with domain evolution, we simply updated our CLI or web UI to match. External systems weren't affected because they interacted with our presentation layer, not directly with these models.

In an API-first system, however, these models become directly exposed as the public contract:

```python
# API Request DTO - now a public contract
class CreateTaskRequest:
    title: str
    description: str
    project_id: Optional[str] = None
```

Notice how the API system version of the `CreateTaskRequest` class appears simpler. The `to_execution_params` method is notably absent. This difference reflects a fundamental distinction between UI-centric and API systems. In our original task management application, this method handled the complex translation between user interface formats and domain concepts. It needed to process form data, handle string-to-UUID conversions, and manage validation before domain processing could begin.

In API systems, many of these presentation concerns disappear entirely. The client handles UI rendering and initial input formatting, submitting data already structured according to our API contract. This shifts responsibility away from our system, allowing the request model to focus solely on defining the structure of valid inputs rather than transforming them. The actual transformation between API contracts and domain objects still happens, but often through simpler, more standardized mechanisms provided by API frameworks.

Clean Architecture's Interface Adapters layer proves its value precisely in this challenging context. Within this layer, controllers continue to fulfill their essential translation role, but with adaptations specific to an API context. They now perform a critical balancing act, maintaining their fundamental responsibility of isolating the domain from external concerns while also ensuring API contract stability for external consumers.

In API systems, the nature of these external concerns shifts significantly. Rather than managing presentation details like form handling or template rendering, controllers now focus on maintaining boundaries that ensure:

- Our domain model can adapt to changing business needs without breaking API contracts

- We can version our API contracts without restructuring our entire domain

- We can provide multiple interface variants for different client needs while sharing the same core logic

Meanwhile, the outer Frameworks and Drivers layer also adapts to this API-focused context. Rather than managing multiple presentation technologies such as CLI and web interfaces, it now specializes in HTTP protocol handling, request routing, and content negotiation. This outermost layer continues its role of handling framework-specific concerns, but with greater focus on API delivery mechanisms rather than user interface technologies.

With proper architectural boundaries, pure API systems leverage the same fundamental Clean Architecture principles we've applied throughout this book. The separation of concerns, dependency inversion, and explicit interfaces work just as effectively in this context, albeit with different emphasis. All layers continue their essential roles, now adapted to the unique requirements of public API contracts.

Modern API frameworks provide specialized tools to support these architectural patterns, offering features that can simplify implementation while maintaining clean boundaries. Let's examine how these frameworks can complement our Clean Architecture approach.

Framework considerations with FastAPI

Just as we leveraged Flask for our task management web interface in *Chapter 9*, the Python ecosystem offers specialized frameworks for building APIs. **FastAPI** is one popular example that has gained significant traction for its performance, automatic documentation generation, and strong typing integration.

While Flask focuses on general web development with template rendering and session management, FastAPI specializes in building high-performance APIs with automatic OpenAPI documentation. **Pydantic**, a core component of FastAPI, offers data validation, serialization, and documentation through Python type annotations, conceptually similar to the dataclasses we've used throughout our task management implementation, but with additional validation capabilities.

API systems often leverage these specialized frameworks, which presents us with an interesting architectural decision regarding their role in our Clean Architecture implementation. The powerful validation, serialization, and documentation capabilities they provide creates an opportunity to simplify our architecture compared to our original task management implementation.

Transformation of data in request and response models becomes much more streamlined. In our original task management system, we created distinct request and response models with manual validation to manage the boundary between layers:

```python
# Task management - manual validation
class CreateTaskRequest:
    """Request data for creating a new task."""
```

```python
    title: str
    description: str

    def __post_init__(self):
        if not self.title.strip():
            raise ValueError("Title cannot be empty")

    def to_execution_params(self) -> dict:
        return {"title": self.title.strip(),
                "description": self.description.strip()}
```

This manual validation approach requires explicit checks and transformation methods in our task management system. By contrast, Pydantic integrates these capabilities directly into the model definition:

```python
# FastAPI/Pydantic - automatic validation
from pydantic import BaseModel, Field


class CreateTaskRequest(BaseModel):
    title: str = Field(..., min_length=1)
    description: str
```

Here `CreateTaskRequest` extends Pydantic's `BaseModel`. This change not only removes validation boilerplate, but also handles validation automatically through field constraints such as `min_length=1`.

When using this model with FastAPI, validation happens automatically:

```python
# How validation works with FastAPI/Pydantic
@app.post("/tasks/")
def create_task(task_data: CreateTaskRequest):
    # FastAPI has already validated all fields
    # Invalid requests are rejected with 422 Unprocessable Entity

    result = task_controller.handle_create(
        title=task_data.title,
        description=task_data.description
    )
    return result.success
```

Suppose a client sends invalid data, such as an empty title:

```
{
  "title": "",
  "description": "Test description"
}
```

FastAPI automatically responds with a validation error:

```
{
  "detail": [
    {
      "loc": ["body", "title"],
      "msg": "ensure this value has at least 1 characters",
      "type": "value_error.any_str.min_length",
      "ctx": {"limit_value": 1}
    }
  ]
}
```

This validation occurs before your route handler executes, eliminating the need for manual validation code.

This declarative approach significantly reduces the boilerplate needed in our task management system. However, it raises an important architectural question: should we allow Pydantic, a third-party library, to penetrate our inner layers? Clean Architecture's Dependency Rule warns against this.

To maintain strict adherence to Clean Architecture principles, we would need to do this:

```python
# Pure Clean Architecture approach with FastAPI
@app.post("/tasks/")
def create_task(task_data: CreateTaskRequest):  # Using Pydantic here is
fine - we're in the Frameworks Layer
    # Transform the Pydantic model to our internal domain model
    # to avoid letting Pydantic penetrate inner layers
    request = InternalCreateTaskRequest(
        title=task_data.title.strip(),
        description=task_data.description.strip()
    )
```

```python
# Pass our internal model to the controller
result = task_controller.handle_create(request)
return result.success
```

This approach maintains Clean Architecture's Dependency Rule but introduces significant duplication. We'd need to:

- Define Pydantic models for external validation (FastAPI layer)
- Define nearly identical internal models for our Application layer
- Create transformations between these parallel models
- Maintain both model types as the API evolves

This duplication would violate the **Don't Repeat Yourself (DRY)** principle and would introduce a maintenance burden, requiring synchronized updates to both sets of models whenever requirements changed.

A pragmatic alternative would be to treat Pydantic as a stable extension to Python's core capabilities rather than a volatile third-party library. Its wide adoption, stability, and focused purpose make it less likely to undergo breaking changes that would significantly impact our domain logic.

Ultimately, each team must weigh these considerations for their specific context:

- How critical is strict architectural purity to your project goals?
- What is the maintenance cost of duplicate models in your specific domain?
- How stable and established are the external dependencies in question?
- What precedent does this decision set for other architectural boundaries?

There is no universally correct answer. Some teams will prioritize strict adherence to Clean Architecture principles, accepting the additional maintenance burden to ensure complete separation of concerns. Others will make a calculated compromise for specific, well-justified cases like Pydantic, treating it as a foundational dependency similar to Python's standard library.

The key is to make this decision explicitly, documenting it in your architectural decision records, and ensuring the team understands the reasoning. Whether you choose strict separation or pragmatic compromise, what matters most is that the decision is intentional, consistent, and aligned with your project's specific needs and constraints. This explicit decision-making preserves architectural integrity even when practical considerations lead to controlled exceptions to the rules.

Applying Clean Architecture with FastAPI

To illustrate how these architectural principles translate to API systems, let's look at a concise implementation using FastAPI. This example demonstrates how the same Clean Architecture patterns we used with Flask apply in an API context:

```python
# Framework layer (infrastructure/api/routes.py)
@app.post("/tasks/", response_model=TaskResponse, status_code=201)
def create_task(task_data: CreateTaskRequest):
    """Create a new task."""
    # The controller handles translation between API and domain
    result = task_controller.handle_create(
        title=task_data.title,
        description=task_data.description,
        project_id=task_data.project_id
    )

    if not result.is_success:
        # Error handling at the framework boundary
        raise HTTPException(status_code=400, detail=result.error.message)

    return result.success  # Automatic serialization to TaskResponse
```

This route handler follows the same Clean Architecture principles as our Flask routes from *Chapter 9*, but with API-specific adaptations. Both implementations:

1. Keep framework-specific code at the system edge
2. Delegate to controllers for business operations
3. Transform between external and internal formats
4. Handle errors at the appropriate boundary

The primary differences lie in how the frameworks handle request processing and response formatting. In Flask, route handlers extract form data and render templates, while in FastAPI, route handlers leverage Pydantic models for validation and serialization. Yet the architectural boundaries remain intact in both cases. The route handler serves as a thin adapter between the framework and our application core.

This consistency across different interface types demonstrates Clean Architecture's adaptability. Whether implementing a web UI, CLI, or API, the same architectural principles guide our design decisions. Each interface type brings its own specific concerns and optimizations, but the fundamental pattern of keeping business logic independent from delivery mechanisms remains constant.

Event-driven architectures and Clean Architecture

Event-driven architecture represents another paradigm shift from our task management system's request/response model. While our original task management application processed direct commands like *create task* or *complete task*, event-driven systems instead react to events—facts that have occurred, such as *task created* or *deadline approached*.

This fundamental change in interaction patterns introduces new architectural challenges that Clean Architecture is uniquely positioned to address. While a comprehensive exploration of event-driven architecture would require a book of its own, we'll focus on how Clean Architecture principles can be applied in this context, highlighting key patterns and considerations that maintain architectural boundaries in event-driven systems.

Core concepts of event-driven architecture

In event-driven systems, the central organizing principle is the event, a significant occurrence that the system either generates or consumes. The event-driven paradigm introduces several architectural elements that weren't present in our task management system:

- **Event producers** that generate events when significant state changes occur
- **Event consumers** that react to events by performing appropriate operations
- **Message brokers** that facilitate reliable event delivery between producers and consumers
- **Event stores** that maintain event histories for replay and audit purposes

These elements create new architectural boundaries that must be managed while maintaining Clean Architecture's Dependency Rule and separation of concerns.

Applying Clean Architecture for event-driven systems

When applying Clean Architecture to event-driven systems, the Domain layer remains largely unchanged, our business entities and core rules stay the same. The significant adaptations occur primarily in the Application and Interface layers.

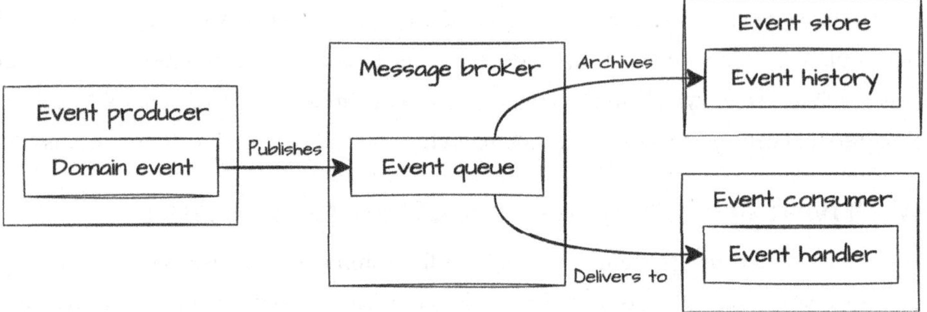

Figure 12.1: Components of an event-driven system

The Application layer in event-driven systems typically evolves to include:

- **Event handlers** that react to incoming events, similar to use cases but triggered by events rather than direct commands
- **Event generators** that produce domain events when significant state changes occur

The Interface Adapters layer transforms to include:

- **Event serializers** that translate between domain events and the message format used by the message broker
- **Message broker adapters** that abstract the specific messaging technology from the application core

Within our task management context, an event-driven implementation might react to events like *TaskCreated*, *DeadlineApproaching*, or *ProjectCompleted*. These events would flow through the system, triggering appropriate handling logic while maintaining Clean Architecture's boundaries.

Domain events as first-class citizens in Clean Architecture

One of the most significant adaptations in event-driven Clean Architecture is elevating domain events to first-class citizens in your architecture. In our original task management system, events might have existed implicitly, perhaps a notification triggered when a task was completed, but they weren't central architectural components.

In an event-driven architecture, domain events become explicit, named objects that represent meaningful business occurrences. These events aren't just messages; they're part of your ubiquitous language and domain model. They capture what happened in business terms, serving as the communication mechanism between bounded contexts while maintaining clean architectural boundaries.

Let's examine how Clean Architecture helps tame the complexity of event-driven systems by providing clear boundaries and responsibilities. The following anti-pattern demonstrates what happens without these boundaries:

```python
# Anti-pattern: Domain entity directly publishing events
class Task:
    def complete(self, user_id: UUID):
        self.status = TaskStatus.DONE
        self.completed_at = datetime.now()
        self.completed_by = user_id

        # Direct dependency on messaging system -
        # violates Clean Architecture
        kafka_producer = KafkaProducer(bootstrap_servers='kafka:9092')
        event_data = {
            "task_id": str(self.id),
            "completed_by": str(user_id),
            "completed_at": self.completed_at.isoformat()
        }
        kafka_producer.send(
            'task_events',
            json.dumps(event_data).encode()
        )
```

This anti-pattern violates Clean Architecture principles by directly coupling domain entities to infrastructure concerns (Kafka messaging). It makes the Domain layer dependent on external technologies, compromising testability and flexibility.

A clean implementation maintains proper separation of concerns across all architectural layers. Let's examine each layer individually.

First, the domain entity remains focused solely on business logic with no awareness of event publishing:

```python
# Clean domain entity - no messaging dependencies
class Task:
    def complete(self, user_id: UUID) > None:
        if self.status == TaskStatus.DONE:
            raise ValueError("Task is already completed")
```

```python
    self.status = TaskStatus.DONE
    self.completed_at = datetime.now()
    self.completed_by = user_id
```

Notice how the `Task` entity handles only the business logic of task completion. It performs its state change and validation but has no knowledge of events or messaging. This maintains pure domain logic that can be tested in isolation.

Moving to the Application layer, the use case takes responsibility for orchestrating the domain operation and event creation:

```python
# Application layer handles event creation
@dataclass
class CompleteTaskUseCase:
    task_repository: TaskRepository
    # Abstract interface, not implementation:
    event_publisher: EventPublisher

    def execute(self, task_id: UUID, user_id: UUID) -> Result:
        try:
            task = self.task_repository.get_by_id(task_id)
            task.complete(user_id)
            self.task_repository.save(task)

            # Create domain event and publish through abstract interface
            event = TaskCompletedEvent.from_task(task, user_id)
            self.event_publisher.publish(event)

            return Result.success(task)
        except ValueError as e:
            return Result.failure(Error(str(e)))
```

The use case coordinates multiple operations: retrieving the task, executing the domain operation, persisting the updated state, and publishing the event. Critically, it depends only on the abstract `EventPublisher` interface, not any specific implementation.

Finally, in the Interface Adapters layer, concrete implementations like `KafkaEventPublisher` class would handle the technical details of event delivery. Similar to how our `SQLiteTaskRepository` class implemented the abstract `TaskRepository` interface in previous chapters, these event publishers implement the abstract `EventPublisher` interface while encapsulating all messaging-specific details. This maintains Clean Architecture's consistent pattern of keeping infrastructure implementations in the outermost layer while the application core interacts only with abstractions.

This clean implementation provides several key benefits for event-driven systems:

- **Testability**: Domain logic can be tested without message brokers or event infrastructure
- **Flexibility**: Messaging technology can be changed without modifying domain or application logic
- **Clarity**: Event flow becomes explicit and traceable through well-defined boundaries
- **Evolution**: New event types and handlers can be added without disrupting existing components

In addition, at a broader level, Clean Architecture provides clear guidance on where each event-related concern belongs in our system. Domain events find their natural home in the Domain layer as value objects representing significant business occurrences. Event publishing logic resides in the Application layer as part of use case coordination, while event serialization belongs in the Interface Adapters layer where it translates between domain concepts and technical formats. Finally, all messaging infrastructure remains properly contained in the outermost Frameworks and Drivers layer, keeping these technical details completely isolated from core business logic. This clear separation brings order to the potential complexity of event-driven systems while enabling the specific interaction patterns this architectural style requires.

By maintaining these clean separations, event-driven systems become more manageable despite their inherent complexity. The domain model remains focused on business concepts, the Application layer coordinates operations and event flow, and the outer layers handle technical concerns without contaminating the core.

This demonstrates Clean Architecture's adaptability to different architectural styles. Whether building request/response APIs or event-driven reactive systems, the core principles remain consistent, keeping business logic pure and isolated from technical concerns while enabling the specific interaction patterns each style requires.

Architectural leadership and community engagement

Throughout this book, we've focused on technical implementation of Clean Architecture in Python. Technical knowledge alone isn't enough to create lasting architectural impact. Successful architectural adoption requires leadership, communication, and community building.

Clean Architecture isn't just a set of technical patterns; it's a philosophy that challenges conventional approaches to software design. Implementing it effectively often requires organizational change, team alignment, and cultural shifts. As you master the technical aspects of Clean Architecture, your ability to influence these broader factors becomes increasingly important.

In this section, we'll explore how to lead architectural change, contribute to the broader community, and build sustainable architectural practices within your organization. These skills will complement your technical knowledge, enabling you to create lasting impact beyond individual implementations.

Leading architectural change

Architectural leadership rarely comes with formal authority. Whether you're a senior developer, technical lead, or architect, implementing Clean Architecture typically requires influencing decisions across teams and departments. This influence-based leadership presents both challenges and opportunities.

Building the case for Clean Architecture

The first step in leading architectural change is making a compelling case for Clean Architecture principles. As we explored in *Chapter 11* when discussing legacy system transformation, this requires translating technical benefits into business value that stakeholders care about:

Clean Architecture benefit	Business value
Separation of concerns	Faster feature delivery after initial investment
Clear boundaries	Reduced regression issues, more stable releases
Framework independence	Longer system lifespan, reduced rewrite necessity
Testability	Higher quality, fewer production incidents

When presenting Clean Architecture to different stakeholders, adapt your message to their specific concerns:

- For product managers, emphasize how architectural clarity supports rapid feature iteration after the initial investment
- For engineering managers, highlight how Clean Architecture improves maintainability and reduces technical debt
- For developers, focus on how clear boundaries simplify work and reduce unexpected side effects
- For executives, translate technical benefits into business metrics like reduced time-to-market and ability to pivot to changing market drivers

Remember that Clean Architecture represents a significant investment. Be honest about the upfront costs while emphasizing the long-term benefits. Concrete examples from your organization, such as previous projects that became difficult to maintain, can make your case more compelling than can abstract principles.

Starting small: the power of exemplars

Trying to implement Clean Architecture across an entire organization at once rarely succeeds. Instead, demonstrate its value through small, visible successes:

- Identify a well-bounded component where Clean Architecture can provide clear benefits
- Implement it thoroughly with proper separation of concerns and clear boundaries
- Document both the process and the outcome to share with others
- Measure improvements in metrics like development velocity, defect rates, or onboarding time

These exemplars serve multiple purposes beyond just demonstrating architectural concepts. By showing Clean Architecture in action, they provide concrete evidence of its benefits that abstract discussions cannot match. They also create valuable reference implementations that other teams can study and adapt to their own contexts. As you successfully implement these exemplars, you build credibility as an architectural leader within your organization, enabling greater influence on future decisions. Perhaps most importantly, these implementations create natural opportunities to mentor others in architectural principles through collaborative work and code reviews, spreading knowledge throughout your organization.

The exemplar approach works effectively in both greenfield projects and existing systems. While building a new application from scratch offers the cleanest implementation path, most organizations have substantial existing codebases that can't be immediately replaced. In these environments, you might implement a new feature in an existing system using Clean Architecture principles, clearly separating domain logic from framework concerns. As this component proves easier to test, extend, and maintain than others, it becomes a powerful argument for broader adoption. This targeted approach demonstrates Clean Architecture's value without requiring a complete system overhaul, creating momentum for incremental improvements.

Overcoming resistance to architectural change

Architectural change often faces resistance, which typically falls into predictable patterns. Understanding these common objections helps you address them effectively.

"It's too abstract": People often struggle to see how architectural principles apply to their daily work. The concepts can seem theoretical and disconnected from practical coding tasks. Address this by creating concrete examples using your organization's actual code. Show how Clean Architecture principles solve specific problems the team has encountered, translating abstract concepts into tangible improvements they can immediately recognize.

"It's too much overhead": Teams frequently perceive the upfront cost of architectural discipline as excessive compared to immediate gains. The additional interfaces and separation can appear unnecessary to those focused on short-term delivery. Counter this perception by demonstrating long-term efficiency gains through metrics and examples from previous projects. Share stories of how architectural investment reduced maintenance costs and accelerated feature development in later stages.

"We don't have time": Delivery pressure constantly pushes teams toward expedient solutions over architectural improvements. This time constraint is usually real, not just an excuse. Acknowledge this reality while showing how architectural boundaries actually accelerate development after the initial investment. Start with small, incremental improvements that deliver immediate benefits without disrupting critical deadlines.

"It won't work here": Organizations often believe their problems are uniquely unsuited to established approaches like Clean Architecture. This exceptionalism stems from deep familiarity with internal complexities and challenges. Address this by identifying small areas where the principles can be applied successfully, demonstrating that Clean Architecture can adapt to your specific context. These targeted successes gradually overcome the 'not invented here' resistance.

Most importantly, recognize that resistance often comes from valid concerns rather than simple obstinacy. Listen carefully to specific objections, acknowledge their legitimacy, and address them directly rather than dismissing them.

Balancing pragmatism and principle

In the preceding chapters, we've emphasized that Clean Architecture is a set of principles rather than rigid rules. As we discussed earlier in this chapter when exploring API-first systems and event-driven architectures, practical implementation often requires thoughtful adaptation to specific contexts. This flexibility is even more crucial when leading architectural change. A dogmatic approach that insists on architectural purity in all circumstances will typically fail, while a completely inconsistent approach provides no architectural benefits.

The middle path, principled pragmatism, offers the best chance of success:

- Maintain clarity about core principles that should not be compromised

- Recognize areas where practical compromises might be necessary

- Document architectural decisions and their rationales, including compromises

- Establish clear boundaries for where different standards apply

For example, you might rigorously maintain separation between domain and infrastructure in core business logic, while accepting more coupling in less critical areas. Or you might accept a controlled dependency on a stable library in the Domain layer while strictly prohibiting framework dependencies.

These architectural boundaries and decisions should be explicitly documented and communicated, ideally through **Architectural Decision Records (ADRs)** that capture both the decisions and their context. This documentation builds shared understanding and prevents architectural drift as teams change over time. Here's a concise ADR template for documenting a Clean Architecture decision:

```
# ADR-001. Use of Pydantic Models in Domain Layer

## Status
Accepted

## Context
Our API-first system requires extensive validation and serialization.
Implementing these capabilities manually would require significant effort
and potentially introduce bugs. Pydantic provides robust validation,
```

```
serialization, and documentation through type annotations.

## Decision
We will allow Pydantic models in our domain layer, treating it as a stable
extension to Python's type system rather than a volatile third-party
dependency.

## Consequences
* Positive: Reduced boilerplate, improved validation, better documentation
* Positive: Consistent validation across system boundaries
* Negative: Creates dependency on external library in inner layers
* Negative: May complicate testing of domain entities

## Compliance
When using Pydantic in domain entities:
* Keep models focused on data structure, not behavior
* Avoid Pydantic-specific features that don't relate to validation
* Include comprehensive tests to verify domain rules still apply
```

For more information on creating effective ADRs, see the ADR GitHub organization: `https://adr.github.io/`

This example demonstrates how ADRs formalize architectural decisions, particularly around pragmatic compromises such as allowing certain dependencies into inner layers. The template shows how to document the context, decision, and consequences in a structured format that helps future developers understand not just what was decided, but why.

You can successfully lead architectural change in your organization by combining technical knowledge with leadership skills: making compelling cases, creating exemplars, addressing resistance, and balancing principles with pragmatism. This influence-based leadership extends Clean Architecture's impact beyond individual implementation to create lasting organizational change.

Closing the implementation gap

Despite Clean Architecture's popularity and widespread awareness, a significant gap exists between theoretical understanding and practical implementation. Many developers are familiar with the concepts but struggle to apply them effectively in real-world codebases. This implementation gap represents both a challenge and an opportunity for architectural leaders.

Contributing Clean Architecture examples

As an architectural leader, one of the most valuable contributions you can make is to share your real-world implementations with the broader community. This doesn't necessarily mean open-sourcing entire applications, but rather creating examples, patterns, and references that others can learn from. Beyond helping others, this process of teaching and documenting your implementation approaches provides significant personal benefits. The act of explaining architectural concepts to others validates your own understanding and often reveals subtle gaps in your knowledge. As the saying goes, *To teach is to learn twice.* When you articulate Clean Architecture principles clearly enough for others to understand, you solidify and deepen your own mastery of these concepts.

Consider contributing by producing:

- **Open source reference implementations** that demonstrate Clean Architecture in specific domains
- **Articles or blog posts** that explain how you've applied Clean Architecture to solve real problems
- **Templates or starter kits** that provide foundations for Clean Architecture in Python
- **Code snippets** showing how to handle specific architectural challenges
- **Architectural pattern libraries** that provide reusable solutions for common problems

These contributions help bridge the gap between theory and practice, making Clean Architecture more accessible to the broader development community. They also establish you as a thought leader in architectural design, creating opportunities for further influence and learning.

When creating these examples, focus on the aspects that are most misunderstood or difficult to implement:

- Repository pattern implementations that maintain proper abstraction
- Use case designs that effectively coordinate domain operations
- Interface adapters that cleanly translate between layers
- Dependency injection approaches that support testing and flexibility
- Boundary maintenance between architectural layers

By addressing these specific challenges with concrete code examples, you can significantly accelerate others' Clean Architecture adoption.

Learning from multiple perspectives

While contributing your own implementations, it's equally important to learn from others. Clean Architecture, like any architectural approach, continues to evolve as practitioners apply it to new domains and technologies. By engaging with diverse perspectives, you can refine your understanding and approach.

Seek out varied viewpoints through:

- Reading implementations in languages other than Python to identify language-agnostic patterns
- Examining different interpretations of Clean Architecture to understand tradeoffs
- Participating in architectural forums and discussions to hear diverse experiences
- Studying related architectural styles such as Hexagonal Architecture or Onion Architecture
- Mentoring others and being mentored, as teaching reinforces understanding while learning from experienced practitioners accelerates growth

Remember that this book represents one perspective on Clean Architecture in Python. Other equally valid approaches exist, and the *right* implementation often depends on specific context and constraints. Being open to these diverse perspectives strengthens your architectural thinking and enables more nuanced application of the principles.

By both contributing to and learning from the broader community, you help close the implementation gap while continuing your own architectural growth. This bidirectional engagement creates a virtuous cycle that advances both individual and collective understanding of Clean Architecture principles.

Building your architecture community

While individual architectural leadership is powerful, sustained architectural excellence typically requires community. Building an architecture community, whether within your organization or across the broader development ecosystem, creates momentum that individual efforts cannot match.

Creating communities of practice

Within organizations, **communities of practice** provide powerful structures for architectural learning and alignment. These voluntary, cross-team groups bring together developers interested in architectural excellence to share knowledge, develop standards, and solve common problems.

To establish an architecture community of practice:

- **Start informally** with lunch-and-learns or discussion groups to gauge interest
- **Define a clear purpose** centered on architectural learning and improvement
- **Create regular touchpoints** like weekly meetings or monthly deep dives
- **Rotate leadership** to include diverse perspectives and share the workload
- **Produce tangible outputs** like guidelines, patterns, or reference implementations

These communities serve multiple purposes:

- They create spaces for architectural discussions without immediate delivery pressure
- They build shared vocabulary and understanding across teams
- They identify and address common architectural challenges
- They provide mentoring opportunities for less experienced developers

Most importantly, they distribute architectural knowledge beyond individual experts, creating organizational resilience and continuity even as team members change over time.

By establishing communities of practice within your organization, you create an ecosystem that sustains architectural excellence beyond individual efforts. This community approach transforms Clean Architecture from a personal interest into an organizational capability, ensuring that the benefits we've explored throughout this book can scale across teams and endure over time.

Clean Architecture's lasting impact comes not just from technical implementation but from the communities and cultures that form around it. By leading architectural change, closing implementation gaps, and building sustainable communities, you extend Clean Architecture's benefits far beyond individual systems to create lasting positive change in how software is designed and built.

Summary

In this final chapter, we've expanded our view of Clean Architecture beyond our task management system to its broader applications and adaptations.

We reflected on our Clean Architecture journey, seeing how well-defined architectural layers create flexible, resilient systems. Features of Python like duck typing, type hinting, and abstract base classes have allowed us to build maintainable systems without excessive boilerplate.

We then explored Clean Architecture adaptations for different system types. In API-first systems, frameworks like FastAPI enhance implementation while requiring thoughtful decisions about architectural boundaries. For event-driven architectures, Clean Architecture brings order to event flows while maintaining pure business logic.

We also discussed architectural leadership and community engagement, exploring strategies for advocating Clean Architecture, addressing resistance, and building communities of practice that sustain architectural excellence over time.

As you conclude this book and continue your Clean Architecture journey, remember that the principles we've explored are tools to be applied thoughtfully, not rigid rules to follow dogmatically. The Dependency Rule, clear boundaries, and separation of concerns provide a foundation for creating systems that remain adaptable and maintainable as requirements evolve. How you apply these principles should reflect your specific context, constraints, and goals.

The true power of Clean Architecture lies in its ability to create systems where business logic remains clear and focused, regardless of changing technologies or delivery mechanisms. By establishing proper architectural boundaries and maintaining the discipline to respect them, you create systems that not only work today but can evolve gracefully to meet tomorrow's challenges.

Thank you for joining me on this exploration of Clean Architecture with Python. I hope the patterns, principles, and practices shared throughout this book serve you well in creating systems that stand the test of time.

Further reading

- *FastAPI* (`https://fastapi.tiangolo.com/`). This is a modern, high-performance web framework for building APIs with Python, leveraging standard Python type hints.
- *Pydantic* (`https://docs.pydantic.dev/latest/`). Pydantic is a Python library for data validation and settings management, using Python type annotations.
- *Building Event-Driven Microservices: Leveraging Data Streams for Scale and Resilience* (`https://www.oreilly.com/library/view/building-event-driven-microservices/9781492057888/`). A practical guide to designing and implementing scalable and resilient microservices using event-driven architectures and data streams.
- *Communities of Practice: The Organizational Frontier* (`https://hbr.org/2000/01/communities-of-practice-the-organizational-frontier`). This article introduces and explains the concept of communities of practice, highlighting their role in knowledge sharing, problem-solving, and organizational improvement through examples from various industries.

packtpub.com

Subscribe to our online digital library for full access to over 7,000 books and videos, as well as industry leading tools to help you plan your personal development and advance your career. For more information, please visit our website.

Why subscribe?

- Spend less time learning and more time coding with practical eBooks and Videos from over 4,000 industry professionals

- Improve your learning with Skill Plans built especially for you

- Get a free eBook or video every month

- Fully searchable for easy access to vital information

- Copy and paste, print, and bookmark content

At www.packtpub.com, you can also read a collection of free technical articles, sign up for a range of free newsletters, and receive exclusive discounts and offers on Packt books and eBooks.

Other Books You May Enjoy

If you enjoyed this book, you may be interested in these other books by Packt:

Learn Python Programming, Fourth Edition

Fabrizio Romano, Heinrich Kruger

ISBN: 978-1-83588-294-8

- Install and set up Python on Windows, Mac, and Linux
- Write elegant, reusable, and efficient code
- Avoid common pitfalls such as duplication and over-engineering
- Use functional and object-oriented programming approaches appropriately
- Build APIs with FastAPI and program CLI applications
- Understand data persistence and cryptography for secure applications
- Manipulate data efficiently using Python's built-in data structures
- Package your applications for distribution via the Python Package Index (PyPI)
- Solve competitive programming problems with Python

Clean Code in Python, Second Edition

Mariano Anaya

ISBN: 978-1-80056-021-5

- Set up a productive development environment by leveraging automatic tools
- Leverage the magic methods in Python to write better code, abstracting complexity away and encapsulating details
- Create advanced object-oriented designs using unique features of Python, such as descriptors
- Eliminate duplicated code by creating powerful abstractions using software engineering principles of object-oriented design
- Create Python-specific solutions using decorators and descriptors
- Refactor code effectively with the help of unit tests
- Build the foundations for solid architecture with a clean codebase as its cornerstone

Python Object-Oriented Programming, Fourth Edition

Steven F. Lott, Dusty Phillips

ISBN: 978-1-80107-726-2

- Implement objects in Python by creating classes and defining methods
- Extend class functionality using inheritance
- Use exceptions to handle unusual situations cleanly
- Understand when to use object-oriented features, and more importantly, when not to use them
- Discover several widely used design patterns and how they are implemented in Python
- Uncover the simplicity of unit and integration testing and understand why they are so important
- Learn to statically type check your dynamic code
- Understand concurrency with asyncio and how it speeds up programs

Packt is searching for authors like you

If you're interested in becoming an author for Packt, please visit `authors.packtpub.com` and apply today. We have worked with thousands of developers and tech professionals, just like you, to help them share their insight with the global tech community. You can make a general application, apply for a specific hot topic that we are recruiting an author for, or submit your own idea.

Share your thoughts

Now you've finished *Clean Architecture with Python*, we'd love to hear your thoughts! Scan the QR code below to go straight to the Amazon review page for this book and share your feedback or leave a review on the site that you purchased it from.

`https://packt.link/r/183664289X`

Your review is important to us and the tech community and will help us make sure we're delivering excellent quality content.

Index

Made in the USA
Monee, IL
07 July 2026

56553284R00201